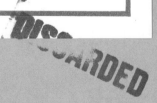

# A GEORGE ELIOT MISCELLANY

# A GEORGE ELIOT MISCELLANY

## A Supplement to her Novels

Edited with Commentary and Notes by

## F. B. PINION

*First published 1982 by*
THE MACMILLAN PRESS LTD
*London and Basingstoke*
*Companies and representatives*
*throughout the world*

ISBN 0 333 29348 7

*Typeset by Computacomp (UK) Ltd, Fort William, Scotland*
*and printed in Hong Kong*

# Contents

v

## V   LATE ESSAYS

# Preface

To realize George Eliot's objectives and achievements in *Scenes of Clerical Life* and her seven novels, a reader needs to have access to her other writings. These are not readily available, and it is primarily for this reason that this miscellany has been prepared. It comprises key passages from her pre-novel essays and reviews, two stories in prose, writings relative to some of her major publications, four poems, and some evaluations of her contemporary English world. The order has the advantage of being almost entirely chronological from start to finish.

The selections from George Eliot's pre-novel prose afford an invaluable, if not indispensable, introduction to her fiction. The two stories form a contrast: one, unusually light and entertaining; the other dark, inventive, and prophetic, a forerunner in its ultimate theme of T. S. Eliot's *The Waste Land*. This minor masterpiece, 'The Lifted Veil', emphasizes by its bleak negations the positive virtues which motivate George Eliot's more familiar fiction. Many readers will have admired the poetry in some of the anonymous chapter epigraphs in her last three novels. They were composed by George Eliot, and exemplify her range to a remarkable degree, above all the union of deep feeling, human understanding or empathy, and originality of poetic expression which characterizes her best work. George Eliot's poetry is undeservedly ignored. 'Stradivarius' would not discredit any poet; it has a bearing on the romantically artistic young Ladislaw in *Middlemarch*. Similarly the biographical significance of the 'Brother and Sister' sonnets holds a special interest for readers of the more fictional childhood experiences in *The Mill on the Floss*.

Apart from its relevance to *Felix Holt*, the 'Address to Working Men', like the two essays included from *Impressions of Theophrastus Such*, has a strikingly undiminished cogency in the present era. Their broader implications are inherent in George Eliot's work generally; the fundamental articles of her belief did not change from *Scenes of Clerical life* to *Daniel Deronda*.

This selection, therefore, may be regarded as a supplement, or even an adult introduction, to her works. The commentaries are supplied in order to establish relationships, and, with the same end in view, quotations are introduced from George Eliot's other writings, including her letters. Some items, among them a story in verse, are included solely for their intrinsic merits.

Grateful acknowledgments are made to Yale University Library, Yale University Press, and Gordon S. Haight for permission to produce the manuscript text of 'How I Came to Write Fiction' and 'History of "Adam Bede" ' from *The George Eliot Letters*; also to Angus Hulton for his assistance with some of the classical references.

The following abbreviations are used:

| | | | |
|---|---|---|---|
| AB | *Adam Bede* | MF | *The Mill on the Floss* |
| DD | *Daniel Deronda* | R | *Romola* |
| FH | *Felix Holt* | SCL | *Scenes of Clerical Life* |
| M | *Middlemarch* | SM | *Silas Marner* |
| | WR | *The Westminster Review* | |

Dates in the form 27.x.60 enable the reader to find passages in either J. W. Cross, *George Eliot's Life* or Gordon S. Haight (ed.), *The George Eliot Letters* (Yale University Press).

# Introduction

Mary Ann Evans (1819–80) chose to live with George Henry Lewes in 1854, and their unofficial marriage proved to be unusually happy and successful, each encouraging the other to the highest authorial endeavour. Lewes, whose versatility as a writer had already been shown, was to enhance his reputation as an editor and biographer, and make important contributions to natural sciences and psychology. Unfortunately, although he and his legal wife had separated by mutual consent, he could not obtain a divorce, having condoned adultery by registering the first of her three illegitimate children as his. 'Marian' Evans, condemned by a Grundyan society for her union with Lewes, adopted 'George Eliot' as her *nom de plume* in 1857, after the publication of her first story, choosing 'George' after her devoted husband, and 'Eliot' because she thought it 'a good mouth-filling, easily pronounced word'.

Years before her birth, her father Robert Evans had become the estate manager for Francis Parker, first at Wootton Hall in Staffordshire, then at West Hallam in Derbyshire. His competence and conscientiousness made him indispensable, so much so that in 1806, when his master succeeded Sir Roger Newdigate at Arbury Hall near Nuneaton, he was given responsbility for the whole estate, his diverse duties including farm maintenance, forestry, roads, the mining of coal, and its transportation by tramroad and canal. After only a few months at South Farm, her birthplace, Mary Evans lived twenty-one years at Griff House, a large farmstead by the Coventry road. She was her father's youngest and favourite child, and he often took her on his rounds in his gig; she observed much and forgot little. After her mother's death and her sister's marriage, she was virtually in charge at Griff House. She had been given the best education that was available for girls, first at Nuneaton, then at Coventry; already proficient in French, she was tutored in German and Italian on leaving school. Highly musical, and a great reader, she was very religious, a fervent Evangelical during her late adolescence, with a pronounced Calvinistic bias at one period.

When Robert Evans retired in 1841, he and Mary Ann (as she preferred to be known at the time) moved to Foleshill near Coventry. In poorer parts of the city she was appalled by the poverty of families engaged in the ribbon industry; she had witnessed it in the Griff–Nuneaton area, but never on such a scale. She continued to receive instruction in German and Italian, had lessons also in Greek and Latin, and read widely, Carlyle's *Sartor Resartus* and the more modern books on astronomy and geology giving her much food for thought. Wordsworth was her favourite poet. At Rosehill, the home of Charles Bray, a ribbon manufacturer and free-thinker, she met some of his more distinguished visitors. Mrs Bray's brother Charles Hennell had independently reached conclusions similar to those of the German historical critics, undermining all that is miraculous and supernatural in the Gospels. His *An Inquiry into the Origins of Christianity* had reached its second edition when Mary Ann bought her copy and inscribed her name on 2 January 1842. Her refusal to attend church with her father led almost to their separation, but mediation prevailed, and Miss Evans began to perceive the truth of what was to become one of her cardinal principles in fiction, that human relationships, active sympathy, and co-operation are more instrumental in creating progress than any form of sectarian discrimination or dogma. When Elizabeth Brabant, who had begun the translation of Strauss's *Das Leben Jesu*, became engaged to Charles Hennell, Miss Evans was persuaded to continued this massive task; the work was published anonymously in 1846. In 1847 she admired Hennell's work more than ever before, and found inspiration in the pantheism of Wordsworth and Spinoza. She read contemporary novels, and was particularly enthusiastic about George Sand's; when Emerson met her at the Brays', and asked what had led her to think most deeply, she answered 'Rousseau's *Confessions*'.

After her father's death, and a period at Geneva, where she resumed her translation of Spinoza's *Tractatus-Theologico-Politicus*, she met John Chapman at Rosehill. Subsequently he bought *The Westminster Review*; being most unbusinesslike himself, he engaged Marian (as she now signed herself) to assist him. When the first number in its new series appeared in January 1852, she had become responsible, without remuneration, for most of the editorial work. She met eminent writers and intellectuals, British and foreign; among them Herbert Spencer, with whom she fell in love. He regarded her as 'the most admirable woman, mentally' he had ever met; they had many philosophical discussions, but it was a relief to him when she became friendly with George Henry Lewes. By this time, she had begun her translation of Feuerbach's *The Essence of Christianity*, a work which, unlike the Strauss, appealed to her throughout. In its apotheosis of human love she found a warm expression of the new religion which she felt mankind needed for its amelioration and happiness. The translation appeared in July 1854, soon after she and Lewes had left for Weimar, where she helped him to prepare his biography of Goethe.

On their return Marian accepted Chapman's invitation to take charge of the Belles Lettres section of *The Westminster* at a salary of £50 per annum. She read assiduously, and became a writer in earnest, producing for this and other journals a series of reviews and essays which demonstrated high critical sagacity and literary talent. Both Lewes and Spencer had urged her to turn to fiction. This she was persuaded to do, after thinking of the story which became the first in *Scenes of Clerical Life*. Lewes recommended it to his publisher John Blackwood, and with its appearance in *Blackwood's Magazine* at the beginning of 1857 George Eliot's career began.

# I    Pre-Novel Writings

---

## i    A LITTLE FABLE WITH A GREAT MORAL

(Appearing in February 1847, this is the fourth of a series of original articles 'from the Notebook of an Eccentric' which Mary Ann Evans, after contributing anonymous reviews, wrote for *The Herald and Observer*, a Coventry weekly newspaper acquired by Charles Bray in June 1846 for the promotion of ideas on reform.)

In very early times indeed, when no maidens had looking-glasses, except the mermaidens, there lived in a deep valley two beautiful Hamadryads. Now the Hamadryads are a race of nymphs that inhabit the forests. Whenever a little acorn, or a beech nut, or any other seed of a forest tree, begins to sprout, a little Hamadryad is born, and grows up, and lives and dies with the tree. So, you see, the Hamadryads, the daughters of the trees, live far longer than the daughters of men, – some of them even a thousand years; still, they do at last get old, and faded, and shrivelled. Now the two Hamadryads of whom I spoke lived in a forest by the side of a clear lake, and they loved better than anything to go down to the brink of the lake, and look into the mirror of waters; but not for the same reason. Idione loved to look into the lake because she saw herself there; she would sit on the bank, weaving leaves and flowers in her silken hair, and smiling at her own image all the day long, and if the pretty water-lilies or any other plants began to spread themselves on the surface below her, and spoil her mirror, she would tear them up in anger. But Hieria cared not to look at herself in the lake; she only cared about watching the heavens as they were reflected in its bosom – the foamy clouds on the clear blue by day, and the moon and the stars by night. She did not mind that the water-lilies grew below her, for she was always looking farther off, into the deep part of the lake; she only thought the lilies pretty, and loved them. So, in the course of time, these two Hamadryads grew old, and Idione began to be angry with the lake, and to hate it, because it no longer gave back a

1

pleasant image of herself, and she would carry little stones to the margin, and dash them into the lake for vengeance; but she only tired herself, and did not hurt the lake. And as she was frowning and looking spiteful all the day, the lake only went on giving her an uglier and uglier picture of herself, till at last she ran away from it into the hollow of her tree, and sat there lonely and sad till she died. But Hieria grew old without finding it out, for she never looked for herself in the lake; – only as, in the centuries she had lived, some of the thick forests had been cleared away from the earth, and men had begun to build and to plough, the sky was less often obscured by vapours, so that the lake was more and more beautiful to her, and she loved better and better the water-lilies that grew below her. Until one morning, after she had been watching the stars in the lake, she went home to her tree, and lying down, she fell into a gentle sleep, and dreamed that she had left her mouldering tree, and had been carried up to live in a star, from which she could still look down on her lake that she had loved so long. And while she was dreaming this, men came and cut down her tree, and Hieria died without knowing that she had become old.

*       *       *

The story has its variants in George Eliot's novels. Hetty Sorrel, self-centred and vain, performs her narcissistic rites in front of a mirror, while Dinah Morris looks out of the window in the next bedroom, and thinks of all the people out there whom she has learned to love and care for (AB.xv). The beauty of the lake for Hieria has its counterpart in the autumnal sunshine which outwardly expresses the mellowing of Adam Bede's humanitarian self as a result of suffering and the awakening of a deeper love than that inspired by Hetty. Transome Court spells tragedy for the proud, withdrawn, self-pitying Mrs Transome, and Esther Lyon rejects its 'silken bondage'; she yearns for a more purposive life, and finds it in Felix Holt's self-dedication to the cause of his fellow-workers. Both women look out on the same scene at night; where one sees no relief (a black boundary of trees and the long line of the river), the other notices the bending movement of the trees, the forever flowing river, and veiled glimmerings of moonlight (FH.xlix–l). Life goes on for Esther, and hope returns, just as when Dorothea, after self-pitying grief, recovers her better self, draws the curtains, and sees the pearly light of dawn, with signs of 'the manifold wakings of men to endurance and labour' (M.lxxx). *Daniel Deronda* illustrates the association of distant

illuminated prospects with such altruistic causes as are to be found
in Mordecai's zeal for Zionism (xxxviii) and the hero's yearning to
be useful to humanity, July evening scenes serving to contrast the
latter with the self-seeking hedonism of Gwendolen Harleth
(xi,xvii). Hieria's finding the lake more beautiful as a result of
men's labour is an earnest of the value attached by George Eliot to
improvements in housing, land-cultivation, industry, and
transport for the benefit of the public and the future (AB.i;
M.xxiv,xl,lvi).


## ii FROM THE REVIEW OF R. W. MACKAY'S
## *THE PROGRESS OF THE INTELLECT*

(The book was published by John Chapman, and he and the
author met Mary Evans at Charles Bray's. She agreed to review the
book, and the result was her first contribution to *The Westminster
Review*, where it appeared in January 1851.

There are many, and those not the least powerful thinkers and
efficient workers amongst us, who are prone to under-rate critical
research into ancient modes of life and forms of thought, alleging
that what it behoves us chiefly to ascertain is the truth which
comes home to men's business and bosoms[1] in these our days, and
not by-gone speculations and beliefs which we can never fully
comprehend, and with which we can only yet more imperfectly
sympathise. Holding, with Auguste Comte, that theological and
metaphysical speculation have reached their limit, and that the
only hope of extending man's sources of knowledge and
happiness is to be found in positive science, and in the universal
application of its principles; they urge that the thinkers who are in
the van of human progress should devote their energies to the
actual rather than to the retrospective.

There is, undeniably, truth in this view. It is better to discover
and apply improved methods of draining our own towns, than to
be able to quote Aristophanes in proof that the streets of Athens
were in a state of unmacadamized muddiness – better to reason
justly on some point of immediate concern, than to know the
fallacies of the ancient sophists – better to look with 'awful eye'[2] at
the starry heavens, and, under the teaching of Newton and
Herschel,[3] feel the immensity, the order, the sublimity of the
universe, and of the forces by which it subsists, than to pore over
the grotesque symbols, whereby the Assyrian or Egyptian

shadowed forth his own more vague impressions of the same great facts. But it would be a very serious mistake to suppose that the study of the past and the labours of criticism have no important practical bearing on the present. Our civilization, and, yet more, our religion, are an anomalous blending of lifeless barbarisms, which have descended to us like so many petrifactions from distant ages,[4] with living ideas, the offspring of a true process of development. We are in bondage to terms and conceptions which, having had their root in conditions of thought no longer existing, have ceased to possess any vitality, and are for us as spells which have lost their virtue. The endeavour to spread enlightened ideas is perpetually counteracted by these *idola theatri*,[5] which have allied themselves, on the one hand with men's better sentiments, and on the other with institutions in whose defence are arrayed the passions and the interests of dominant classes. Now, though the teaching of positive truth is the grand means of expelling error, the process will be very much quickened if the negative argument serve as its pioneer; if, by a survey of the past, it can be shown how each age and each race has had a faith and a symbolism suited to its need and its stage of development, and that for succeeding ages to dream of retaining the spirit along with the forms of the past, is as futile as the embalming of the dead body in the hope that it may one day be resumed by the living soul.

But apart from this objective utility of critical research, it has certain highly advantageous influences on the mind which pursues it. There is so far justice in the common sarcasms against men of erudition *par excellence*, that they have rarely been distinguished for warmth of moral sympathy, or for fertility and grandeur of conception; but your eminently practical thinker is often beset by a narrowness of another kind. It may be doubted, whether a mind which has no susceptibility to the pleasure of changing its point of view, of mastering a remote form of thought, of perceiving identity of nature under variety of manifestation – a perception which resembles an expansion of one's own being, a pre-existence in the past – can possess the flexibility, the ready sympathy, or the tolerance, which characterizes a truly philosophic culture. Now and then, however, we meet with a nature which combines the faculty for amassing minute erudition with the largeness of view necessary to give it a practical bearing; a high appreciation of the genius of antiquity, with a profound belief in the progressive character of human development – in the eternal freshness of the founts of inspiration, a wonderful intuition of the mental conditions of past ages with an ardent participation in the most advanced ideas and most hopeful efforts of the present; a nature like some mighty river, which, in its long windings through unfrequented regions, gathers mineral and earthy treasures only more effectually to enrich and fertilize the cultivated valleys and busy cities which form the habitation of man.

Of such a nature . . . we have evidence in the work before us. . . . We believe Mr Mackay's work is unique in its kind. England has been slow to use or to emulate the immense labours of Germany in the departments of mythology and biblical criticism; but when once she does so, the greater solidity and directness of the English mind ensure a superiority of treatment. . . . It is Mr Mackay's faith that divine revelation is not contained exclusively or pre-eminently in the facts and inspirations of any one age or nation, but is co-extensive with the history of human development, and is perpetually unfolding itself to our widened experience and investigation, as firmament upon firmament becomes visible to us in proportion to the power and range of our exploring instruments. The master key to this revelation, is the recognition of the presence of undeviating law in the material and moral world – of that invariability of sequence which is acknowledged to be the basis of physical science, but which is still perversely ignored in our social organization, our ethics and our religion. It is this invariability of sequence which can alone give value to experience and render education in the true sense possible. The divine yea and nay, the seal of prohibition and of sanction, are effectually impressed on human deeds and aspirations, not by means of Greek and Hebrew, but by that inexorable law of consequences, whose evidence is confirmed instead of weakened as the ages advance; and human duty is comprised in the earnest study of this law and patient obedience to its teaching. While this belief sheds a bright beam of promise on the future career of our race, it lights up what once seemed the dreariest region of history with new interest; every past phase of human development is part of that education of the race in which we are sharing; every mistake, every absurdity into which poor human nature has fallen, may be looked on as an experiment of which we may reap the benefit. A correct generalization gives significance to the smallest detail, just as the great inductions of geology demonstrate in every pebble the working of laws by which the earth has become adapted for the habitation of man. In this view, religion and philosophy are not merely conciliated, they are identical; or rather, religion is the crown and consummation of philosophy – the delicate corolla, which can only spread out its petals in all their symmetry and brillance to the sun, when root and branch exhibit the conditions of a healthy and vigorous life.

*             *             *

Perhaps the above provides one reason for George Eliot's conclusion that Positivism is 'one-sided' (12.vii.61), for her writings are in accord with the basic principles of 'the religion of humanity' which emanated from the philosophy and doctrines of Auguste Comte (1798–1857). She did not agree with all his teaching, but acknowledged her 'great debt' to him; it was greater (as far as J. W. Cross could remember her acknowledging) than to any other writer. Believing that 'other-worldliness' is a distraction from the real centre of human endeavour, she and Comte held that education and science are fundamental to progress, that religion needs to be at one with scientific truth, and that self-interest should be subordinated to altruism and general welfare. Above all, Comte emphasized the necessity for stimulating humanitarian feeling and moral energy, if social justice is to be achieved and maintained (cf. pp. 170–2).

The width of Mary Evans' outlook is seen not only in terms of evolutionary religion and civilization, but also in her scientific allusions, and in her insistence on the 'undeviating law' of cause-effect (the 'inexorable law of consequences') in human affairs. Any religion that ignores it is inadequate. It may be seen in the rise and fall of nations. George Eliot illustrates it in her novels: in Arthur Donnithorne (AB), Godfrey Cass (SM), Tito Melema (R), Lydgate, Bulstrode (M), and Gwendolen Harleth (DD); also in more successful characters such as Adam Bede, Silas Marner, and Dorothea Brooke. The importance of not breaking violently away from tradition is one of the interrelated themes of *Felix Holt.*

### iii   FROM 'WOMAN IN FRANCE: MADAME DE SABLÉ'

(Devoted principally to Victor Cousin's *Madame de Sablé: études sur les femmes illustres et la société du XVII^e siècle*, this was the first review Marian Evans contributed to *The Westminster Review* after she had chosen to live with George Henry Lewes; it appeared in October 1854. The happy relationship and intellectual interdependence of these two writers contributed much to the cogency of this article.)

Such was Madame de Sablé,[6] whose name is, perhaps, new to some of our readers, so far does it lie from the surface of literature and history. We have seen, too, that she was only one amongst a crowd – one in a firmament of feminine stars which, when once the biographical telescope is turned upon them, appear scarcely less remarkable and interesting. Now, if the reader recollects what was the position and average intellectual character of women in the high society of England during the reigns of James the First and the two Charleses – the period through which Madame de Sablé's career extends – we think he will admit our position as to the early superiority of womanly development in France: and this fact, with its causes, has not merely an historical interest, it has an important bearing on the culture of women in the present day. Women become superior in France by being admitted to a common fund of ideas, to common objects of interest with men; and this must ever be the essential condition at once of true womanly culture and of true social well-being. We have no faith in feminine conversazioni, where ladies are eloquent on Apollo and Mars; though we sympathize with the yearning activity of faculties which, deprived of their proper material, waste themselves in weaving fabrics out of cobwebs. Let the whole field of reality be laid open to woman as well as to man, and then that which is peculiar in her mental modification, instead of being, as it is now, a source of discord and repulsion between the sexes, will be found to be a necessary complement to the truth and beauty of life. Then we shall have that marriage of minds which alone can blend all the hues of thought and feeling in one lovely rainbow of promise[6] for the harvest of human happiness.

*     *     *

With the above, one should consider the typically masculine views expressed by Bardo (R.v) and Mr Brooke (M.vii), and the kind of education which, on the one hand, fails to prepare Maggie Tulliver (MF) and Dorothea Brooke for life and, on the other, adds to Rosamond's superficial attractiveness, yet makes her a handicap in marriage to the exceptionally talented Lydgate (M). Coincidentally, the rainbow image of promise was used by D. H. Lawrence in *The Rainbow*, as a sign of women's coming self-responsibility, at a time when he believed he would do more for their emancipation than the suffragette movement could ever achieve.

## iv FROM 'EVANGELICAL TEACHING: DR CUMMING'

(WR October 1855. Dr John Cumming was minister of the Scottish National Church at Crown Court, Covent Garden, from 1832 to 1879. A popular preacher, prolific writer, and interpreter of the Apocalypse, he was strong in his denunciation of heterodoxy based on science and historical criticism, and even more of Roman Catholicism. Marian Evans describes him as 'the Boanerges of Crown-court', and Tennyson in 'Sea Dreams', after reading her article, as 'Our Boanerges with his threats of doom,/ And loud-lung'd Antibabylonianisms'.)

Dr. Cumming's theory, as we have seen, is that actions are good or evil according as they are prompted or not prompted by an exclusive reference to the 'glory of God'. God, then, in Dr. Cumming's conception, is a being who has no pleasure in the exercise of love and truthfulness and justice, considered as effecting the well-being of his creatures; He has satisfaction in us only in so far as we exhaust our motives and dispositions of all relation to our fellow-beings, and replace sympathy with men by anxiety for the 'glory of God'. The deed of Grace Darling, when she took a boat in the storm to rescue drowning men and women[7] was not good if it was only compassion that nerved her arm and impelled her to brave death for the chance of saving others; it was only good if she asked herself – Will this redound to the glory of God? The man who endures tortures rather than betray a trust, the man who spends years in toil in order to discharge an obligation from which the law declares him free, must be animated not by the spirit of fidelity to his fellow-man, but by a desire to make 'the name of God more known'. The sweet charities of domestic life – the ready hand and the soothing word in sickness, the forbearance towards frailties, the prompt helpfulness in all efforts and sympathy in all joys, are simply evil if they result from a 'constitutional tendency', or from dispositions disciplined by the experience of suffering and the perception of moral loveliness. A wife is not to devote herself to her husband out of love to him and a sense of the duties implied by a close relation – she is to be a faithful wife for the glory of God; if she feels her natural affections welling up too strongly, she is to repress them; it will not do to act from natural affection – she must think of the glory of God. A man is to guide his affairs with energy and discretion, not from an honest desire to fulfil his responsibilities as a member of society and a father, but – that 'God's praise may be sung'. Dr. Cumming's Christian pays his debts for the glory of God; were it not for the coercion of that supreme motive, it would be evil to pay them. A man is not to be just from a feeling of justice; he is not to help his fellow-men out of good-will to his fellow-men; he is not to be a tender husband and father out of affection: all these natural muscles and fibres are to be torn away and replaced by a patent steel-spring – anxiety for the 'glory of God'.

Happily, the constitution of human nature forbids the complete prevalence of such a theory. Fatally powerful as religious systems have been, human nature is stronger and wider than religious systems, and though dogmas may hamper, they cannot absolutely repress its growth: build walls round the living tree as you will, the bricks and mortar have by and bye to give way before the slow and sure operation of the sap. But next to that hatred to the enemies of God which is the principle of persecution, there perhaps has been no perversion more obstructive of true moral development than this substitution of a reference to the glory of God for the direct promptings of the sympathetic feelings. Benevolence and justice are strong only in proportion as they are directly and inevitably called into activity by their proper objects: pity is strong only because we are strongly impressed by suffering; and only in proportion as it is compassion that speaks through the eyes when we soothe, and moves the arm when we succour, is a deed strictly benevolent. If the soothing or the succour be given because another being wishes or approves it, the deed ceases to be one of benevolence, and becomes one of deference, of obedience, of self-interest, or vanity. Accessory motives may aid in producing an *action*, but they pre-suppose the weakness of the direct motive; and conversely, when the direct motive is strong, the action of accessory motives will be excluded. If then, as Dr. Cumming inculcates, the glory of God is to be 'the absorbing and the influential aim' in our thoughts and actions, this must tend to neutralize the human sympathies; the stream of feeling will be diverted from its natural current in order to feed an artificial canal. The idea of God is really moral in its influence – it really cherishes all that is best and loveliest in man – only when God is contemplated as sympathizing with the pure elements of human feeling, as possessing infinitely all those attributes which we recognize to be moral in humanity. In this light, the idea of God and the sense of His presence intensify all noble feeling, and encourage all noble effort, on the same principle that human sympathy is found a source of strength: the brave man feels braver when he knows that another stout heart is beating time with his; the devoted woman who is wearing out her years in patient effort to alleviate suffering or save vice from the last stages of degradation, finds aid in the pressure of a friendly hand which tells her that there is one who understands her deeds, and in her place would do the like. The idea of a God who not only sympathizes with all we feel and endure for our fellow-men, but who will pour new life into our too languid love, and give firmness to our vacillating purpose, is an extension and multiplication of the effects produced by human sympathy; and it has been intensified for the better spirits who have been under the influence of orthodox Christianity, by the contemplation of Jesus as 'God manifest in the flesh'. But Dr. Cumming's God is the very opposite of all this: he is a God who instead of sharing and aiding our human sympathies, is directly in collision with them; who instead of strengthening the bond between man and man, by encouraging the sense that they are both alike the objects of His love and care, thrusts himself between them and forbids them to feel for each other except as they have relation to Him. He is a God, who, instead of adding his solar force to swell the tide of those impulses that tend to give humanity a common life in which the good of one is the good of all, commands us to check those impulses, lest they should prevent us from thinking of His glory. It is in vain for Dr. Cumming to say that we are to love man for God's sake: with the conception of God which his teaching presents, the love of man for God's sake involves, as his writings abundantly show, a strong principle of hatred. We can only love one being for the sake of another when there is an habitual delight in associating the idea of those two beings – that is, when the object of our indirect love is a source of joy and honour to the object of our direct love: but, according to Dr. Cumming's theory, the majority of mankind – the majority of his neighbours – are in precisely the opposite relation to God. His soul has no pleasure in them, they belong more to Satan than to Him, and if they contribute to His glory, it is against their will. Dr. Cumming then can only love *some* men for God's sake; the rest he must in consistency *hate* for God's sake.

*          *          *

The emphasis placed on human feeling in religion was partly inspired by Feuerbach (p. xi). Marian's creed is above sectarianism; she can sympathize with any religion which promotes kindness and welfare (cf. 6.xii.59). Believing (as she writes in her conclusion) in 'the tendency towards good in human nature' which 'no creed can utterly counteract', she appeals for a living, everyday religion in this world, not the imagined ('the stream of feeling' in its 'natural current' as opposed to the artificial). The examples she gives of this practical religion recall 'Janet's Repentance' (SCL). The essay, which anticipates that on Young, convinced Lewes that his wife was a writer of genius.

## v  FROM 'THE NATURAL HISTORY OF GERMAN LIFE'

(WR July 1856. In this review of third editions of the first two volumes of Wilhelm Heinrich Riehl's *Naturgeschichte des Volks*, Marian extols the faithful depiction of life in art, as she did when she reviewed the third volume of Ruskin's *Modern Painters* earlier in the year.)

How little the real characteristics of the working-classes are known to those who are outside them, how little their natural history has been studied, is sufficiently disclosed by our Art as well as by our political and social theories. Where, in our picture exhibitions, shall we find a group of true peasantry? What English artist even attempts to rival in truthfulness such studies of popular life as the pictures of Teniers or the ragged boys of Murillo?[8] Even one of the greatest painters of the pre-eminently realistic school, while, in his picture of 'The Hireling Shepherds',[9] he gave us a landscape of marvellous truthfulness, placed a pair of peasants in the foreground who were not much more real than the idyllic swains and damsels of our chimney ornaments. Only a total absence of acquaintance and sympathy with our peasantry, could give a moment's popularity to such a picture as 'Cross Purposes', where we have a peasant girl who looks as if she knew L. E. L.'s poems by heart, and English rustics, whose costume seems to indicate that they are meant for ploughmen, with exotic features that remind us of a handsome *primo tenore*.[10] Rather than such cockney sentimentality as this, as an education for the taste and sympathies, we prefer the most crapulous group of boors that Teniers ever painted. But even those among our painters who aim at giving the rustic type of features, who are far above the effeminate feebleness of the 'Keepsake' style, treat their subjects under the influence of traditions and prepossessions rather than of direct observation. The notion that peasants are joyous, that the typical moment to represent a man in a smock-frock is when he is cracking a joke and showing a row of sound teeth, that cottage matrons are usually buxom, and village children necessarily rosy and merry, are prejudices difficult to dislodge from the artistic mind, which looks for its subjects into literature instead of life. The painter is still under the influence of idyllic literature, which has always expressed the imagination of the cultivated and town-bred, rather than the truth of rustic life. Idyllic ploughmen are jocund when they drive their team afield; idyllic shepherds make bashful love under hawthorn bushes; idyllic villagers dance in the chequered shade and refresh themselves, not immoderately, with spicy nut-brown ale.[11] But no one who has seen much of actual ploughmen thinks them jocund; no one who is well acquainted with the English peasantry can pronounce them merry. The slow gaze, in which no sense of beauty beams, no humour twinkles, – the slow utterance, and the heavy slouching walk, remind one rather of that melancholy animal the camel, than of the sturdy countryman, with striped stockings, red waistcoat, and hat aside, who represents the traditional English peasant. Observe a company of haymakers. When you see them at a distance, tossing up the forkfuls of hay in the golden light, while the wagon creeps slowly with its increasing burthen over the meadow, and the bright green space which tells of work done gets larger and larger, you pronounce the scene 'smiling', and you think these companions in labour must be as bright and cheerful as the picture to which they give animation. Approach nearer, and you will certainly find that haymaking time is a time for joking, especially if there are women among the labourers; but the coarse laugh that bursts out every now and then, and expresses the triumphant taunt, is as far as possible from your conception of idyllic merriment. That delicious effervescence of the mind which we call fun, has no equivalent for the northern peasant, except tipsy revelry; the only realm of fancy and imagination for the English clown exists at the bottom of the third quart pot.

The conventional countryman of the stage, who picks up pocket-books and never looks into them, and who is too simple even to know that honesty has its opposite, represents the still lingering mistake, that an unintelligible dialect is a guarantee for ingenuousness, and that slouching shoulders indicate an upright disposition. It is quite true that a thresher is likely to be innocent of any adroit arithmetical cheating, but he is not the less likely to carry home his master's corn in his shoes and pocket; a reaper is not given to writing begging-letters, but he is quite capable of cajolling the dairymaid into filling his small-beer bottle with ale. The selfish instincts are not subdued by the sight of buttercups, nor is integrity in the least established by that classic rural

occupation, sheep-washing. To make men moral, something
more is requisite than to turn them out to grass.

Opera peasants, whose unreality excites Mr.
Ruskin's indignation,[12] are surely too frank an idealization to be mis-
leading; and since popular chorus is one of the most effective
elements of the opera, we can hardly object to lyric rustics in
elegant laced boddices and picturesque motley, unless we are
prepared to advocate a chorus of colliers in their pit costume, or a
ballet of char-women and stocking-weavers. But our social novels
profess to represent the people as they are, and the unreality of
their representations is a grave evil. The greatest benefit we owe to
the artist, whether painter, poet, or novelist, is the extension of
our sympathies. Appeals founded on generalizations and statistics
require a sympathy ready-made, a moral sentiment already in
activity; but a picture of human life such as a great artist can give,
surprises even the trivial and the selfish into that attention to what
is apart from themselves, which may be called the raw material of
moral sentiment. When Scott takes us into Luckie Mucklebackit's
cottage, or tells the story of 'The Two Drovers', – when
Wordsworth sings to us the reverie of 'Poor Susan', – when
Kingsley shows us Alton Locke gazing yearningly over the gate
which leads from the highway into the first wood he ever saw, –
when Hornung paints a group of chimney-sweepers,[13] – more is
done towards linking the higher classes with the lower, towards
obliterating the vulgarity of exclusiveness, than by hundreds of
sermons and philosophical dissertations. Art is the nearest thing
to life; it is a mode of amplifying experience and extending our
contact with our fellowmen beyond the bounds of our personal
lot. All the more sacred is the task of the artist when he undertakes
to paint the life of the People. Falsification here is far more
pernicious than in the more artificial aspects of life. It is not so
very serious that we should have false ideas about evanescent
fashions – about the manners and conversation of beaux and
duchesses; but it *is* serious that our sympathy with the perennial
joys and struggles, the toil, the tragedy, and the humour in the life
of our more heavily-laden fellow-men, should be perverted, and
turned towards a false object instead of the true one.

This perversion is not the less fatal because the
misrepresentation which gives rise to it has what the artist
considers a moral end. The thing for mankind to know is, not what
are the motives and influences which the moralist thinks *ought* to
act on the labourer or the artisan, but what are the motives and
influences which *do* act on him. We want to be taught to feel, not
for the heroic artisan or the sentimental peasant, but for the

peasant in all his coarse apathy, and the artisan in all his suspicious selfishness.

\*     \*     \*

Marian Evans wrote the above at Ilfracombe, where her co-operation in Lewes's research for his *Seaside Studies* reinforced her desire 'to escape from all vagueness and inaccuracy' of expression. Believing that the artist's greatest function is 'the extension of our sympathies', she lays stress on truthful presentation, especially of the great majority, the labouring poor. Hence her admiration of Dutch paintings (AB.xvii) and her Crabbe-like correction of idyllic literature. She does not avoid this kind of realism (cf. AB.xix,liii), but it is not characteristic of her novels, which, while true to life generally, are directed by ennobling ends, 'an endeavour to see what our thought and emotion may be capable of – what stores of motive, actual or hinted as possible, give promise of a better after which we may strive' (25.i.76).

## vi  FROM 'SILLY NOVELS BY LADY NOVELISTS'

(WR October 1856. This was written just before Marian Evans began her first essay in fiction, 'The Sad Fortunes of the Rev. Amos Barton'. Although the extract throws clear light on one type of silly novel favoured by contemporary authoresses, its main importance lies in its statement on the classes among which the 'real drama' of Evangelicalism was to be found, as she demonstrates particularly in her first story and 'Janet's Repentance' (SCL).

The Orlando of Evangelical literature is the young curate, looked at from the point of view of the middle class, where cambric bands are understood to have as thrilling an effect on the hearts of young ladies as epaulettes have in the classes above and below it. In the ordinary type of these novels, the hero is almost sure to be a young curate, frowned upon, perhaps, by worldly mammas, but carrying captive the hearts of their daughters, who can 'never forget *that* sermon'; tender glances are seized from the pulpit stairs instead of the opera-box; *tête-à-têtes* are seasoned with quotations from Scripture, instead of quotations from the poets; and questions as to the state of the heroine's affections are mingled with anxieties as to the state of her soul. The young curate always has a background of well-dressed and wealthy, if not fashionable society; – for Evangelical silliness is as snobbish as any other kind of silliness; and the Evangelical lady novelist, while she explains to you the type of the scapegoat on one page, is ambitious on another to represent the manners and conversation of aristocratic people. Her pictures of fashionable society are often curious studies considered as efforts of the Evangelical imagination; but in one particular the novels of the White Neck-cloth School are meritoriously realistic, – their favourite hero, the Evangelical young curate is always rather an insipid personage.

The most recent novel of this species that we happen to have before us, is 'The Old Grey Church'.[14] It is utterly tame and feeble; there is no one set of objects on which the writer seems to have a stronger grasp than on any other; and we should be entirely at a loss to conjecture among what phases of life her experience has been gained, but for certain vulgarisms of style which sufficiently indicate that she has had the advantage, though she has been unable to use it, of mingling chiefly with men and women whose manners and characters have not had all their bosses and angles rubbed down by refined conventionalism. It is less excusable in an Evangelical novelist, than in any other, gratuitously to seek her subjects among titles and carriages. The real drama of Evangelicalism – and it has abundance of fine drama for any one who has genius enough to discern and reproduce it – lies among the middle and lower classes; and are not Evangelical opinions understood to give an especial interest in the weak things of the earth, rather than in the mighty? Why then, cannot our Evangelical lady novelists show us the operation of their religious views among people (there really are many such in the world) who keep no carriage, 'not so much as a brassbound gig', who even manage to eat their dinner without a silver fork, and in whose mouths the authoress's questionable English would be strictly consistent? Why can we not have pictures of religious life among the industrial classes in England, as interesting as Mrs. Stowe's pictures of religious life among the negroes?[15] Instead of this, pious ladies nauseate us with novels which remind us of what we sometimes see in a worldly woman recently 'converted'; – she is as fond of a fine dinner table as before, but she invites clergymen instead of beaux; she thinks as much of her dress as before, but she adopts a more sober choice of colours and patterns; her conversation is as trivial as before, but the triviality is flavoured with gospel instead of gossip. In 'The Old Grey Church', we have

the same sort of Evangelical travesty of the fashionable novel, and
of course the vicious, intriguing baronet is not wanting.

## vii  FROM 'WORLDLINESS AND OTHER-WORLDLINESS: THE POET YOUNG'

(WR January 1857. This essay, the last of Marian's to appear in *The
Westminster Review*, was begun in April 1856, laid aside for the
articles on Riehl and 'silly novels', then for 'Amos Barton'. It was
resumed in November, and finished a month later. She alludes to
her early enthusiasm for Young's *Night Thoughts*, and returns to the
viewpoint, founded on Positivism and Feuerbach's gospel, which
she vigorously expressed in her essay on Dr Cumming.)

Young's biographers and critics have usually set out from the
position that he was a great religious teacher, and that his poetry is
morally sublime; and they have toned down his failings into
harmony with their conception of the divine and the poet. For our
own part, we set out from precisely the opposite conviction –
namely, that the religious and moral spirit of Young's poetry is
low and false; and we think it of some importance to show that
the 'Night Thoughts' are the reflex of a mind in which the higher
human sympathies were inactive. This judgment is entirely
opposed to our youthful predilections and enthusiasm. The sweet
garden-breath of early enjoyment lingers about many a page of
the 'Night Thoughts', and even of the 'Last Day',[16] giving an
extrinsic charm to passages of stilted rhetoric and false sentiment;
but the sober and repeated reading of maturer years has
convinced us that it would hardly be possible to find a more
typical instance than Young's poetry, of the mistake which
substitutes interested obedience for sympathetic emotion, and
baptizes egoism as religion. . . .

Seeing that we are about to be severe on Young's failings and
failures, we ought, if a reviewer's space were elastic, to dwell also
on his merits, – on the startling vigour of his imagery, – on the
occasional grandeur of his thought, – on the piquant force of that
grave satire into which his meditations continually run. But, since
our 'limits' are rigorous, we must content ourselves with the less
agreeable half of the critic's duty; and we may the rather do so,
because it would be difficult to say anything new of Young, in the
way of admiration, while we think there are many salutary lessons
remaining to be drawn from his faults.

One of the most striking characteristics of Young is his *radical insincerity as a poetic artist*. This, added to the thin and artificial texture of his wit, is the true explanation of the paradox – that a poet who is often inopportunely witty has the opposite vice of a bombastic absurdity. The source of all grandiloquence is the want of taking for a criterion the true qualities of the object described, or the emotion expressed. The grandiloquent man is never bent on saying what he feels or what he sees, but on producing a certain effect on his audience; hence he may float away into utter inanity without meeting any criterion to arrest him. Here lies the distinction between grandiloquence and genuine fancy or bold imaginativeness. The fantastic or the boldly imaginative poet may be as sincere as the most realistic: he is true to his own sensibilities or inward vision, and in his wildest flights he never breaks loose from his criterion – the truth of his own mental state. Now, this disruption of language from genuine thought and feeling is what we are constantly detecting in Young; and his insincerity is the more likely to betray him into absurdity, because he habitually treats of abstractions, and not of concrete objects or specific emotions. He descants perpetually on virtue, religion, 'the good man', life, death, immortality, eternity – subjects which are apt to give a factitious grandeur to empty wordiness. When a poet floats in the empyrean, and only takes a bird's-eye view of the earth, some people accept the mere fact of his soaring for sublimity, and mistake his dim vision of earth for proximity to heaven. . . .

Again:


Far beneath
A soul immortal is a mortal joy.


Happily for human nature, we are sure no man really believes that. Which of us has the impiety not to feel that our souls are only too narrow for the joy of looking into the trusting eyes of our children, of reposing on the love of a husband or wife, – nay, of listening to the divine voice of music, or watching the calm brightness of autumn afternoons? But Young could utter this falsity without detecting it, because, when he spoke of 'mortal joys', he rarely had in his mind any object to which he could attach sacredness. He was thinking of bishoprics and benefices, of smiling monarchs, patronizing prime ministers, and a 'much indebted muse'. Of anything between these and eternal bliss, he was but rarely and moderately conscious. Often, indeed, he sinks very much below even the bishopric, and seems to have no notion of earthly pleasure, but such as breathes gas-light and the fumes of wine. His picture of life is precisely such as you would expect from a man who has risen from his bed at two o'clock in the afternoon with a headache, and a dim remembrance that he has added to his 'debts of honour':

> What wretched repetition cloys us here!
> What periodic potions for the sick,
> Distemper'd bodies, and distemper'd minds!

And then he flies off to his usual antithesis:

> In an eternity what scenes shall strike!
> Adventures thicken, novelties surprise!

'Earth' means lords and levees, duchesses and Dalilahs, South-Sea dreams[17] and illegal percentage; and the only things distinctly preferable to these are, eternity and the stars. Deprive Young of this antithesis, and more than half his eloquence would be shrivelled up. Place him on a breezy common, where the furze is in its golden bloom, where children are playing, and horses are standing in the sunshine with fondling necks, and he would have nothing to say. Here are neither depths of guilt, nor heights of glory; and we doubt whether in such a scene he would be able to pay his usual compliment to the Creator:

> Where'er I turn, what claim on all applause!

It is true that he sometimes – not often – speaks of virtue as capable of sweetening life, as well as of taking the sting from death and winning heaven; and, lest we should be guilty of any unfairness to him, we will quote the two passages[18] which convey this sentiment the most explicitly. . . . Even here, where he is in his most amiable mood, you see at what a telescopic distance he stands from mother Earth and simple human joys – 'Nature's circle rolls beneath.' Indeed, we remember no mind in poetic literature that seems to have absorbed less of the beauty and the healthy breath of the common land-scape than Young's. . . .

The adherence to abstractions, or to the personification of abstractions, is closely allied in Young to the *want of genuine emotion*. He sees Virtue sitting on a mount serene, far above the mists and storms of earth: he sees Religion coming down from the skies, with this world in her left hand and the other world in her right: but we never find him dwelling on virtue or religion as it really exists – in the emotions of a man dressed in an ordinary coat, and seated by his fire-side of an evening, with his hand resting on the head of his little daughter; in courageous effort for unselfish ends, in the internal triumph of justice and pity over personal resentments, in all the sublime self-renunciation and sweet charities which are found in the details of ordinary life. Now, emotion links itself with particulars, and only in a faint and secondary manner with abstractions. An orator may discourse very eloquently on injustice in general, and leave his audience cold; but let him state a special case of oppression, and every heart will throb. The most untheoretic persons are aware of this relation between true emotion and particular facts, as opposed to general terms, and implicitly recognise it in the repulsion they feel towards any one who professes strong feeling about abstractions, – in the interjectional 'humbug!' which immediately rises to their lips. Wherever abstractions appear to excite strong emotion, this occurs in men of active intellect and imagination, in whom the abstract term rapidly and vividly calls up the particulars it represents, these particulars being the true source of the emotion; and such men, if they wished to express their feeling, would be infallibly prompted to the presentation of details. Strong emotion can no more be directed to generalities apart from particulars, than skill in figures can be directed to arithmetic apart from numbers. Generalities are the refuge at once of deficient intellectual activity and deficient feeling. . . .

This remarkable negation of sympathy is in perfect consistency with Young's theory of ethics:

> Virtue is a crime,
> A crime to reason, if it costs us pain
> Unpaid . . .[19]

If there is no immortality for man,

Sense! take the rein; blind Passion, drive us on;
And Ignorance! befriend us on our way. . . .
Yes; give the pulse full empire; live the Brute,
Since as the brute we die. The sum of man,
Of godlike man, to revel and to rot.
. . . . . . . . . . . . . . . . . .

If this life's gain invites him to the deed,
Why not his country sold, his father slain?
. . . . . . . . . . . . . . . . . .

Ambition, avarice, by the wise disdain'd,
Is perfect wisdom, while mankind are fools,
And think a turf or tombstone covers all.
. . . . . . . . . . . . . . . . . .

Die for thy country, thou romantic fool!
Seize, seize the plank thyself, and let her sink.
. . . . . . . . . . . . . . . . . .

As in the dying parent dies the child,
Virtue with Immortality expires.
Who tells me he denies his soul immortal,
*Whate'er his boast, has told me he's a knave.*
*His duty 'tis to love himself alone,*
*Nor care though mankind perish, if he smiles.*

We can imagine the man who 'denies his soul immortal',
replying, 'It is quite possible that *you* would be a knave, and love
yourself alone, if it were not for your belief in immortality; but
you are not to force upon me what would result from your own
utter want of moral emotion. I am just and honest, not because I
expect to live in another world, but because, having felt the pain
of injustice and dishonesty towards myself, I have a fellow-feeling
with other men, who would suffer the same pain if I were unjust
or dishonest towards them. Why should I give my neighbour short
weight in this world, because there is not another world in which I
should have nothing to weigh out to him? I am honest, because I
don't like to inflict evil on others in this life, not because I'm
afraid of evil to myself in another. The fact is I do *not* love myself
alone, whatever logical necessity there may be for that in your
mind. I have a tender love for my wife, and children, and friends,
and through that love I sympathize with like affections in other
men. It is a pang to me to witness the suffering of a fellow-being,
and I feel his suffering the more acutely because he is *mortal* –
because his life is so short, and I would have it, if possible, filled
with happiness and not misery. Through my union and fellowship

with the men and women I *have* seen, I feel a like, though a fainter, sympathy with those I have *not* seen; and I am able so to live in imagination with the generations to come, that their good is not alien to me, and is a stimulus to me to labour for ends which may not benefit myself, but will benefit them. It is possible that you might prefer to "live the brute", to sell your country, or to slay your father, if you were not afraid of some disagreeable consequences from the criminal laws of another world; but even if I could conceive no motive but by my own worldly interest or the gratification of my animal desires, I have not observed that beastliness, treachery, and parricide, are the direct way to happiness and comfort on earth. And I should say, that if you feel no motive to common morality but your fear of a criminal bar in heaven, you are decidedly a man for the police on earth to keep their eye upon, since it is a matter of world-old experience that fear of distant consequences is a very insufficient barrier against the rush of immediate desire. Fear of consequences is only one form of egoism, which will hardly stand against half-a-dozen other forms of egoism bearing down upon it. And in opposition to your theory that a belief in immortality is the only source of virtue, I maintain that, so far as moral action is dependent on that belief, so far the emotion which prompts it is not truly moral – is still in the stage of egoism, and has not yet attained the higher development of sympathy. In proportion as a man would care less for the rights and the welfare of his fellow, if he did not believe in a future life, in that proportion is he wanting in the genuine feelings of justice and benevolence; as the musician who would care less to play a sonata of Beethoven's finely in solitude than in public, where he was to be paid for it, is wanting in genuine enthusiasm for music.'

Thus far the man who 'denies himself immortal' might give a warrantable reply to Young's assumption of peculiar loftiness in maintaining that 'virtue with immortality expires'.[20] We may admit, indeed, that if the better part of virtue consists, as Young appears to think, in contempt for mortal joys, in 'meditation of our own decease', and in 'applause' of God in the style of a congratulatory address to Her Majesty – all which has small relation to the well-being of mankind on this earth – the motive to it must be gathered from something that lies quite outside the sphere of human sympathy. But, for certain other elements of virtue, which are of more obvious importance to untheological minds, – a delicate sense of our neighbour's rights, an active participation in the joys and sorrows of our fellow-men, a magnanimous acceptance of privation or suffering for ourselves

when it is the condition of good to others, in a word, the extension and intensification of our sympathetic nature, – we
think it of some importance to contend, that they have no more
direct relation to the belief in a future state than the interchange
of gases in the lungs has to the plurality of worlds. Nay, to us it is
conceivable that in some minds the deep pathos lying in the
thought of human mortality – that we are here for a little while
and then vanish away, that this earthly life is all that is given to our
loved ones and to our many suffering fellow-men – lies nearer the
fountains of moral emotion than the conception of extended
existence. And surely it ought to be a welcome fact, if the thought
of *mortality*, as well as of immortality, be favourable to virtue. . . .

It is this pedagogic tendency, this sermonizing attitude of
Young's mind, which produces the wearisome monotony of his
pauses. After the first two or three Nights, he is rarely singing,
rarely pouring forth any continuous melody inspired by the
spontaneous flow of thought or feeling. He is rather occupied with
argumentative insistance, with hammering in the proofs of his
propositions by disconnected verses, which he puts down at
intervals. The perpetual recurrence of the pause at the end of the
line throughout long passages, makes them as fatiguing to the ear
as a monotonous chant, which consists of the endless repetition of
one short musical phrase. . . .

How different from the easy, graceful melody of Cowper's
blank verse! Indeed, it is hardly possible to criticise Young,
without being reminded at every step of the contrast presented to
him by Cowper. And this contrast urges itself upon us the more
from the fact that there is, to a certain extent, a parallelism
between the 'Night Thoughts' and the 'Task'. In both poems, the
author achieves his greatest in virtue of the new freedom
conferred by blank verse; both poems are professedly didactic,
and mingle much satire with their graver meditations; both
poems are the productions of men whose estimate of this life was
formed by the light of a belief in immortality, and who were
intensely attached to Christianity. On some grounds, we might
have anticipated a more morbid view of things from Cowper than
from Young. Cowper's religion was dogmatically the more
gloomy, for he was a Calvinist; while Young was a 'low'
Arminian, believing that Christ died for all, and that the only
obstacle to any man's salvation lay in his will, which he could
change if he chose.[21] There was real and deep sadness involved in
Cowper's personal lot; while Young, apart from his ambitious
and greedy discontent, seems to have had no great sorrow.

Yet, see how a lovely, sympathetic nature manifests itself in

spite of creed and circumstance! Where is the poem that surpasses
the 'Task' in the genuine love it breathes, at once towards
inanimate and animate existence – in truthfulness of perception
and sincerity of presentation – in the calm gladness that springs
from a delight in objects for their own sake, without self-reference
– in divine sympathy with the lowliest pleasures, with the most
short-lived capacity for pain. Here is no railing at the earth's
'melancholy map', but the happiest lingering over her simplest
scenes with all the fond minuteness of attention that belongs to
love; no prompous rhetoric about the inferiority of the 'brutes',
but a warm plea on their behalf against man's inconsiderateness
and cruelty, and a sense of enlarged happiness from their
companionship in enjoyment; no vague rant about human
misery and human virtue, but that close and vivid presentation of
particular sorrows and privations, of particular deeds and
misdeeds, which is the direct road to the emotions. How Cowper's
exquisite mind falls with the mild warmth of morning sunlight on
the commonest objects, at once disclosing every detail and
investing every detail with beauty! . . . And then he passes into
reflection, not with curt apophthegm and snappish reproof, but
with that melodious flow of utterance which belongs to thought
when it is carried along in a stream of feeling:

> The heart is hard in nature, and unfit
> For human fellowship, as being void
> Of sympathy, and therefore dead alike
> To love and friendship both, that is not pleased
> With sight of animals enjoying life,
> Nor feels their happiness augment his own.

His large and tender heart embraces the most every-day forms of
human life – the carter driving his team through the wintry
storm; the cottager's wife who, painfully nursing the embers on
her hearth, while her infants 'sit cowering o'er the sparks',

> Retires, content to quake, so they be warm'd;

or the villager, with her little ones, going out to pick

> A cheap but wholesome salad from the brook;

and he compels our colder natures to follow his in its manifold sympathies, not by exhortations, not by telling us to meditate at midnight, to 'indulge' the thought of death, or to ask ourselves how we shall 'weather an eternal night', *but by presenting to us the object of his compassion truthfully and lovingly.* And when he handles greater themes, when he takes a wider survey, and considers the men or the deeds which have a direct influence on the welfare of communities and nations, there is the same unselfish warmth of feeling, the same scrupulous truthfulness. He is never vague in his remonstrance or his satire; but puts his finger on some particular vice or folly, which excites his indignation or 'dissolves his heart in pity', because of some specific injury it does to his fellow-man or to a sacred cause. And when he is asked why he interests himself about the sorrows and wrongs of others, hear what is the reason he gives. Not, like Young, that the movements of the planets show a mutual dependence, and that

> Thus man his soveriegn duty learns in this
> Material picture of benevolence –

or that,

> More generous sorrow while it sinks, exalts,
> And conscious virtue mitigates the pang.

What is Cowper's answer, when he imagines some 'sage erudite, profound', asking him 'What's the world to you?' –

> Much. *I was born of woman, and drew milk*
> *As sweet as charity from human breasts.*
> I think, articulate, I laugh and weep,
> And exercise all functions of a man.
> How then should I and any man that lives
> Be strangers to each other?

Young is astonished that men can make war on each other – that any one can 'seize his brother's throat', while

The Planets cry, 'Forbear.'

Cowper weeps because –

> There is no flesh in man's obdurate heart;
> *It does not feel for man.*

Young applauds God as a monarch with an empire and a court quite superior to the English, or as an author who produces 'volumes for man's perusal. Cowper sees his Father's love in all the gentle pleasures of the home fire-side, in the charms even of the wintry landscape, and thinks –

> Happy who walks with him! whom what he finds
> Of flavour or of scent in fruit or flower,
> Or what he views of beautiful or grand
> In nature, from the broad, majestic oak
> To the green blade that twinkles in the sun
> *Prompts with remembrance of a present God.*

To conclude – for we must arrest ourselves in a contrast that would lead us beyond our bounds: Young flies for his utmost consolation to the day of judgment, when

> Final Ruin fiercely drives
> Her ploughshare o'er Creation;

when earth, stars, and suns are swept aside,

> And now, all dross removed, Heaven's own pure day
> Full on the confines of our ether, flames:
> While (dreadful contrast!) far (how far!) beneath,
> Hell, bursting, belches forth her blazing seas,
> And storms sulphureous; her voracious jaws
> Expanding wide, and roaring for her prey, –

Dr. Young, and similar 'ornaments of religion and virtue', passing, of course, with grateful 'applause' into the upper region. Cowper finds his highest inspiration in the Millennium – in the restoration of this our beloved home of earth to perfect holiness and bliss, when the Supreme

> Shall visit earth in mercy; shall descend
> Propitious in his chariot paved with love;
> And what his storms have blasted and defaced
> For man's revolt, shall with a smile repair.

And into what delicious melody his song flows at the thought of that blessedness to be enjoyed by future generations on earth! –

> The dwellers in the vales and on the rocks
> Shout to each other, and the mountain tops
> From distant mountains catch the flying joy;
> Till, nation after nation taught the strain,
> Earth rolls the rapturous Hosanna round!

The sum of our comparison is this – In Young we have the type of that deficient human sympathy, that impiety towards the present and the visible, which flies for its motives, its sanctities, and its religion, to the remote, the vague, and the unknown: in Cowper we have the type of that genuine love which cherishes things in proportion to their nearness, and feels its reverence grow in proportion to the intimacy of its knowledge.

\*     \*     \*

The essay reveals literary sensitivity in its comments on the stylistic evidence of Cowper's sincerity and Young's 'radical insincerity as a poetic artist'. Young's conclusion that man would be immorally selfish without a belief in immortality indicates facile reasoning and a lack of intrinsic faith and manhood. Matthew Arnold's aptly entitled sonnet 'Anti-Desperation' provides an answer to this kind of Pauline pessimism. Man acquires a moral sense from the evolutionary civilization of the centuries, as is implied in the review of Mackay's *The Progress of the Intellect*. George Eliot did not lose faith in human nature, but the depressing thought of a loveless people in a godless world is at the very heart of her theme in 'The Lifted Veil'. Her conviction is succinctly expressed in the passage 'Nay, to us it is conceivable . . . favourable to virtue' (p. 22). In this we have a view of life shared by Thomas Hardy, and inherent in his tragedy of *Tess of the d'Urbervilles*, which seemed like 'a Positive allegory' to the distinguished Positivist Frederic Harrison. In George Eliot's novels criticism of one kind of egoism (pp. 2–3) or another is continually implicit; it is always designed to awaken the humanitarian sympathies which she found deficient in Young.

# II  Two Contrasting Stories

## i  'THE LIFTED VEIL'

(So great was the immediate success of *Adam Bede* when it made its first appearance – in volume form, in February 1859 – that its publisher John Blackwood asked George Eliot if she had a story for his magazine. She had almost completed 'The Lifted Veil', and sent it a month later; it appeared in the July number of *Blackwood's Magazine*. Her 'private critic' Lewes aptly described it as 'very striking and original', whereas she referred to it as 'a slight story of an outré kind – not a *jeu d'esprit* but a *jeu de mélancolie*'. She had begun it during a period of depression after starting *The Mill on the Floss*. The opening chapters of this novel had awakened memories of a childhood in which so much of her happiness had depended on the goodwill and approval of her brother Isaac (as may be seen in the 'Brother and Sister' sonnets). Strictly religious, he had refused to recognise her marriage, simply because it could not be sanctified by the church; and it was from this severance of ties, and the ache to renew them, that the crux of her novel was to develop. The *mélancolie* which made her 'too stupid' to continue her 'more important work' was the inspiration of 'The Lifted Veil', and it is clearly expressed at a personal level in the conclusion which introduces it. The story has a significance beyond this, the author's depression having led her to face up to the possibility of a civilization without love or sympathy, in a secular era without the new religion which she felt essential for enlightened progress. To present this vision of the future (anticipating T. S. Eliot's *The Waste Land* in some respects), George Eliot's invention is of the 'outré kind'; the hero's prevision is the one departure from the natural in all her fiction.

Although he admired the excellence of its style, John Blackwood did not appreciate the story, finding it 'horribly painful'. For this reason he was not anxious to include it in a uniform edition of George Eliot's works, and in 1873 suggested that it should form part of a miscellany, the first in a series of *Tales from Blackwood*. The proposal was declined. The author liked the creative idea of the story more than ever, and wrote the epigraph as much for her publisher's enlightenment as for the reader's.)

> Give me no light, great heaven, but such as turns
> To energy of human fellowship;
> No powers beyond the growing heritage
> That makes completer manhood.[1]

### *Chapter I*

The time of my end approaches. I have lately been subject to attacks of *angina pectoris*; and in the ordinary course of things, my physician tells me, I may fairly hope that my life will not be protracted many months. Unless, then, I am cursed with an exceptional physical constitution, as I am cursed with an exceptional mental character, I shall not much longer groan under the wearisome burthen of this earthly existence. If it were to be otherwise – if I were to live on to the age most men desire and provide for – I should for once have known whether the miseries of delusive expectation can outweigh the miseries of true prevision. For I foresee when I shall die, and everything that will happen in my last moments.

Just a month from this day, on the 20 September 1850, I shall be sitting in this chair, in this study, at ten o'clock at night, longing to die, weary of incessant insight and foresight, without delusions and without hope. Just as I am watching a tongue of blue flame rising in the fire, and my lamp is burning low, the horrible contraction will begin at my chest. I shall only have time to reach the bell, and pull it violently, before the sense of suffocation will come. No one will answer my bell. I know why. My two servants are lovers, and will have quarrelled. My housekeeper will have rushed out of the house in a fury, two hours before, hoping that Perry will believe she has gone to drown herself. Perry is alarmed at last, and is gone out after her. The little scullery-maid is asleep on a bench: she never answers the bell; it does not wake her. The sense of suffocation increases: my lamp goes out with a horrible stench: I make a great effort, and snatch at the bell again. I long for life, and there is no help. I thirsted for the unknown: the thirst is gone. O God, let me stay with the known, and be weary of it: I am content. Agony of pain and suffocation – and all the while the earth, the fields, the pebbly brook at the bottom of the rookery, the fresh scent after the rain, the light of the morning through my chamber-window, the warmth of the hearth after the frosty air – will darkness close over them for ever?

Darkness – darkness – no pain – nothing but darkness: but I am passing on and on through the darkness: my thought stays in the darkness, but always with a sense of moving onward. . . .

Before that time comes, I wish to use my last hours of ease and strength in telling the strange story of my experience. I have never fully unbosomed myself to any human being; I have never been encouraged to trust much in the sympathy of my fellow-men. But we have all a chance of meeting with some pity, some tenderness, some charity, when we are dead: it is the living only who cannot be forgiven – the living only from whom men's indulgence and reverence are held off, like the rain by the hard east wind. While the heart beats, bruise it – it is your only opportunity; while the eye can still turn towards you with moist timid entreaty, freeze it with an icy unanswering gaze; while the ear, that delicate messenger to the inmost sanctuary of the soul, can still take in the tones of kindness, put it off with hard civility, or sneering compliment, or envious affectation of indifference; while the creative brain can still throb with the sense of injustice, with the yearning for brotherly recognition – make haste – oppress it with your ill-considered judgments, your trivial comparisons, your careless misrepresentations. The heart will by-and-by be still – *ubi saeva indignatio ulterius cor lacerare nequit*;[2] the eye will cease to entreat; the ear will be deaf; the brain will have ceased from all wants as well as from all work. Then your charitable speeches may find vent; then you may remember and pity the toil and the struggle and the failure; then you may give due honour to the work achieved; then you may find extenuation for errors, and may consent to bury them.

That is a trivial schoolboy text; why do I dwell on it? It has little reference to me, for I shall leave no works behind me for men to honour. I have no near relatives who will make up, by weeping over my grave, for the wounds they inflicted on me when I was among them. It is only the story of my life that will perhaps win a little more sympathy from strangers when I am dead, than I ever believed it would obtain from my friends while I was living.

My childhood perhaps seems happier to me than it really was, by contrast with all the after-years. For then the curtain of the future was as impenetrable to me as to other children: I had all their delight in the present hour, their sweet indefinite hopes for the morrow; and I had a tender mother: even now, after the dreary lapse of long years, a slight trace of sensation accompanies the remembrance of her caress as she held me on her knee – her arms round my little body, her cheek pressed on mine. I had a complaint of the eyes that made me blind for a little while, and she kept me on her knee from morning till night. That unequalled love soon vanished out of my life, and even to my childish consciousness it was as if that life had become more chill. I rode my little white pony with the groom by my side as before, but there were no loving eyes looking at me as I mounted, no glad arms opened to me when I came back. Perhaps I missed my mother's love more than most children of seven or eight would have done, to whom the other pleasures of life remained as before; for I was certainly a very sensitive child. I remember still the mingled trepidation and delicious excitement with which I was affected by the tramping of the horses on the pavement in the echoing stables, by the loud resonance of the grooms' voices, by the booming bark of the dogs as my father's carriage thundered under the archway of the courtyard, by the din of the gong as it gave notice of luncheon and dinner. The measured tramp of soldiery which I sometimes heard – for my father's house lay near a county town where there were large barracks – made me sob and tremble; and yet when they were gone past, I longed for them to come back again.

I fancy my father thought me an odd child, and had little fondness for me; though he was very careful in fulfilling what he regarded as a parent's duties. But he was already past the middle of life, and I was not his only son. My mother had been his second wife, and he was five-and-forty when he married her. He was a firm, unbending, intensely orderly man, in root and stem a banker, but with a flourishing graft of the active landholder, aspiring to county influence: one of those people who are always like themselves from day to day, who are uninfluenced by the weather, and neither know melancholy nor high spirits. I held him in great awe, and appeared more timid and sensitive in his presence than at other times; a circumstance which, perhaps, helped to confirm him in the intention to educate me on a different plan from the prescriptive one with which he had complied in the case of my elder brother, already a tall youth at Eton. My brother was to be his representative and successor; he must go to Eton and Oxford, for the sake of making connections, of course: my father was not a man to under-rate the bearing of Latin satirists or Greek dramatists on the attainment of an aristocratic position. But, intrinsically, he had slight esteem for 'those dead but sceptred spirits';[3] having qualified himself for forming an independent opinion by reading Potter's 'Aeschylus' and dipping into Francis's 'Horace'.[4] To this negative view he added a positive one, derived from a recent connection with mining speculations; namely, that a scientific education was the really useful training for a younger son. Moreover, it was clear that a shy, sensitive boy like me was not fit to encounter the rough experience of a public school. Mr Letherall had said so very decidedly. Mr Letherall was a large man in spectacles, who one day took my small head between his large hands, and pressed it here and there in an exploratory, suspicious manner – then placed each of his great thumbs on my temples, and pushed me a little way from him, and stared at me with glittering spectacles. The contemplation appeared to displease him, for he frowned sternly, and said to my father, drawing his thumbs across my eyebrows –

'The deficiency is there, sir – there; and here,' he added, touching the upper sides of my head, 'here is the excess. That must be brought out, sir, and this must be laid to sleep.'[5]

I was in a state of tremor, partly at the vague idea that I was the object of reprobation, partly in the agitation of my first hatred – hatred of this big, spectacled man, who pulled my head about as if he wanted to buy and cheapen it.

I am not aware how much Mr Letherall had to do with the system afterwards adopted towards me, but it was presently clear that private tutors, natural history, science, and the modern languages, were the appliances by which the defects of my organisation were to be remedied. I was very stupid about machines, so I was to be greatly occupied with them; I had no memory for classification, so it was particularly necessary that I should study systematic zoology and botany; I was hungry for human deeds and human emotions, so I was to be plentifully crammed with the mechanical powers, the elementary bodies, and the phenomena of electricity and magnetism. A better-constituted boy would certainly have profited under my intelligent tutors, with their scientific apparatus; and would, doubtless, have found the phenomena of electricity and magnetism as fascinating as I was, every Thursday, assured they were. As it was, I could have paired off, for ignorance of whatever was taught me, with the worst Latin scholar that was ever turned out of a classical academy. I read Plutarch, and Shakespeare, and Don Quixote by the sly, and supplied myself in that way with wandering thoughts, while my tutor was assuring me that 'an improved man, as distinguished from an ignorant one, was a man who knew the reason why water ran downhill.' I had no desire to be this improved man; I was glad of the running water; I could watch it and listen to it gurgling among the pebbles, and bathing the bright green water-plants, by the hour together. I did not want to know *why* it ran; I had perfect confidence that there were good reasons for what was so very beautiful.

There is no need to dwell on this part of my life. I have said enough to indicate that my nature was of the sensitive, unpractical order, and that it grew up in an uncongenial medium, which could never foster it into happy, healthy development. When I was sixteen I was sent to Geneva to complete my course of education; and the change was a very happy one to me, for the first sight of the Alps, with the setting sun on them, as we descended the Jura, seemed to me like an entrance into heaven; and the three years of my life there were spent in a perpetual sense of exaltation, as if from a draught of delicious wine, at the presence of Nature in all her awful loveliness. You will think, perhaps, that I must have been a poet, from this early sensibility to Nature. But my lot was not so happy as that. A poet pours forth his song and *believes* in the listening ear and answering soul, to which his song will be floated sooner or later. But the poet's sensibility without his voice – the poet's sensibility that finds no vent but in silent tears on the sunny bank, when the noonday light sparkles on the water, or in an inward shudder at the sound of harsh human tones, the sight of a cold human eye – this dumb passion brings with it a fatal solitude of soul in the society of one's fellow-men. My least solitary moments were those in which I pushed off in my boat, at evening, towards the centre of the lake; it seemed to me that the sky, and the glowing mountain-tops, and the wide blue water, surrounded me with a cherishing love such as no human face had shed on me since my mother's love had vanished out of my life. I used to do as Jean Jacques[6] did – lie down in my boat and let it glide where it would, while I looked up at the departing glow leaving one mountain-top after the other, as if the prophet's chariot of fire[7] were passing over them on its way to the home of light. Then, when the white summits were all sad and corpse-like, I had to push homeward, for I was under careful surveillance, and was allowed no late wanderings. This disposition of mine was not favourable to the formation of intimate friendships among the numerous youths of my own age who are always to be found studying at Geneva. Yet I made *one* such friendship; and, singularly enough, it was with a youth whose intellectual tendencies were the very reverse of my own. I shall call him Charles Meunier; his real surname – an English one, for he was of English extraction – having since become celebrated. He was an orphan, who lived on a miserable pittance while he pursued the medical studies for which he had a special genius. Strange! that

with my vague mind, susceptible and unobservant, hating inquiry
and given up to contemplation, I should have been drawn towards
a youth whose strongest passion was science. But the bond was not
an intellectual one; it came from a source that can happily blend
the stupid with the brilliant, the dreamy with the practical: it
came from community of feeling. Charles was poor and ugly,
derided by Genevese *gamins*, and not acceptable in drawing-
rooms. I saw that he was isolated, as I was, though from a different
cause, and, stimulated by a sympathetic resentment, I made timid
advances towards him. It is enough to say that there sprang up as
much comradeship between us as our different habits would
allow; and in Charles's rare holidays we went up the Salève
together, or took the boat to Vevay, while I listened dreamily to
the monologues in which he unfolded his bold conceptions of
future experiment and discovery. I mingled them confusedly in
my thought with glimpses of blue water and delicate floating
cloud, with the notes of birds and the distant glitter of the glacier.
He knew quite well that my mind was half absent, yet he liked to
talk to me in this way; for don't we talk of our hopes and our
projects even to dogs and birds, when they love us? I have
mentioned this one friendship because of its connection with a
strange and terrible scene which I shall have to narrate in my
subsequent life.

   This happier life at Geneva was put an end to by a severe illness,
which is partly a blank to me, partly a time of dimly-remembered
suffering, with the presence of my father by my bed from time to
time. Then came the languid monotony of convalescence, the
days gradually breaking into variety and distinctness as my
strength enabled me to take longer and longer drives. On one of
these more vividly remembered days, my father said to me, as he
sat beside my sofa –

   'When you are quite well enough to travel, Latimer, I shall take
you home with me. The journey will amuse you and do you good,
for I shall go through the Tyrol and Austria, and you will see many
new places. Our neighbours, the Filmores, are come; Alfred will
join us at Basle, and we shall all go together to Vienna, and back
by Prague . . .'

   My father was called away before he had finished his sentence,
and he left my mind resting on the word *Prague*, with a strange
sense that a new and wondrous scene was breaking upon me: a
city under the broad sunshine, that seemed to me as if it were the
summer sunshine of a long-past century arrested in its course –
unrefreshed for ages by the dews of night, or the rushing rain-
cloud; scorching the dusty, weary, time-eaten grandeur of a

people doomed to live on in the stale repetition of memories, like deposed and superannuated kings in their regal gold-inwoven tatters. The city looked so thirsty that the broad river seemed to me a sheet of metal; and the blackened statues, as I passed under their blank gaze, along the unending bridge, with their ancient garments and their saintly crowns, seemed to me the real inhabitants and owners of this place, while the busy, trivial men and women, hurrying to and fro, were a swarm of ephemeral visitants infesting it for a day. It is such grim, stony beings as these, I thought, who are the fathers of ancient faded children, in those tanned time-fretted dwellings that crowd the steep before me; who pay their court in the worn and crumbling pomp of the palace which stretches its monotonous length on the height; who worship wearily in the stifling air of the churches, urged by no fear or hope, but compelled by their doom to be ever old and undying, to live on in the rigidity of habit, as they live on in perpetual mid-day, without the repose of night or the new birth of morning.

A stunning clang of metal suddenly thrilled through me, and I became conscious of the objects in my room again: one of the fire-irons had fallen as Pierre opened the door to bring me my draught. My heart was palpitating violently, and I begged Pierre to leave my draught beside me; I would take it presently.

As soon as I was alone again, I began to ask myself whether I had been sleeping. Was this a dream – this wonderfully distinct vision – minute in its distinctness down to a patch of rainbow light on the pavement, transmitted through a coloured lamp in the shape of a star – of a strange city, quite unfamiliar to my imagination? I had seen no picture of Prague: it lay in my mind as a mere name, with vaguely-remembered historical associations – ill-defined memories of imperial grandeur and religious wars.

Nothing of this sort had ever occurred in my dreaming experience before, for I had often been humiliated because my dreams were only saved from being utterly disjointed and commonplace by the frequent terrors of nightmare. But I could not believe that I had been asleep, for I remembered distinctly the gradual breaking-in of the vision upon me, like the new images in a dissolving view, or the growing distinctness of the landscape as the sun lifts up the veil of the morning mist. And while I was conscious of this incipient vision, I was also conscious that Pierre came to tell my father Mr Filmore was waiting for him, and that my father hurried out of the room. No, it was not a dream; was it – the thought was full of tremulous exultation – was it the poet's nature in me, hitherto only a troubled yearning sensibility, now manifesting itself suddenly as spontaneous creation? Surely it was in this way that Homer saw the plain of Troy, that Dante saw the abodes of the departed, that Milton saw the earthward flight of the Tempter. Was it that my illness had wrought some happy change in my organisation – given a firmer tension to my nerves – carried off some dull obstruction? I had often read of such effects – in works of fiction at least. Nay; in genuine biographies I had read of the subtilising or exalting influence of some diseases on the mental powers. Did not Novalis[8] feel his inspiration intensified under the progress of consumption?

When my mind had dwelt for some time on this blissful idea, it seemed to me that I might perhaps test it by an exertion of my will. The vision had begun when my father was speaking of our going to Prague. I did not for a moment believe it was really a representation of that city; I believed – I hoped it was a picture that my newly-liberated genius had painted in fiery haste, with the colours snatched from lazy memory. Suppose I were to fix my mind on some other place – Venice, for example, which was far more familiar to my imagination than Prague: perhaps the same sort of result would follow. I concentrated my thoughts on Venice; I stimulated my imagination with poetic memories, and strove to feel myself present in Venice, as I had felt myself present in Prague. But in vain. I was only colouring the Canaletto[9] engravings that hung in my old bedroom at home; the picture was a shifting one, my mind wandering uncertainly in search of more vivid images; I could see no accident of form or shadow without conscious labour after the necessary conditions. It was all prosaic effort, not rapt passivity, such as I had experienced half an hour before. I was discouraged; but I remembered that inspiration was fitful.

For several days I was in a state of excited expectation, watching for a recurrence of my new gift. I sent my thoughts ranging over my world of knowledge, in the hope that they would find some object which would send a re-awakening vibration through my slumbering genius. But no; my world remained as dim as ever, and that flash of strange light refused to come again, though I watched for it with palpitating eagerness.

My father accompanied me every day in a drive, and a gradually lengthening walk as my powers of walking increased; and one evening he had agreed to come and fetch me at twelve the next day, that we might go together to select a musical box, and other purchases rigorously demanded of a rich Englishman visiting Geneva. He was one of the most punctual of men and bankers, and I was always nervously anxious to be quite ready for him at the appointed time. But, to my surprise, at a quarter-past twelve he had not appeared. I felt all the impatience of a convalescent who has nothing particular to do, and who has just taken a tonic in the prospect of immediate exercise that would carry off the stimulus.

Unable to sit still and reserve my strength, I walked up and down the room, looking out on the current of the Rhone, just where it leaves the dark-blue lake; but thinking all the while of the possible causes that could detain my father.

Suddenly I was conscious that my father was in the room, but not alone: there were two persons with him. Strange! I had heard no footstep, I had not seen the door open; but I saw my father, and at his right hand our neighbour Mrs Filmore, whom I remembered very well, though I had not seen her for five years. She was a commonplace middle-aged woman, in silk and cashmere; but the lady on the left of my father was not more than twenty, a tall, slim, willowy figure, with luxuriant blond hair, arranged in cunning braids and folds that looked almost too massive for the slight figure and the small-featured, thin-lipped face they crowned. But the face had not a girlish expression: the features were sharp, the pale grey eyes at once acute, restless, and sarcastic. They were fixed on me in half-smiling curiosity, and I felt a painful sensation as if a sharp wind were cutting me. The pale-green dress, and the green leaves that seemed to form a border about her pale blond hair, made me think of a Water-Nixie, – for my mind was full of German lyrics, and this pale, fatal-eyed woman, with the green weeds, looked like a birth from some cold sedgy stream, the daughter of an aged river.

'Well, Latimer, you thought me long', my father said. . . .

But while the last word was in my ears, the whole group vanished, and there was nothing between me and the Chinese painted folding-screen that stood before the door. I was cold and trembling; I could only totter forward and throw myself on the sofa. This strange new power had manifested itself again. . . . But *was* it a power? Might it not rather be a disease – a sort of intermittent delirium, concentrating my energy of brain into moments of unhealthy activity, and leaving my saner hours all the more barren? I felt a dizzy sense of unreality in what my eye rested on; I grasped the bell convulsively, like one trying to free himself from nightmare, and rang it twice. Pierre came with a look of alarm in his face.

'Monsieur ne se trouve pas bien?' he said, anxiously.

'I'm tired of waiting, Pierre', I said, as distinctly and emphatically as I could, like a man determined to be sober in spite of wine; 'I'm afraid something has happened to my father – he's usually so punctual. Run to the Hôtel des Bergues and see if he is there.'

Pierre left the room at once, with a soothing 'Bien, Monsieur'; and I felt the better for this scene of simple, waking prose. Seeking to calm myself still further, I went into my bedroom, adjoining the *salon*, and opened a case of eau-de-Cologne; took out a bottle; went through the process of taking out the cork very neatly, and then rubbed the reviving spirit over my hands and forehead, and under my nostrils, drawing a new delight from the scent because I had procured it by slow details of labour, and by no strange sudden madness. Already I had begun to taste something of the horror that belongs to the lot of a human being whose nature is not adjusted to simple human conditions.

Still enjoying the scent, I returned to the *salon*, but it was not unoccupied, as it had been before I left it. In front of the Chinese folding-screen there was my father, with Mrs Filmore on his right hand, and on his left – the slim blond-haired girl, with the keen face and the keen eyes fixed on me in half-smiling curiosity.

'Well, Latimer, you thought me long', my father said. . . .

I heard no more, felt no more, till I became conscious that I was lying with my head low on the sofa, Pierre and my father by my side. As soon as I was thoroughly revived, my father left the room, and presently returned, saying –

'I've been to tell the ladies how you are, Latimer. They were waiting in the next room. We shall put off our shopping expedition to-day.'

Presently he said, 'That young lady is Bertha Grant, Mrs Filmore's orphan niece. Filmore has adopted her, and she lives with them, so you will have her for a neighbour when we go home – perhaps for a near relation; for there is a tenderness between her and Alfred, I suspect, and I should be gratified by the match, since Filmore means to provide for her in every way as if she were his daughter. It had not occurred to me that you knew nothing about her living with the Filmores.'

He made no further allusion to the fact of my having fainted at the moment of seeing her, and I would not for the world have told him the reason: I shrank from the idea of disclosing to any one what might be regarded as a pitiable peculiarity, most of all from betraying it to my father, who would have suspected my sanity ever after.

I do not mean to dwell with particularity on the details of my experience. I have described these two cases at length, because they had definite, clearly traceable results in my after-lot.

Shortly after this last occurrence – I think the very next day – I began to be aware of a phase in my abnormal sensibility, to which, from the languid and slight nature of my intercourse with others since my illness, I had not been alive before. This was the obtrusion on my mind of the mental process going forward in first one person, and then another, with whom I happened to be in contact: the vagrant, frivolous ideas and emotions of some uninteresting acquaintance – Mrs Filmore, for example – would force themselves on my consciousness like an importunate, ill-played musical instrument, or the loud activity of an imprisoned insect. But this unpleasant sensibility was fitful, and left me moments of rest, when the souls of my companions were once more shut out from me, and I felt a relief such as silence brings to wearied nerves. I might have believed this importunate insight to be merely a diseased activity of the imagination, but that my prevision of incalculable words and actions proved it to have a fixed relation to the mental process in other minds. But this superadded consciousness, wearying and annoying enough when it urged on me the trivial experience of indifferent people, became an intense pain and grief when it seemed to be opening to me the souls of those who were in a close relation to me – when the rational talk, the graceful attentions, the wittily-turned phrases, and the kindly deeds, which used to make the web of their characters, were seen as if thrust asunder by a microscopic vision, that showed all the intermediate frivolities, all the suppressed egoism, all the struggling chaos of puerilities, meanness, vague capricious memories, and indolent make-shift thoughts, from which human words and deeds emerge like leaflets covering a fermenting heap.

At Basle we were joined by my brother Alfred, now a handsome self-confident man of six-and-twenty – a thorough contrast to my fragile, nervous, ineffectual self. I believe I was held to have a sort of half-womanish, half-ghostly beauty; for the portrait-painters, who are thick as weeds at Geneva, had often asked me to sit to them, and I had been the model of a dying minstrel in a fancy picture. But I thoroughly disliked my own *physique*, and nothing but the belief that it was a condition of poetic genius would have reconciled me to it. That brief hope was quite fled, and I saw in my face now nothing but the stamp of a morbid organisation, framed for passive suffering – too feeble for the sublime resistance of poetic production. Alfred, from whom I had been almost constantly separated, and who, in his present stage of character and appearance, came before me as a perfect stranger, was bent on being extremely friendly and brother-like to me. He had the superficial kindness of a good-humoured, self-satisfied nature, that fears no rivalry, and has encountered no contrarieties. I am not sure that my disposition was good enough for me to have been quite free from envy towards him, even if our desires had not clashed, and if I had been in the healthy human condition which admits of generous confidence and charitable construction. There must always have been an antipathy between our natures. As it was, he became in a few weeks an object of intense hatred to me; and when he entered the room, still more when he spoke, it was as if a sensation of grating metal had set my teeth on edge. My diseased consciousness was more intensely and continually occupied with his thoughts and emotions, than with those of any other person who came in my way. I was perpetually exasperated with the petty promptings of his conceit and his love of patronage, with his self-complacent belief in Bertha Grant's passion for him, with his half-pitying contempt for me – seen not in the ordinary indications of intonation and phrase and slight action, which an acute and suspicious mind is on the watch for, but in all their naked skinless complication.

For we were rivals, and our desires clashed, though he was not aware of it. I have said nothing yet of the effect Bertha Grant produced in me on a nearer acquaintance. That effect was chiefly determined by the fact that she made the only exception, among all the human beings about me, to my unhappy gift of insight. About Bertha I was always in a state of uncertainty: I could watch the expression on her face, and speculate on its meaning; I could ask for her opinion with the real interest of ignorance; I could listen for her words and watch for her smile with hope and fear: she had for me the fascination of an unravelled destiny. I say it was this fact that chiefly determined the strong effect she produced on me: for, in the abstract, no womanly character could seem to have less affinity for that of a shrinking, romantic, passionate youth than Bertha's. She was keen, sarcastic, unimaginative, prematurely cynical, remaining critical and unmoved in the most impressive scenes, inclined to dissect all my favourite poems, and especially contemptuous towards the German lyrics which were my pet literature at that time. To this moment I am unable to define my feeling towards her: it was not ordinary boyish admiration, for she was the very opposite, even to the colour of her hair, of the ideal woman who still remained to me the type of loveliness; and she was without that enthusiasm for the great and good, which, even at the moment of her strongest dominion over me, I should have declared to be the highest element of character. But there is no tyranny more complete than that which a self-centred negative nature exercises over a morbidly sensitive nature perpetually craving sympathy and support. The most independent people feel the effect of a man's silence in heightening their value for his opinion – feel an additional triumph in conquering the reverence of a critic habitually captious and satirical: no wonder, then, that an enthusiastic self-distrusting youth should watch and wait before the closed secret of a sarcastic woman's face, as if it were the shrine of the doubtfully benignant deity who ruled his destiny. For a young enthusiast is unable to imagine the total negation in another mind of the emotions which are stirring his own: they may be feeble, latent, inactive, he thinks, but they are there – they may be called forth; sometimes, in moments of happy hallucination, he believes they may be there in all the greater strength because he sees no outward sign of them. And this effect, as I have intimated, was heightened to its utmost intensity in me, because Bertha was the only being who remained for me in the mysterious seclusion of soul that renders such youthful delusion possible. Doubtless there was another sort of fascination at work – that subtle physical attraction which delights in cheating our psychological predictions, and in compelling the men who paint sylphs, to fall in love with some *bonne et brave femme*, heavy-heeled and freckled.

Bertha's behaviour towards me was such as to encourage all my illusions, to heighten my boyish passion, and make me more and more dependent on her smiles. Looking back with my present wretched knowledge, I conclude that her vanity and love of power were intensely gratified by the belief that I had fainted on first seeing her purely from the strong impression her person had produced on me. The most prosaic woman likes to believe herself the object of a violent, a poetic passion; and without a grain of romance in her, Bertha had that spirit of intrigue which gave piquancy to the idea that the brother of the man she meant to marry was dying with love and jealousy for her sake. That she meant to marry my brother, was what at that time I did not believe; for though he was assiduous in his attentions to her, and I knew well enough that both he and my father had made up their minds to this result, there was not yet an understood engagement – there had been no explicit declaration; and Bertha habitually, while she flirted with my brother, and accepted his homage in a way that implied to him a thorough recognition of its intention, made me believe, by the subtlest looks and phrases – feminine nothings which could never be quoted against her – that he was really the object of her secret ridicule; that she thought him, as I did, a coxcomb, whom she would have pleasure in disappointing. Me she openly petted in my brother's presence, as if I were·too young and sickly ever to be thought of as a lover; and that was the view he took of me. But I believe she must inwardly have delighted in the tremors into which she threw me by the coaxing way in which she patted my curls, while she laughed at my quotations. Such caresses were always given in the presence of our friends; for when we were alone together, she affected a much greater distance towards me, and now and then took the opportunity, by words or slight actions, to stimulate my foolish timid hope that she really preferred me. And why should she not follow her inclination? I was not in so advantageous a position as my brother, but I had fortune, I was not a year younger than she was, and she was an heiress, who would soon be of age to decide for herself.

The fluctuations of hope and fear, confined to this one channel, made each day in her presence a delicious torment. There was one deliberate act of hers which especially helped to intoxicate me. When we were at Vienna her twentieth birthday occurred, and as she was very fond of ornaments, we all took the opportunity of the splendid jewellers' shops in that Teutonic Paris to purchase her a birthday present of jewellery. Mine, naturally, was the least expensive; it was an opal ring – the opal was my favourite stone, because it seems to blush and turn pale as if it had a soul. I told Bertha so when I gave it her, and said that it was an emblem of the poetic nature, changing with the changing light of heaven and of woman's eyes. In the evening she appeared elegantly dressed, and wearing conspicuously all the birthday presents except mine. I looked eagerly at her fingers, but saw no opal. I had no opportunity of noticing this to her during the evening; but the next day, when I found her seated near the window alone, after breakfast, I said, 'You scorn to wear my poor opal. I should have remembered that you despised poetic natures, and should have given you coral, or turquoise, or some other opaque unresponsive stone.' 'Do I despise it?' she answered, taking hold of a delicate gold chain which she always wore round her neck and drawing out the end from her bosom with my ring hanging to it; 'it hurts me a little, I can tell you,' she said, with her usual dubious smile, 'to wear it in that secret place; and since your poetical nature is so stupid as to prefer a more public position, I shall not endure the pain any longer.'

She took off the ring from the chain and put it on her finger, smiling still, while the blood rushed to my cheeks, and I could not trust myself to say a word of entreaty that she would keep the ring where it was before.

I was completely fooled by this, and for two days shut myself up in my own room whenever Bertha was absent, that I might intoxicate myself afresh with the thought of this scene and all it implied.

I should mention that during these two months – which seemed a long life to me from the novelty and intensity of the pleasures and pains I underwent – my diseased participation in other people's consciousness continued to torment me; now it was my father, and now my brother, now Mrs Filmore or her husband, and now our German courier, whose stream of thought rushed upon me like a ringing in the ears not to be got rid of, though it allowed my own impulses and ideas to continue their uninterrupted course. It was like a preternaturally heightened sense of hearing, making audible to one a roar of sound where others find perfect stillness. The weariness and disgust of this involuntary intrusion into other souls was counteracted only by my ignorance of Bertha, and my growing passion for her; a passion enormously stimulated, if not produced, by that ignorance. She was my oasis of mystery in the dreary desert of knowledge. It had never allowed my diseased condition to betray itself, or to drive me into any unusual speech or action, except once, when, in a moment of peculiar bitterness against my brother, I had forestalled some words which I knew he was going to utter – a clever observation, which he had prepared beforehand. He had occasionally a slightly-affected hesitation in his speech, and when he paused an instant after the second word, my impatience and jealousy impelled me to continue the speech for him, as if it were something we had both learned by rote. He coloured and looked astonished, as well as annoyed; and the words had no sooner escaped my lips than I felt a shock of alarm lest such an anticipation of words – very far from being words of course, easy to divine – should have betrayed me as an exceptional being, a sort of quiet energumen,[10] whom every one, Bertha above all, would shudder at and avoid. But I magnified, as usual, the impression any word or deed of mine could produce on others; for no one gave any sign of having noticed my interruption as more than a rudeness, to be forgiven me on the score of my feeble nervous condition.

While this superadded consciousness of the actual was almost constant with me, I had never had a recurrence of that distinct prevision which I have described in relation to my first interview with Bertha; and I was waiting with eager curiosity to know whether or not my vision of Prague would prove to have been an instance of the same kind. A few days after the incident of the opal ring, we were paying one of our frequent visits to the Lichtenberg

Palace. I could never look at many pictures in succession; for
pictures, when they are at all powerful, affect me so strongly that
one or two exhaust all my capability of contemplation. This
morning I had been looking at Giorgione's picture of the cruel-
eyed woman, said to be a likeness of Lucrezia Borgia.[11] I had stood
long alone before it, fascinated by the terrible reality of that
cunning, relentless face, till I felt a strange poisoned sensation, as
if I had long been inhaling a fatal odour, and was just beginning
to be conscious of its effects. Perhaps even then I should not have
moved away, if the rest of the party had not returned to this room,
and announced that they were going to the Belvedere Gallery to
settle a bet which had arisen between my brother and Mr Filmore
about a portrait. I followed them dreamily, and was hardly alive to
what occurred till they had all gone up to the gallery, leaving me
below; for I refused to come within sight of another picture that
day. I made my way to the Grand Terrace, since it was agreed that
we should saunter in the gardens when the dispute had been
decided. I had been sitting here a short space, vaguely conscious of
trim gardens, with a city and green hills in the distance, when,
wishing to avoid the proximity of the sentinel, I rose and walked
down the broad stone steps, intending to seat myself farther on in
the gardens. Just as I reached the gravel-walk, I felt an arm slipped
within mine, and a light hand gently pressing my wrist. In the
same instant a strange intoxicating numbness passed over me,
like the continuance or climax of the sensation I was still feeling
from the gaze of Lucrezia Borgia. The gardens, the summer sky,
the consciousness of Bertha's arm being within mine, all
vanished, and I seemed to be suddenly in darkness, out of which
there gradually broke a dim firelight, and I felt myself sitting in
my father's leather chair in the library at home. I knew the
fireplace – the dogs for the wood-fire – the black marble chimney-
piece with the white marble medallion of the dying Cleopatra in
the centre. Intense and hopeless misery was pressing on my soul;
the light became stronger, for Bertha was entering with a candle
in her hand – Bertha, my wife – with cruel eyes, with green jewels
and green leaves on her white ball-dress; every hateful thought
within her present to me. . . . 'Madman, idiot! why don't you kill
yourself, then?' It was a moment of hell. I saw into her pitiless soul
– saw its barren worldliness, its scorching hate – and felt it clothe
me round like an air I was obliged to breathe. She came with her
candle and stood over me with a bitter smile of contempt; I saw
the great emerald brooch on her bosom, a studded serpent with
diamond eyes. I shuddered – I despised this woman with the
barren soul and mean thoughts; but I felt helpless before her, as if

she clutched my bleeding heart, and would clutch it till the last drop of life-blood ebbed away. She was my wife, and we hated each other. Gradually the hearth, the dim library, the candle-light disappeared – seemed to melt away into a background of light, the green serpent with the diamond eyes remaining a dark image on the retina. Then I had a sense of my eyelids quivering, and the living daylight broke in upon me; I saw gardens, and heard voices; I was seated on the steps of the Belvedere Terrace, and my friends were round me.

The tumult of mind into which I was thrown by this hideous vision made me ill for several days, and prolonged our stay at Vienna. I shuddered with horror as the scene recurred to me; and it recurred constantly, with all its minutiæ, as if they had been burnt into my memory; and yet, such is the madness of the human heart under the influence of its immediate desires, I felt a wild hell-braving joy that Bertha was to be mine; for the fulfilment of my former prevision concerning her first appearance before me, left me little hope that this last hideous glimpse of the future was the mere diseased play of my own mind, and had no relation to external realities. One thing alone I looked towards as a possible means of casting doubt on my terrible conviction – the discovery that my vision of Prague had been false – and Prague was the next city on our route.

Meanwhile, I was no sooner in Bertha's society again, than I was as completely under her sway as before. What if I saw into the heart of Bertha, the matured woman – Bertha, my wife? Bertha, the *girl*, was a fascinating secret to me still: I trembled under her touch; I felt the witchery of her presence; I yearned to be assured of her love. The fear of poison is feeble against the sense of thirst. Nay, I was just as jealous of my brother as before – just as much irritated by his small patronising ways; for my pride, my diseased sensibility, were there as they had always been, and winced as inevitably under every offence as my eye winced from an intruding mote. The future, even when brought within the compass of feeling by a vision that made me shudder, had still no more than the force of an idea, compared with the force of present emotion – of my love for Bertha, of my dislike and jealousy towards my brother.

It is an old story,[12] that men sell themselves to the tempter, and sign a bond with their blood, because it is only to take effect at a distant day; then rush on to snatch the cup their souls thirst after with an impulse not the less savage because there is a dark shadow beside them for evermore. There is no short cut, no patent tram-road, to wisdom: after all the centuries of invention, the soul's

path lies through the thorny wilderness[13] which must be still
trodden in solitude, with bleeding feet, with sobs for help, as it was
trodden by them of old time.

My mind speculated eagerly on the means by which I should
become my brother's successful rival, for I was still too timid, in
my ignorance of Bertha's actual feeling, to venture on any step
that would urge from her an avowal of it. I thought I should gain
confidence even for this, if my vision of Prague proved to have
been veracious; and yet, the horror of that certitude! Behind the
slim girl Bertha, whose words and looks I watched for, whose touch
was bliss, there stood continually that Bertha with the fuller form,
the harder eyes, the more rigid mouth, – with the barren selfish
soul laid bare; no longer a fascinating secret, but a measured fact,
urging itself perpetually on my unwilling sight. Are you unable to
give me your sympathy – you who read this? Are you unable to
imagine this double consciousness at work within me, flowing on
like two parallel streams which never mingle their waters and
blend into a common hue? Yet you must have known something
of the presentiments that spring from an insight at war with
passion; and my visions were only like presentiments intensified
to horror. You have known the powerlessness of ideas before the
might of impulse; and my visions, when once they had passed into
memory, were mere ideas – pale shadows that beckoned in vain,
while my hand was grasped by the living and the loved.

In after-days I thought with bitter regret that if I had foreseen
something more or something different – if instead of that hideous
vision which poisoned the passion it could not destroy, or if even
along with it I could have had a foreshadowing of that moment
when I looked on my brother's face for the last time, some
softening influence would have been shed over my feeling towards
him: pride and hatred would surely have been subdued into pity,
and the record of those hidden sins would have been shortened.
But this is one of the vain thoughts with which we men flatter
ourselves. We try to believe that the egoism within us would have
easily been melted, and that it was only the narrowness of our
knowledge which hemmed in our generosity, our awe, our human
piety, and hindered them from submerging our hard indifference
to the sensations and emotions of our fellow. Our tenderness and
self-renunciation seem strong when our egoism has had its day –
when, after our mean striving for a triumph that is to be another's
loss, the triumph comes suddenly, and we shudder at it, because it
is held out by the chill hand of death.

Our arrival in Prague happened at night, and I was glad of this,
for it seemed like a deferring of a terribly decisive moment, to be

in the city for hours without seeing it. As we were not to remain long in Prague, but to go on speedily to Dresden, it was proposed that we should drive out the next morning and take a general view of the place, as well as visit some of its specially interesting spots, before the heat became oppressive – for we were in August, and the season was hot and dry. But it happened that the ladies were rather late at their morning toilet, and to my father's politely-repressed but perceptible annoyance, we were not in the carriage till the morning was far advanced. I thought with a sense of relief, as we entered the Jews' quarter, where we were to visit the old synagogue, that we should be kept in this flat, shut-up part of the city, until we should all be too tired and too warm to go farther, and so we should return without seeing more than the streets through which we had already passed. That would give me another day's suspense – suspense, the only form in which a fearful spirit knows the solace of hope. But, as I stood under the blackened, groined arches of that old synagogue, made dimly visible by the seven thin candles in the sacred lamp, while our Jewish cicerone reached down the Book of the Law, and read to us in its ancient tongue, – I felt a shuddering impression that this strange building, with its shrunken lights, this surviving withered remnant of medieval Judaism, was of a piece with my vision. Those darkened dusty Christian saints, with their loftier arches and their larger candles, needed the consolatory scorn with which they might point to a more shrivelled death-in-life than their own.

As I expected, when we left the Jews' quarter the elders of our party wished to return to the hotel. But now, instead of rejoicing in this, as I had done beforehand, I felt a sudden overpowering impulse to go on at once to the bridge, and put an end to the suspense I had been wishing to protract. I declared, with unusual decision, that I would get out of the carriage and walk on alone; they might return without me. My father, thinking this merely a sample of my usual 'poetic nonsense', objected that I should only do myself harm by walking in the heat; but when I persisted, he said angrily that I might follow my own absurd devices, but that Schmidt (our courier) must go with me. I assented to this, and set off with Schmidt towards the bridge. I had no sooner passed from under the archway of the grand old gate leading on to the bridge, than a trembling seized me, and I turned cold under the mid-day sun; yet I went on; I was in search of something – a small detail which I remembered with special intensity as part of my vision. There it was – the patch of rainbow light on the pavement transmitted through a lamp in the shape of a star.

## Chapter II

Before the autumn was at an end, and while the brown leaves still stood thick on the beeches in our park, my brother and Bertha were engaged to each other, and it was understood that their marriage was to take place early in the next spring. In spite of the certainty I had felt from that moment on the bridge at Prague, that Bertha would one day be my wife, my constitutional timidity and distrust had continued to benumb me, and the words in which I had sometimes premeditated a confession of my love, had died away unuttered. The same conflict had gone on within me as before – the longing for an assurance of love from Bertha's lips, the dread lest a word of contempt and denial should fall upon me like a corrosive acid. What was the conviction of a distant necessity to me? I trembled under a present glance, I hungered after a present joy, I was clogged and chilled by a present fear. And so the days passed on: I witnessed Bertha's engagement and heard her marriage discussed as if I were under a conscious nightmare – knowing it was a dream that would vanish, but feeling stifled under the grasp of hard-clutching fingers.

When I was not in Bertha's presence – and I was with her very often, for she continued to treat me with a playful patronage that wakened no jealousy in my brother – I spent my time chiefly in wandering, in strolling, or taking long rides while the daylight lasted, and then shutting myself up with my unread books; for books had lost the power of chaining my attention. My self-consciousness was heightened to that pitch of intensity in which our own emotions take the form of a drama which urges itself imperatively on our contemplation, and we begin to weep, less under the sense of our suffering than at the thought of it. I felt a sort of pitying anguish over the pathos of my own lot: the lot of being finely organised for pain, but with hardly any fibres that responded to pleasure – to whom the idea of future evil robbed the present of its joy, and for whom the idea of future good did not still the uneasiness of a present yearning or a present dread. I went dumbly through that stage of the poet's suffering, in which he feels the delicious pang of utterance, and makes an image of his sorrows.

I was left entirely without remonstrance concerning this dreamy wayward life: I knew my father's thought about me: 'That lad will never be good for anything in life: he may waste his years in an insignificant way on the income that falls to him: I shall not trouble myself about a career for him.'

One mild morning in the beginning of November, it happened

that I was standing outside the portico patting lazy old Caesar, a Newfoundland almost blind with age, the only dog that ever took any notice of me – for the very dogs shunned me, and fawned on the happier people about me – when the groom brought up my brother's horse which was to carry him to the hunt, and my brother himself appeared at the door, florid, broad-chested, and self-complacent, feeling what a good-natured fellow he was not to behave insolently to us all on the strength of his great advantages.

'Latimer, old boy,' he said to me in a tone of compassionate cordiality, 'what a pity it is you don't have a run with the hounds now and then! The finest thing in the world for low spirits!'

'Low spirits!' I thought bitterly, as he rode away; 'that is the sort of phrase with which coarse, narrow natures like yours think to describe experience of which you can know no more than your horse knows. It is to such as you that the good of this world falls: ready dulness, healthy selfishness, good-tempered conceit – these are the keys to happiness.'

The quick thought came, that my selfishness was even stronger than his – it was only a suffering selfishness instead of an enjoying one. But then, again, my exasperating insight into Alfred's self-complacent soul, his freedom from all the doubts and fears, the unsatisfied yearnings, the exquisite tortures of sensitiveness, that had made the web of my life, seemed to absolve me from all bonds towards him. This man needed no pity, no love; those fine influences would have been as little felt by him as the delicate white mist is felt by the rock it caresses. There was no evil in store for *him*: if he was not to marry Bertha, it would be because he had found a lot pleasanter to himself.

Mr Filmore's house lay not more than half a mile beyond our own gates, and whenever I knew my brother was gone in another direction, I went there for the chance of finding Bertha at home. Later on in the day I walked thither. By a rare accident she was alone, and we walked out in the grounds together, for she seldom went on foot beyond the trimly-swept gravel-walks. I remember what a beautiful sylph she looked to me as the low November sun shone on her blond hair, and she tripped along teasing me with her usual light banter, to which I listened half fondly, half moodily; it was all the sign Bertha's mysterious inner self ever made to me. To-day perhaps the moodiness predominated, for I had not yet shaken off the access of jealous hate which my brother had raised in me by his parting patronage. Suddenly I interrupted and startled her by saying, almost fiercely, 'Bertha, how can you love Alfred?'

She looked at me with surprise for a moment, but soon her light smile came again, and she answered sarcastically, 'Why do you suppose I love him?'

'How can you ask that, Bertha?'

'What! your wisdom thinks I must love the man I'm going to marry? The most unpleasant thing in the world. I should quarrel with him; I should be jealous of him; our *ménage* would be conducted in a very ill-bred manner. A little quiet contempt contributes greatly to the elegance of life.'

'Bertha, that is not your real feeling. Why do you delight in trying to deceive me by inventing such cynical speeches?'

'I need never take the trouble of invention in order to deceive you, my small Tasso'[14] – (that was the mocking name she usually gave me). 'The easiest way to deceive a poet is to tell him the truth.'

She was testing the validity of her epigram in a daring way, and for a moment the shadow of my vision – the Bertha whose soul was no secret to me – passed between me and the radiant girl, the playful sylph whose feelings were a fascinating mystery. I suppose I must have shuddered, or betrayed in some other way my momentary chill of horror.

'Tasso!' she said, seizing my wrist, and peeping round into my face, 'are you really beginning to discern what a heartless girl I am? Why, you are not half the poet I thought you were; you are actually capable of believing the truth about me.'

The shadow passed from between us, and was no longer the object nearest to me. The girl whose light fingers grasped me, whose elfish charming face looked into mine – who, I thought, was betraying an interest in my feelings that she would not have directly avowed, – this warm-breathing presence again possessed my senses and imagination like a returning siren melody which had been overpowered for an instant by the roar of threatening waves. It was a moment as delicious to me as the waking up to a consciousness of youth after a dream of middle age. I forgot everything but my passion, and said with swimming eyes –

'Bertha, shall you love me when we are first married? I wouldn't mind if you really loved me only for a little while.'

Her look of astonishment, as she loosed my hand and started away from me, recalled me to a sense of my strange, my criminal indiscretion.

'Forgive me,' I said, hurriedly, as soon as I could speak again; 'I did not know what I was saying.'

'Ah, Tasso's mad fit has come on, I see', she answered quietly, for she had recovered herself sooner than I had. 'Let him go home and keep his head cool. I must go in, for the sun is setting.'

I left her – full of indignation against myself. I had let slip words which, if she reflected on them, might rouse in her a suspicion of my abnormal mental condition – a suspicion which of all things I dreaded. And besides that, I was ashamed of the apparent baseness I had committed in uttering them to my brother's betrothed wife. I wandered home slowly, entering our park through a private gate instead of by the lodges. As I approached the house, I saw a man dashing off at full speed from the stable-yard across the park. Had any accident happened at home? No; perhaps it was only one of my father's peremptory business errands that required this headlong haste. Nevertheless I quickened my pace without any distinct motive, and was soon at the house. I will not dwell on the scene I found there. My brother was dead – had been pitched from his horse, and killed on the spot by a concussion of the brain.

I went up to the room where he lay, and where my father was seated beside him with a look of rigid despair. I had shunned my father more than any one since our return home, for the radical antipathy between our natures made my insight into his inner self a constant affliction to me. But now, as I went up to him, and stood beside him in sad silence, I felt the presence of a new element that blended us as we had never been blent before. My father had been one of the most successful men in the money-getting world: he had had no sentimental sufferings, no illness. The heaviest trouble that had befallen him was the death of his first wife. But he married my mother soon after; and I remember he seemed exactly the same, to my keen childish observation, the week after her death as before. But now, at last, a sorrow had come – the sorrow of old age, which suffers the more from the crushing of its pride and its hopes, in proportion as the pride and hope are narrow and prosaic. His son was to have been married soon – would probably have stood for the borough at the next election. That son's existence was the best motive that could be alleged for making new purchases of land every year to round off the estate. It is a dreary thing to live on doing the same things year after year, without knowing why we do them. Perhaps the tragedy of disappointed youth and passion is less piteous than the tragedy of disappointed age and worldliness.

As I saw into the desolation of my father's heart, I felt a movement of deep pity towards him, which was the beginning of a new affection – an affection that grew and strengthened in spite of the strange bitterness with which he regarded me in the first month or two after my brother's death. If it had not been for the softening influence of my compassion for him – the first deep compassion I had ever felt – I should have been stung by the perception that my father transferred the inheritance of an eldest son to me with a mortified sense that fate had compelled him to the unwelcome course of caring for me as an important being. It was only in spite of himself that he began to think of me with anxious regard. There is hardly any neglected child for whom death has made vacant a more favoured place, who will not understand what I mean.

Gradually, however, my new deference to his wishes, the effect of that patience which was born of my pity for him, won upon his affection, and he began to please himself with the endeavour to make me fill my brother's place as fully as my feebler personality would admit. I saw that the prospect which by-and-by presented itself of my becoming Bertha's husband was welcome to him, and he even contemplated in my case what he had not intended in my brother's – that his son and daughter-in-law should make one household with him. My softened feeling towards my father made this the happiest time I had known since childhood; – these last months in which I retained the delicious illusion of loving Bertha, of longing and doubting and hoping that she might love me. She behaved with a certain new consciousness and distance towards me after my brother's death; and I too was under a double constraint – that of delicacy towards my brother's memory, and of anxiety as to the impression my abrupt words had left on her mind. But the additional screen this mutual reserve erected between us only brought me more completely under her power: no matter how empty the adytum, so that the veil be thick enough. So absolute is our soul's need of something hidden and uncertain for the maintenance of that doubt and hope and effort which are the breath of its life, that if the whole future were laid bare to us beyond to-day, the interest of all mankind would be bent on the hours that lie between; we should pant after the uncertainties of our one morning and our one afternoon; we should rush fiercely to the Exchange for our last possibility of speculation, of success, of disappointment; we should have a glut of political prophets foretelling a crisis or a no-crisis within the only twenty-four hours left open to prophecy. Conceive the condition of the human mind if all propositions whatsoever were self-evident except one, which was to become self-evident at the close of a summer's day, but in the meantime might be the subject of question, of hypothesis, of debate. Art and philosophy, literature and science, would fasten like bees on that one proposition which had the honey of probability in it, and be the more eager because their enjoyment would end with sunset. Our impulses, our spiritual activities, no more adjust themselves to the idea of their future nullity, than the beating of our heart, or the irritability of our muscles.

Bertha, the slim, fair-haired girl, whose present thoughts and emotions were an enigma to me amidst the fatiguing obviousness of the other minds around me, was as absorbing to me as a single unknown to-day – as a single hypothetic proposition to remain problematic till sunset; and all the cramped, hemmed-in belief and disbelief, trust and distrust, of my nature, welled out in this one narrow channel.

And she made me believe that she loved me. Without ever quitting her tone of *badinage* and playful superiority, she intoxicated me with the sense that I was necessary to her, that she was never at ease unless I was near her, submitting to her playful tyranny. It costs a woman so little effort to besot us in this way! A half-repressed word, a moment's unexpected silence, even an easy fit of petulance on our account, will serve us as *hashish* for a long while. Out of the subtlest web of scarcely perceptible signs, she set me weaving the fancy that she had always unconsciously loved me better than Alfred, but that, with the ignorant fluttered sensibility of a young girl, she had been imposed on by the charm that lay for her in the distinction of being admired and chosen by a man who made so brilliant a figure in the world as my brother. She satirised herself in a very graceful way for her vanity and ambition. What was it to me that I had the light of my wretched prevision on the fact that now it was I who possessed at least all but the personal part of my brother's advantages? Our sweet illusions are half of them conscious illusions, like effects of colour that we know to be made up of tinsel, broken glass, and rags.

We were married eighteen months after Alfred's death, one cold, clear morning in April, when there came hail and sunshine both together; and Bertha, in her white silk and pale-green leaves, and the pale hues of her hair and face, looked like the spirit of the morning. My father was happier than he had thought of being again: my marriage, he felt sure, would complete the desirable modification of my character, and make me practical and worldly enough to take my place in society among sane men. For he delighted in Bertha's tact and acuteness, and felt sure she would be mistress of me, and make me what she chose: I was only twenty-one, and madly in love with her. Poor father! He kept that hope a little while after our first year of marriage, and it was not quite extinct when paralysis came and saved him from utter disappointment.

I shall hurry through the rest of my story, not dwelling so much as I have hitherto done on my inward experience. When people are well known to each other, they talk rather of what befalls them externally, leaving their feelings and sentiments to be inferred.

We lived in a round of visits for some time after our return home, giving splendid dinner-parties, and making a sensation in our neighbourhood by the new lustre of our equipage, for my father had reserved this display of his increased wealth for the period of his son's marriage; and we gave our acquaintances liberal opportunity for remarking that it was a pity I made so poor a figure as an heir and a bridegroom. The nervous fatigue of this existence, the insincerities and platitudes which I had to live through twice over – through my inner and outward sense – would have been maddening to me, if I had not had that sort of intoxicated callousness which came from the delights of a first passion. A bride and bridegroom, surrounded by all the appliances of wealth, hurried through the day by the whirl of society, filling their solitary moments with hastily-snatched caresses, are prepared for their future life together as the novice is prepared for the cloister – by experiencing its utmost contrast.

Through all these crowded excited months, Bertha's inward self remained shrouded from me, and I still read her thoughts only through the language of her lips and demeanour: I had still the human interest of wondering whether what I did and said pleased her, of longing to hear a word of affection, of giving a delicious exaggeration of meaning to her smile. But I was conscious of a growing difference in her manner towards me; sometimes strong enough to be called haughty coldness, cutting and chilling me as the hail had done that came across the sunshine on our marriage morning;[15] sometimes only perceptible in the dexterous avoidance of a *tête-à-tête* walk or dinner to which I had been looking forward. I had been deeply pained by this – had even felt a sort of crushing of the heart, from the sense that my brief day of happiness was near its setting; but still I remained dependent on Bertha, eager for the last rays of a bliss that would soon be gone for ever, hoping and watching for some after-glow more beautiful from the impending night.

I remember – how should I not remember? – the time when that dependence and hope utterly left me, when the sadness I had felt in Bertha's growing estrangement became a joy that I looked back upon with longing, as a man might look back on the last pains in a paralysed limb. It was just after the close of my father's last illness, which had necessarily withdrawn us from society and thrown us more upon each other. It was the evening of my father's death. On that evening the veil which had shrouded

Bertha's soul from me – had made me find in her alone among my fellow-beings the blessed possibility of mystery, and doubt, and expectation – was first withdrawn. Perhaps it was the first day since the beginning of my passion for her, in which that passion was completely neutralised by the presence of an absorbing feeling of another kind. I had been watching by my father's deathbed: I had been witnessing the last fitful yearning glance his soul had cast back on the spent inheritance of life – the last faint consciousness of love he had gathered from the pressure of my hand. What are all our personal loves when we have been sharing in that supreme agony? In the first moments when we come away from the presence of death, every other relation to the living is merged, to our feeling, in the great relation of a common nature and a common destiny.

In that state of mind I joined Bertha in her private sitting-room. She was seated in a leaning posture on a settee, with her back towards the door; the great rich coils of her pale blond hair surmounting her small neck, visible above the back of the settee. I remember, as I closed the door behind me, a cold tremulousness seizing me, and a vague sense of being hated and lonely – vague and strong, like a presentiment. I know how I looked at that moment, for I saw myself in Bertha's thought as she lifted her cutting grey eyes, and looked at me: a miserable ghost-seer, surrounded by phantoms in the noonday, trembling under a breeze when the leaves were still, without appetite for the common objects of human desire, but pining after the moonbeams. We were front to front with each other, and judged each other. The terrible moment of complete illumination had come to me, and I saw that the darkness had hidden no landscape from me, but only a blank prosaic wall: from that evening forth, through the sickening years which followed, I saw all round the narrow room of this woman's soul – saw petty artifice and mere negation where I had delighted to believe in coy sensibilities and in wit at war with latent feeling – saw the light floating vanities of the girl defining themselves into the systematic coquetry, the scheming selfishness, of the woman – saw repulsion and antipathy harden into cruel hatred, giving pain only for the sake of wreaking itself.

For Bertha too, after her kind, felt the bitterness of disillusion. She had believed that my wild poet's passion for her would make me her slave; and that, being her slave, I should execute her will in all things. With the essential shallowness of a negative, unimaginative nature, she was unable to conceive the fact that sensibilities were anything else than weaknesses. She had thought my weaknesses would put me in her power, and she found them unmanageable forces. Our positions were reversed. Before marriage she had completely mastered my imagination, for she was a secret to me; and I created the unknown thought before which I trembled as if it were hers. But now that her soul was laid open to me, now that I was compelled to share the privacy of her motives, to follow all the petty devices that preceded her words and acts, she found herself powerless with me, except to produce in me the chill shudder of repulsion – powerless, because I could be acted on by no lever within her reach. I was dead to worldly ambitions, to social vanities, to all the incentives within the compass of her narrow imagination, and I lived under influences utterly invisible to her.

She was really pitiable to have such a husband, and so all the world thought. A graceful, brilliant woman, like Bertha, who smiled on morning callers, made a figure in ball-rooms, and was capable of that light repartee which, from such a woman, is accepted as wit, was secure of carrying off all sympathy from a husband who was sickly, abstracted, and, as some suspected, crack-brained. Even the servants in our house gave her the balance of their regard and pity. For there were no audible quarrels between us; our alienation, our repulsion from each other, lay within the silence of our own hearts; and if the mistress went out a great deal, and seemed to dislike the master's society, was it not natural, poor thing? The master was odd. I was kind and just to my dependents, but I excited in them a shrinking, half-contemptuous pity; for this class of men and women are but slightly determined in their estimate of others by general considerations, or even experience, of character. They judge of persons as they judge of coins, and value those who pass current at a high rate.

After a time I interfered so little with Bertha's habits, that it might seem wonderful how her hatred towards me could grow so intense and active as it did. But she had begun to suspect, by some involuntary betrayals of mine, that there was an abnormal power of penetration in me – that fitfully, at least, I was strangely cognisant of her thoughts and intentions, and she began to be haunted by a terror of me, which alternated every now and then with defiance. She meditated continually how the incubus could be shaken off her life – how she could be freed from this hateful bond to a being whom she at once despised as an imbecile, and dreaded as an inquisitor. For a long while she lived in the hope that my evident wretchedness would drive me to the commission of suicide; but suicide was not in my nature. I was too completely swayed by the sense that I was in the grasp of unknown forces, to believe in my power of self-release. Towards my own destiny I had become entirely passive; for my one ardent desire had spent itself, and impulse no longer predominated over knowledge. For this reason I never thought of taking any steps towards a complete separation, which would have made our alienation evident to the world. Why should I rush for help to a new course, when I was only suffering from the consequences of a deed which had been the act of my intensest will? That would have been the logic of one who had desires to gratify, and I had no desires. But Bertha and I lived more and more aloof from each other. The rich find it easy to live married and apart.

That course of our life which I have indicated in a few sentences filled the space of years. So much misery – so slow and hideous a growth of hatred and sin, may be compressed into a sentence! And men judge of each other's lives through this summary medium. They epitomise the experience of their fellow-mortal, and pronounce judgment on him in neat syntax, and feel themselves wise and virtuous – conquerors over the temptations they define in well-selected predicates. Seven years of wretchedness glide glibly over the lips of the man who has never counted them out in moments of chill disappointment, of head and heart throbbings, of dread and vain wrestling, of remorse and despair. We learn *words* by rote, but not their meaning; *that* must be paid for with our life-blood, and printed in the subtle fibres of our nerves.

But I will hasten to finish my story. Brevity is justified at once to those who readily understand, and to those who will never understand.

Some years after my father's death, I was sitting by the dim firelight in my library one January evening – sitting in the leather chair that used to be my father's – when Bertha appeared at the door, with a candle in her hand, and advanced towards me. I knew the ball-dress she had on – the white ball-dress, with the green jewels, shone upon by the light of the wax candle which lit up the medallion of the dying Cleopatra on the mantelpiece. Why did she come to me before going out? I had not seen her in the library, which was my habitual place, for months. Why did she stand before me with the candle in her hand, with her cruel contemptuous eyes fixed on me, and the glittering serpent, like a familiar demon, on her breast? For a moment I thought this fulfilment of my vision at Vienna marked some dreadful crisis in my fate, but I saw nothing in Bertha's mind, as she stood before me, except scorn for the look of overwhelming misery with which

I sat before her. . . . 'Fool, idiot, why don't you kill yourself, then?' – that was her thought. But at length her thoughts reverted to her errand, and she spoke aloud. The apparently indifferent nature of the errand seemed to make a ridiculous anticlimax to my prevision and my agitation.

'I have had to hire a new maid. Fletcher is going to be married, and she wants me to ask you to let her husband have the public-house and farm at Molton. I wish him to have it. You must give the promise now, because Fletcher is going to-morrow morning – and quickly, because I'm in a hurry.'

'Very well; you may promise her', I said, indifferently, and Bertha swept out of the library again.

I always shrank from the sight of a new person, and all the more when it was a person whose mental life was likely to weary my reluctant insight with wordly ignorant trivialities. But I shrank especially from the sight of this new maid, because her advent had been announced to me at a moment to which I could not cease to attach some fatality: I had a vague dread that I should find her mixed up with the dreary drama of my life – that some new sickening vision would reveal her to me as an evil genius. When at last I did unavoidably meet her, the vague dread was changed into definite disgust. She was a tall, wiry, dark-eyed woman, this Mrs Archer, with a face handsome enough to give her coarse hard nature the odious finish of bold, self-confident coquetry. That was enough to make me avoid her, quite apart from the contemptuous feeling with which she contemplated me. I seldom saw her; but I perceived that she rapidly became a favourite with her mistress, and, after the lapse of eight or nine months, I began to be aware that there had arisen in Bertha's mind towards this woman a mingled feeling of fear and dependence, and that this feeling was associated with ill-defined images of candle-light scenes in her dressing-room, and the locking-up of something in Bertha's cabinet. My interviews with my wife had become so brief and so rarely solitary, that I had no opportunity of perceiving these images in her mind with more definiteness. The recollections of the past become contracted in the rapidity of thought till they sometimes bear hardly a more distinct resemblance to the external reality than the forms of an oriental alphabet to the objects that suggested them.

Besides, for the last year or more a modification had been going forward in my mental condition, and was growing more and more marked. My insight into the minds of those around me was becoming dimmer and more fitful, and the ideas that crowded my double consciousness became less and less dependent on any personal contact. All that was personal in me seemed to be suffering a gradual death, so that I was losing the organ through which the personal agitations and projects of others could affect me. But along with this relief from wearisome insight, there was a new development of what I concluded – as I have since found rightly – to be a prevision of external scenes. It was as if the relation between me and my fellow-men was more and more deadened, and my relation to what we call the inanimate was quickened into new life. The more I lived apart from society, and in proportion as my wretchedness subsided from the violent throb of agonised passion into the dulness of habitual pain, the more frequent and vivid became such visions as that I had had of Prague – of strange cities, of sandy plains, of gigantic ruins, of midnight skies with strange bright constellations, of mountain-passes, of grassy nooks flecked with the afternoon sunshine through the boughs: I was in the midst of such scenes, and in all of them one presence seemed to weigh on me in all these mighty shapes – the presence of something unknown and pitiless. For continual suffering had annihilated religious faith within me: to the utterly miserable – the unloving and the unloved – there is no religion possible, no worship but a worship of devils. And beyond all these, and continually recurring, was the vision of my death – the pangs, the suffocation, the last struggle, when life would be grasped at in vain.

Things were in this state near the end of the seventh year. I had become entirely free from insight, from my abnormal cognisance of any other consciousness than my own, and instead of intruding involuntarily into the world of other minds, was living continually in my own solitary future. Bertha was aware that I was greatly changed. To my surprise she had of late seemed to seek opportunities of remaining in my society, and had cultivated that kind of distant yet familiar talk which is customary between a husband and wife who live in polite and irrevocable alienation. I bore this with languid submission, and without feeling enough interest in her motives to be roused into keen observation; yet I could not help perceiving something triumphant and excited in her carriage and the expression of her face – something too subtle to express itself in words or tones, but giving one the idea that she lived in a state of expectation or hopeful suspense. My chief feeling was satisfaction that her inner self was once more shut out from me; and I almost revelled for the moment in the absent melancholy that made me answer her at cross purposes, and betray utter ignorance of what she had been saying. I remember well the look and the smile with which she one day said, after a mistake of this kind on my part: 'I used to think you were a clairvoyant, and that was the reason why you were so bitter against other clairvoyants, wanting to keep your monopoly; but I see now you have become rather duller than the rest of the world.'

I said nothing in reply. It occurred to me that her recent obtrusion of herself upon me might have been prompted by the wish to test my power of detecting some of her secrets; but I let the thought drop again at once: her motives and her deeds had no interest for me, and whatever pleasures she might be seeking, I had no wish to balk her. There was still pity in my soul for every living thing, and Bertha was living – was surrounded with possibilities of misery.

Just at this time there occurred an event which roused me somewhat from my inertia, and gave me an interest in the passing moment that I had thought impossible for me. It was a visit from Charles Meunier, who had written me word that he was coming to England for relaxation from too strenuous labour, and would like to see me. Meunier had now a European reputation; but his letter to me expressed that keen remembrance of an early regard, an early debt of sympathy, which is inseparable from nobility of character: and I too felt as if his presence would be to me like a transient resurrection into a happier pre-existence.

He came, and as far as possible, I renewed our old pleasure of making *tête-à-tête* excursions, though, instead of mountains and glaciers and the wide blue lake, we had to content ourselves with mere slopes and ponds and artificial plantations. The years had changed us both, but with what different result! Meunier was now a brilliant figure in society, to whom elegant women pretended to listen, and whose acquaintance was boasted of by noblemen ambitious of brains. He repressed with the utmost delicacy all betrayal of the shock which I am sure he must have received from our meeting, or of a desire to penetrate into my condition and circumstances, and sought by the utmost exertion of his charming social powers to make our reunion agreeable. Bertha was much struck by the unexpected fascinations of a visitor whom she had expected to find presentable only on the score of his celebrity, and put forth all her coquetries and accomplishments. Apparently she succeeded in attracting his admiration, for his manner towards her was attentive and flattering. The effect of his presence on me was so benignant, especially in those renewals of our old *tête-à-tête* wanderings, when he poured forth to me wonderful narratives of his professional experience, that more than once, when his talk turned on the psychological relations of disease, the thought crossed my mind that, if his stay with me were long enough, I might possibly bring myself to tell this man the secrets of my lot. Might there not lie some remedy for *me*, too, in his science? Might there not at least lie some comprehension and sympathy ready for me in his large and susceptible mind? But the thought only flickered feebly now and then, and died out before it could become a wish. The horror I had of again breaking in on the privacy of another soul, made me, by an irrational instinct, draw the shroud of concealment more closely around my own, as we automatically perform the gesture we feel to be wanting in another.

When Meunier's visit was approaching its conclusion, there happened an event which caused some excitement in our household, owing to the surprisingly strong effect it appeared to produce on Bertha – on Bertha, the self-possessed, who usually seemed inaccessible to feminine agitations, and did even her hate in a self-restrained hygienic manner. This event was the sudden severe illness of her maid, Mrs Archer. I have reserved to this moment the mention of a circumstance which had forced itself on my notice shortly before Meunier's arrival, namely, that there had been some quarrel between Bertha and this maid, apparently during a visit to a distant family, in which she had accompanied her mistress. I had overheard Archer speaking in a tone of bitter insolence, which I should have thought an adequate reason for immediate dismissal. No dismissal followed; on the contrary, Bertha seemed to be silently putting up with personal inconveniences from the exhibitions of this woman's temper. I was the more astonished to observe that her illness seemed a cause of strong solicitude to Bertha; that she was at the bedside night and day, and would allow no one else to officiate as head-nurse. It happened that our family doctor was out on a holiday, an accident which made Meunier's presence in the house doubly welcome, and he apparently entered into the case with an interest which seemed so much stronger than the ordinary professional feeling, that one day when he had fallen into a long fit of silence after visiting her, I said to him –

'Is this a very peculiar case of disease, Meunier?'

'No', he answered, 'it is an attack of peritonitis, which will be fatal, but which does not differ physically from many other cases that have come under my observation. But I'll tell you what I have on my mind. I want to make an experiment on this woman, if you will give me permission. It can do her no harm – will give her no pain – for I shall not make it until life is extinct to all purposes of sensation. I want to try the effect of transfusing blood into her arteries after the heart has ceased to beat for some minutes. I have tried the experiment again and again with animals that have died of this disease, with astounding results, and I want to try it on a human subject. I have the small tubes necessary, in a case I have with me, and the rest of the apparatus could be prepared readily. I should use my own blood – take it from my own arm. This woman won't live through the night, I'm convinced, and I want you to promise me your assistance in making the experiment. I can't do without another hand, but it would perhaps not be well to call in a medical assistant from among your provincial doctors. A disagreeable foolish version of the thing might get abroad.'

'Have you spoken to my wife on the subject?' I said, 'because she appears to be peculiarly sensitive about this woman: she has been a favourite maid.'

'To tell you the truth,' said Meunier, 'I don't want her to know about it. There are always insuperable difficulties with women in these matters, and the effect on the supposed dead body may be startling. You and I will sit up together, and be in readiness. When certain symptoms appear I shall take you in, and at the right moment we must manage to get every one else out of the room.'

I need not give our farther conversation on the subject. He entered very fully into the details, and overcame my repulsion from them, by exciting in me a mingled awe and curiosity concerning the possible results of his experiment.

We prepared everything, and he instructed me in my part as assistant. He had not told Bertha of his absolute conviction that Archer would not survive through the night, and endeavoured to persuade her to leave the patient and take a night's rest. But she was obstinate, suspecting the fact that death was at hand, and supposing that he wished merely to save her nerves. She refused to leave the sick-room. Meunier and I sat up together in the library, he making frequent visits to the sick-room, and returning with the information that the case was taking precisely the course he expected. Once he said to me, 'Can you imagine any cause of ill feeling this woman has against her mistress, who is so devoted to her?'

'I think there was some misunderstanding between them before her illness. Why do you ask?'

'Because I have observed for the last five or six hours – since, I fancy, she has lost all hope of recovery – there seems a strange prompting in her to say something which pain and failing strength forbid her to utter; and there is a look of hideous meaning in her eyes, which she turns continually towards her mistress. In this disease the mind often remains singularly clear to the last.'

'I am not surprised at an indication of malevolent feeling in her', I said. 'She is a woman who has always inspired me with distrust and dislike, but she managed to insinuate herself into her mistress's favour.' He was silent after this, looking at the fire with an air of absorption, till he went up-stairs again. He stayed away longer than usual, and on returning, said to me quietly, 'Come now.'

I followed him to the chamber where death was hovering. The dark hangings of the large bed made a background that gave a strong relief to Bertha's pale face as I entered. She started forward as she saw me enter, and then looked at Meunier with an expression of angry inquiry; but he lifted up his hands as if to impose silence, while he fixed his glance on the dying woman and felt her pulse. The face was pinched and ghastly, a cold perspiration was on the forehead, and the eyelids were lowered so as almost to conceal the large dark eyes. After a minute or two, Meunier walked round to the other side of the bed where Bertha stood, and with his usual air of gentle politeness towards her begged her to leave the patient under our care – everything should be done for her – she was no longer in a state to be conscious of an affectionate presence. Bertha was hesistating, apparently almost willing to believe his assurance and to comply. She looked round at the ghastly dying face, as if to read the confirmation of that assurance, when for a moment the lowered eyelids were raised again, and it seemed as if the eyes were looking towards Bertha, but blankly. A shudder passed through Bertha's frame, and she returned to her station near the pillow, tacitly implying that she would not leave the room.

The eyelids were lifted no more. Once I looked at Bertha as she watched the face of the dying one. She wore a rich *peignoir*, and her blond hair was half covered by a lace cap: in her attire she was, as always, an elegant woman, fit to figure in a picture of modern aristocratic life: but I asked myself how that face of hers could ever have seemed to me the face of a woman born of woman, with memories of childhood, capable of pain, needing to be fondled? The features at that moment seemed so preternaturally sharp, the eyes were so hard and eager – she looked like a cruel immortal, finding her spiritual feast in the agonies of a dying race. For across those hard features there came something like a flash when the last hour had been breathed out, and we all felt that the dark veil had completely fallen. What secret was there between Bertha and this woman? I turned my eyes from her with a horrible dread lest my insight should return, and I should be obliged to see what had been breeding about two unloving women's hearts. I felt that

Bertha had been watching for the moment of death as the sealing of her secret: I thanked Heaven it could remain sealed for me.

Meunier said quietly, 'She is gone.' He then gave his arm to Bertha, and she submitted to be led out of the room.

I suppose it was at her order that two female attendants came into the room, and dismissed the younger one who had been present before. When they entered, Meunier had already opened the artery in the long thin neck that lay rigid on the pillow, and I dismissed them, ordering them to remain at a distance till we rang: the doctor, I said, had an operation to perform – he was not sure about the death. For the next twenty minutes I forgot everything but Meunier and the experiment in which he was so absorbed, that I think his senses would have been closed against all sounds or sights which had no relation to it. It was my task at first to keep up the artificial respiration in the body after the transfusion had been effected, but presently Meunier relieved me, and I could see the wondrous slow return of life; the breast began to heave, the inspirations became stronger, the eyelids quivered, and the soul seemed to have returned beneath them. The artificial respiration was withdrawn: still the breathing continued, and there was a movement of the lips.

Just then I heard the handle of the door moving: I suppose Bertha had heard from the women that they had been dismissed: probably a vague fear had arisen in her mind, for she entered with a look of alarm. She came to the foot of the bed and gave a stifled cry.

The dead woman's eyes were wide open, and met hers in full recognition – the recognition of hate. With a sudden strong effort, the hand that Bertha had thought for ever still was pointed towards her, and the haggard face moved. The gasping eager voice said –

'You mean to poison your husband ... the poison is in the black cabinet ... I got if for you ... you laughed at me, and told lies about me behind my back, to make me disgusting ... because you were jealous ... are you sorry ... now?'

The lips continued to murmur, but the sounds were no longer distinct. Soon there was no sound – only a slight movement: the flame had leaped out, and was being extinguished the faster. The wretched woman's heart-strings had been set to hatred and vengeance; the spirit of life had swept the chords for an instant, and was gone again for ever. Great God! Is this what it is to live again ... to wake up with our unstilled thirst upon us, with our unuttered curses rising to our lips, with our muscles ready to act out their half-committed sins?

Bertha stood pale at the foot of the bed, quivering and helpless, despairing of devices, like a cunning animal whose hiding-places are surrounded by swift-advancing flame. Even Meunier looked paralysed; life for that moment ceased to be a scientific problem to him. As for me, this scene seemed of one texture with the rest of my existence: horror was my familiar, and this new revelation was only like an old pain recurring with new circumstances.

. . . . . . . .

Since then Bertha and I have lived apart – she in her own neighbourhood, the mistress of half our wealth, I as a wanderer in foreign countries, until I came to this Devonshire nest to die. Bertha lives pitied and admired; for what had I against that charming woman, whom every one but myself could have been happy with? There had been no witness of the scene in the dying room except Meunier, and while Meunier lived his lips were sealed by a promise to me.

Once or twice, weary of wandering, I rested in a favourite spot, and my heart went out towards the men and women and children whose faces were becoming familiar to me: but I was driven away again in terror at the approach of my old insight – driven away to live continually with the one Unknown Presence revealed and yet hidden by the moving curtain of the earth and sky. Till at last disease took hold of me and forced me to rest here – forced me to live in dependence on my servants. And then the curse of insight – of my double consciousness, came again, and has never left me. I know all their narrow thoughts, their feeble regard, their half-wearied pity.

. . . . . . . .

It is the 20th of September 1850. I know these figures I have just written, as if they were a long familiar inscription. I have seen them on this page in my desk unnumbered times, when the scene of my dying struggle has opened upon me. . . .

\*       \*       \*

The story contains some of the author's recollections of Geneva (where she stayed from July 1849 to March 1850) and of Vienna and Prague (both visited in the summer of 1858). Her feelings of rejection by kindred and friends are implicit in the hero's bitterness (p. 30); and her own religion, as opposed to the other-wordly religion of Dr Young, is heard in the brief overtone of 'I thirsted for the unknown: the thirst is gone. O God, let me stay with the known.' The writing shows ease and mastery throughout, with admirable art in creating larger narrative effects as well as in such detail as the contextual appropriateness of the Lucrezia Borgia picture (p. 44) or the more sensitive image of mist and rock in close association (p. 49).

The hero's double consciousness, 'flowing on like two parallel streams which never mingle', derives, as the title of the story confirms, from Shelley's sonnet 'Lift not the painted veil'. Prevision gives Latimer warnings which he ignores; love (and hope) get the better of him, and he becomes Bertha's willing victim:

> no matter how empty the adytum, so that the veil be thick enough. So absolute is our soul's need of something hidden and uncertain for the maintenance of that doubt and hope and effort which are the breath of its life, that if the whole future were laid bare to us beyond to-day, the interest of all mankind would be bent on the hours that lie between . . .

Shelley's sonnet, which has ideas and dimensions beyond those adapted by George Eliot in her story, begins:

> Lift not the painted veil which those who live
> Call Life: though unreal shapes be pictured there,
> And it but mimic all we would believe
> With colours idly spread, – behind, lurk Fear
> And Hope, twin Destinies; who ever weave
> Their shadows, o'er the chasm, sightless and drear.
> I knew one who had lifted it – he sought,
> For his lost heart was tender, things to love,
> But found them not, alas!. . .

At the heart of the story, in the vision of Prague, lies the more generalized fear of an era when the old, other-worldly religion is dead, and people, without a new religion, pursue their activities mechanically, with no high purpose. It is noticeable that, the more spiritually deadened Latimer becomes through being cut off from his fellow-men, the more subject he is to visions like that of Prague. It does more than reflect his negativism when all that is loving and personal dies within him. The arrested sunshine is like the desert of *The Waste Land*; it makes the city look thirsty, and the river (which might have been 'the river of life') a sheet of metal.

The bridge along which the visionary walks (in the brief transit of life) seems unending, and its blackened statues, with their blank gaze, ancient garments, and saintly crowns, appear to be the real inhabitants and proprietors of the place, 'while the busy, trivial men and women, hurrying to and fro' are 'a swarm of ephemeral visitants infesting it for a day'. It might be thought that the occupants of the time-fretted buildings were descended from those statues; 'urged by no fear or hope', they worship wearily in stifling churches, and remain doomed 'to live on in the rigidity of habit', without 'the repose of night or the new birth of morning'. The scene epitomizes a state of spiritual deadness ('death-in-life') amid the memorials of a past religious age; it presents, in the words of *Romola* (end xxxvi), the 'arrest' of spiritual 'inaction and death'.

Latimer's illusions cast an ironical light on the romantic, idealizing kind of poetry with which he is associated, and this is to be expected of an author who believed with Ruskin, as she wrote in her review of *Modern Painters* (vol. III, WR April 1856), that 'all truth and beauty are to be attained by a humble and faithful study of nature, and not by substituting vague forms, bred by imagination on the mists of feeling, in place of definite, substantial reality'. She expressed the same point of view much later (DD.xix, first paragraph, and xxxiii, 'Here undoubtedly lies the chief poetic energy: – in the force of imagination that pierces or exalts the solid fact, instead of floating among cloud-pictures').

## ii  'BROTHER JACOB'

(Written for the fun of it in the summer of 1860, when she was unable to settle and pursue her researches for *Romola*, this, like 'The Lifted Veil', is an exceptional George Eliot story; despite a respectable epigraph and conclusion, and an unworthy hero, it has no serious aim. The author regarded it as slight, but it was offered to Sampson Low for £250. George Smith, who had secured *Romola* at a very high fee, offered the same sum in February 1863 when serial publication of the novel had to be postponed. After the disappointing sales of *Romola*, George Eliot presented the story in compensation, and it appeared in the July 1864 number of *The Cornhill Magazine*. John Blackwood, to whom she returned with her next novel *Felix Holt*, decided in December 1866 not to include 'The Lifted Veil' and 'Brother Jacob' in his 'recognised series' of George Eliot works; only in 1877 did he give way, after receiving her request that they should augment *Silar Marner* on the new Cabinet Edition.)

Trompeurs, c'est pour vous que j'écris,
Attendez vous à la pareille.[16]
La Fontaine

*Chapter I*

Among the many fatalities attending the bloom of young desire, that of blindly taking to the confectionery line has not, perhaps, been sufficiently considered. How is the son of a British yeoman, who has been fed principally on salt pork and yeast dumplings, to know that there is satiety for the human stomach even in a paradise of glass jars full of sugared almonds and pink lozenges, and that the tedium of life can reach a pitch where plum-buns at discretion cease to offer the slightest enticement? Or how, at the tender age when a confectioner seems to him a very prince whom all the world must envy, – who breakfasts on macaroons, dines on marengs, sups on twelfth-cake, and fills up the intermediate hours with sugar-candy or peppermint, – how is he to foresee the day of sad wisdom, when he will discern that the confectioner's calling is not socially influential, or favourable to a soaring ambition? I have known a man who turned out to have a metaphysical genius, incautiously, in the period of youthful buoyancy, commence his career as a dancing-master; and you may imagine the use that was made of this initial mistake by opponents who felt themselves bound to warn the public against his doctrine of the Inconceivable. He could not give up his dancing-lessons, because he made his bread by them, and metaphysics would not have found him in so much as salt to his bread. It was really the same with Mr David Faux and the confectionery business. His uncle, the butler at the great house close by Brigford, had made a pet of him in his early boyhood, and it was on a visit to this uncle that the confectioners' shops in that brilliant town had, on a single day, fired his tender imagination. He carried home the pleasing illusion that a confectioner must be at once the happiest and the foremost of men, since the things he made were not only the most beautiful to behold, but the very best eating, and such as the Lord Mayor must always order largely for his private recreation; so that when his father declared he must be put to a trade, David chose his line without a moment's hesitation; and, with a rashness inspired by a sweet tooth, wedded himself irrevocably to confectionery. Soon, however, the tooth lost its relish and fell into blank indifference; and all the while, his mind expanded, his ambition took new shapes, which could hardly be satisfied within the sphere his youthful ardour had chosen. But what was he to do? He was a young man of much mental activity, and, above all, gifted with a spirit of contrivance; but then, his faculties would not tell with great effect in any other medium than that of candied sugars, conserves, and pastry. Say what you will about the identity of the reasoning process in all branches of thought, or about the advantage of coming to subjects with a fresh mind, the adjustment of butter to flour, and of heat to pastry, is *not* the best preparation for the office of prime minister; besides, in the present imperfectly-organised state of society, there are social barriers. David could invent delightful things in the way of drop-cakes, and he had the widest views of the sugar department; but in other directions he certainly felt hampered by the want of knowledge and practical skill; and the world is so inconveniently constituted, that the vague consciousness of being a fine fellow is no guarantee of success in any line of business.

This difficulty pressed with some severity on Mr David Faux, even before his apprenticeship was ended. His soul swelled with an impatient sense that he ought to become something very remarkable – that it was quite out of the question for him to put up with a narrow lot as other men did: he scorned the idea that he could accept an average. He was sure there was nothing average about him: even such a person as Mrs Tibbits, the washerwoman, perceived it, and probably had a preference for his linen. At that particular period he was weighing out gingerbread-nuts; but such an anomaly could not continue. No position could be suited to Mr David Faux that was not in the highest degree easy to the flesh and flattering to the spirit. If he had fallen on the present times, and enjoyed the advantages of a Mechanics' Institute,[17] he would certainly have taken to literature and have written reviews; but his education had not been liberal. He had read some novels from the adjoining circulating library, and had even bought the story of 'Inkle and Yarico',[18] which had made him feel very sorry for poor Mr Inkle; so that his ideas might not have been below a certain mark of the literary calling; but his spelling and diction were too unconventional.

When a man is not adequately appreciated or comfortably placed in his own country, his thoughts naturally turn towards foreign climes; and David's imagination circled round and round the utmost limits of his geographical knowledge, in search of a country where a young gentleman of pasty visage, lipless mouth, and stumpy hair, would be likely to be received with the hospitable enthusiasm which he had a right to expect. Having a general idea of America as a country where the population was chiefly black, it appeared to him the most propitious destination for an emigrant who, to begin with, had the broad and easily recognisable merit of whiteness; and this idea gradually took such strong possession of him that Satan seized the opportunity of suggesting to him that he might emigrate under easier circumstances, if he supplied himself with a little money from his master's till. But that evil spirit, whose understanding, I am convinced, has been much overrated, quite wasted his time on this occasion. David would certainly have liked well to have some of his master's money in his pocket, if he had been sure his master would have been the only man to suffer for it; but he was a cautious youth, and quite determined to run no risks on his own account. So he stayed out his apprenticeship, and committed no act of dishonesty that was at all likely to be discovered, reserving his plan of emigration for a future opportunity. And the circumstances under which he carried it out were in this wise. Having been at home a week or two partaking of the family beans,[19] he had used his leisure in ascertaining a fact which was of considerable importance to him, namely, that his mother had a small sum in guineas painfully saved from her maiden perquisites, and kept in the corner of a drawer where her baby-linen had reposed for the last twenty years – ever since her son David had taken to his feet, with a slight promise of bow-legs which had not been altogether unfulfilled. Mr Faux, senior, had told his son very frankly, that he must not look to being set-up in business by *him*: with seven sons, and one of them a very healthy and well-developed idiot, who consumed a dumpling about eight inches in diameter every day, it was pretty well if they got a hundred apiece at his death. Under these circumstances, what was David to do? It was certainly hard that he should take his mother's money; but he saw no other ready means of getting any, and it was not to be expected that a young man of his merit should put up with inconveniences that could be avoided. Besides, it is not robbery to take property belonging to your mother: she doesn't prosecute you. And David was very well behaved to his mother; he comforted her by speaking highly of himself to her, and assuring her that he never fell into the vices he saw practised by other youths of his own age, and that he was particularly fond of honesty. If his mother would have given him her twenty guineas as a reward of this noble disposition, he really would not have

stolen them from her, and it would have been more agreeable to
his feelings. Nevertheless, to an active mind like David's, ingenuity
is not without its pleasures: it was rather an interesting
occupation to become stealthily acquainted with the wards of his
mother's simple key (not in the least like Chubb's patent),[20] and to
get one that would do its work equally well; and also to arrange a
little drama by which he would escape suspicion, and run no risk
of forfeiting the prospective hundred at his father's death, which
would be convenient in the improbable case of his *not* making a
large fortune in the 'Indies'.

First, he spoke freely of his intention to start shortly for
Liverpool and take ship for America; a resolution which cost his
good mother some pain, for, after Jacob the idiot, there was not
one of her sons to whom her heart clung more than to her
youngest-born, David. Next, it appeared to him that Sunday
afternoon, when everybody was gone to church except Jacob and
the cow-boy, was so singularly favourable an opportunity for sons
who wanted to appropriate their mothers' guineas, that he half
thought it must have been kindly intended by Providence for such
purposes. Especially the third Sunday in Lent; because Jacob had
been out on one of his occasional wanderings for the last two
days; and David, being a timid young man, had a considerable
dread and hatred of Jacob, as of a large personage who went about
habitually with a pitchfork in his hand.

Nothing could be easier, then, than for David on this Sunday
afternoon to decline going to church, on the ground that he was
going to tea at Mr Lunn's, whose pretty daughter Sally had been
an early flame of his, and, when the church-goers were at a safe
distance, to abstract the guineas from their wooden box and slip
them into a small canvas bag – nothing easier than to call to the
cow-boy that he was going, and tell him to keep an eye on the
house for fear of Sunday tramps. David thought it would be easy,
too, to get to a small thicket and bury his bag in a hole he had
already made and covered up under the roots of an old hollow ash,
and he had, in fact, found the hole without a moment's difficulty,
had uncovered it, and was about gently to drop the bag into it,
when the sound of a large body rustling towards him with
something like a bellow was such a surprise to David, who, as a
gentleman gifted with much contrivance, was naturally only
prepared for what he expected, that instead of dropping the bag
gently he let it fall so as to make it untwist and vomit forth the
shining guineas. In the same moment he looked up and saw his
dear brother Jacob close upon him, holding the pitchfork so that
the bright smooth prongs were a yard in advance of his own body,

and about a foot off David's. (A learned friend, to whom I once narrated this history, observed that it was David's guilt which made these prongs formidable, and that the *mens nil conscia sibi*[21] strips a pitchfork of all terrors. I thought this idea so valuable, that I obtained his leave to use it on condition of suppressing his name.) Nevertheless, David did not entirely lose his presence of mind; for in that case he would have sunk on the earth or started backward; whereas he kept his ground and smiled at Jacob, who nodded his head up and down, and said, 'Hoich, Zavy!' in a painfully equivocal manner. David's heart was beating audibly, and if he had had any lips they would have been pale; but his mental activity, instead of being paralysed, was stimulated. While he was inwardly praying (he always prayed when he was much frightened), – 'Oh, save me this once, and I'll never get into danger again!' – he was thrusting his hand into his pocket in search of a box of yellow lozenges, which he had brought with him from Brigford among other delicacies of the same portable kind, as a means of conciliating proud beauty, and more particularly the beauty of Miss Sarah Lunn. Not one of these delicacies had he ever offered to poor Jacob, for David was not a young man to waste his jujubes and barley-sugar in giving pleasure to people from whom he expected nothing. But an idiot with equivocal intentions and a pitchfork is as well worth flattering and cajoling as if he were Louis Napoleon.[22] So David, with a promptitude equal to the occasion, drew out his box of yellow lozenges, lifted the lid, and performed a pantomime with his mouth and fingers, which was meant to imply that he was delighted to see his dear brother Jacob, and seized the opportunity of making him a small present, which he would find particularly agreeable to the taste. Jacob, you understand, was not an intense idiot, but within a certain limited range knew how to choose the good and reject the evil: he took one lozenge, by way of test, and sucked it as if he had been a philosopher; then, in as great an ecstasy at its new and complex savour as Caliban at the taste of Trinculo's wine,[23] chuckled and stroked this suddenly beneficent brother, and held out his hand for more; for, except in fits of anger, Jacob was not ferocious or needlessly predatory. David's courage half returned, and he left off praying; pouring a dozen lozenges into Jacob's palm, and trying to look very fond of him. He congratulated himself that he had formed the plan of going to see Miss Sally Lunn this afternoon, and that, as a consequence, he had brought with him these propitiatory delicacies: he was certainly a lucky fellow; indeed, it was always likely Providence should be fonder of him than of other apprentices, and since he *was* to be interrupted, why, an idiot was preferable to any other sort of witness. For the first time in his life, David thought he saw the advantage of idiots.

As for Jacob, he had thrust his pitchfork into the ground, and had thrown himself down beside it, in thorough abandonment to the unprecedented pleasure of having five lozenges in his mouth at once, blinking meanwhile, and making inarticulate sounds of gustative content. He had not given any sign of noticing the guineas, but in seating himself he had laid his broad right hand on them, and unconsciously kept it in that position, absorbed in the sensations of his palate. If he could only be kept so occupied with the lozenges as not to see the guineas before David could manage to cover them! That was David's best hope of safety; for Jacob knew his mother's guineas; it had been part of their common experience as boys to be allowed to look at these handsome coins, and rattle them in their box on high days and holidays, and among all Jacob's narrow experiences as to money, this was likely to be the most memorable.

'Here, Jacob,' said David, in an insinuating tone, handing the box to him, 'I'll give 'em all to you. Run! – make haste! – else somebody'll come and take 'em.'

David, not having studied the psychology of idiots, was not aware that they are not to be wrought upon by imaginative fears. Jacob took the box with his left hand, but saw no necessity for running away. Was ever a promising young man wishing to lay the foundation of his fortune by appropriating his mother's guineas obstructed by such a day-mare as this? But the moment must come when Jacob would move his right hand to draw off the lid of the tin box, and then David would sweep the guineas into the hole with the utmost address and swiftness, and immediately seat himself upon them. Ah, no! It's of no use to have foresight when you are dealing with an idiot: he is not to be calculated upon. Jacob's right hand was given to vague clutching and throwing; it suddenly clutched the guineas as if they had been so many pebbles, and was raised in an attitude which promised to scatter them like seed over a distant bramble, when, from some prompting or other – probably of an unwonted sensation – it paused, descended to Jacob's knee, and opened slowly under the inspection of Jacob's dull eyes. David began to pray again, but immediately desisted – another resource having occurred to him.

'Mother! zinnies!' exclaimed the innocent Jacob. Then, looking at David, he said, interrogatively, 'Box?'

'Hush! hush!' said David, summoning all his ingenuity in this severe strait. 'See, Jacob!' He took the tin box from his brother's hand, and emptied it of the lozenges, returning half of them to

Jacob, but secretly keeping the rest in his own hand. Then he held out the empty box, and said, 'Here's the box, Jacob! The box for the guineas!' gently sweeping them from Jacob's palm into the box.

This procedure was not objectionable to Jacob; on the contrary, the guineas clinked so pleasantly as they fell, that he wished for a repetition of the sound, and seizing the box, began to rattle it very gleefully. David, seizing the opportunity, deposited his reserve of lozenges in the ground and hastily swept some earth over them. 'Look, Jacob!' he said, at last. Jacob paused from his clinking, and looked into the hole, while David began to scratch away the earth, as if in doubtful expectation. When the lozenges were laid bare, he took them out one by one, and gave them to Jacob. 'Hush!' he said, in a loud whisper, 'Tell nobody — all for Jacob — hush — sh — sh! Put guineas in the hole — they'll come out like this!' To make the lesson more complete, he took a guinea, and lowering it into the hole, said 'Put in *so*.' Then, as he took the last lozenge out, he said, 'Come out *so*', and put the lozenge into Jacob's hospitable mouth.

Jacob turned his head on one side, looked first at his brother and then at the hole, like a reflective monkey, and, finally, laid the box of guineas in the hole with much decision. David made haste to add every one of the stray coins, put on the lid, and covered it well with earth, saying in his most coaxing tone—

'Take 'm out to-morrow, Jacob; all for Jacob! Hush — sh — sh!'

Jacob, to whom this once indifferent brother had all at once become a sort of sweet-tasted fetish, stroked David's best coat with his adhesive fingers, and then hugged him with an accompaniment of that mingled chuckling and gurgling by which he was accustomed to express the milder passions. But if he had chosen to bite a small morsel out of his beneficent brother's cheek, David would have been obliged to bear it.

And here I must pause, to point out to you the short-sighted-ness of human contrivance. This ingenious young man, Mr David Faux, thought he had achieved a triumph of cunning when he had associated himself in his brother's rudimentary mind with the flavour of yellow lozenges. But he had yet to learn that it is a dreadful thing to make an idiot fond of you, when you yourself are not of an affectionate disposition: especially an idiot with a pitchfork — obviously a difficult friend to shake off by rough usage.

It may seem to you rather a blundering contrivance for a clever young man to bury the guineas. But, if everything had turned out as David had calculated, you would have seen that his plan was worthy of his talents. The guineas would have lain safely in the earth while the theft was discovered, and David, with the calm of conscious innocence, would have lingered at home, reluctant to say goodbye to his dear mother while she was in grief about her guineas; till at length, on the eve of his departure, he would have disinterred them in the strictest privacy, and carried them on his own person without inconvenience. But David, you perceive, had reckoned without his host, or, to speak more precisely, without his idiot brother – an item of so uncertain and fluctuating a character, that I doubt whether he would not have puzzled the astute heroes of M. de Balzac,[24] whose foresight is so remarkably at home in the future.

It was clear to David now that he had only one alternative before him: he must either renounce the guineas, by quietly putting them back in his mother's drawer (a course not unattended with difficulty); or he must leave more than a suspicion behind him, by departing early the next morning without giving notice, and with the guineas in his pocket. For if he gave notice that he was going, his mother, he knew, would insist on fetching from her box of guineas the three she had always promised him as his share; indeed, in his original plan, he had counted on this as a means by which the theft would be discovered under circumstances that would themselves speak for his innocence; but now, as I need hardly explain, that well-combined plan was completely frustrated. Even if David could have bribed Jacob with perpetual lozenges, an idiot's secrecy is itself betrayal. He dared not even go to tea at Mr Lunn's, for in that case he would have lost sight of Jacob, who, in his impatience for the crop of lozenges, might scratch up the box again while he was absent, and carry it home – depriving him at once of reputation and guineas. No! he must think of nothing all the rest of this day, but of coaxing Jacob and keeping him out of mischief. It was a fatiguing and anxious evening to David; nevertheless, he dared not go to sleep without tying a piece of string to his thumb and great toe, to secure his frequent waking; for he meant to be up with the first peep of dawn, and be far out of reach before breakfast-time. His father, he thought, would certainly cut him off with a shilling; but what then? Such a striking young man as he would be sure to be well received in the West Indies: in foreign countries there are always openings – even for cats. It was probable that some Princess Yarico would want him to marry her, and make him presents of very large jewels beforehand; after which, he needn't marry her unless he liked. David had made up his mind not to steal any more, even from people who were fond of him: it was an unpleasant way of making your fortune in a world where you were likely to be surprised in the act by brothers. Such alarms did not agree with David's constitution, and he had felt so much nausea this evening that no doubt his liver was affected. Besides, he would have been greatly hurt not to be thought well of in the world: he always meant to make a figure, and be thought worthy of the best seats and the best morsels.

Ruminating to this effect on the brilliant future in reserve for him, David by the help of his check-string kept himself on the alert to seize the time of earliest dawn for his rising and departure. His brothers, of course, were early risers, but he should anticipate them by at least an hour and a half, and the little room which he had to himself as only an occasional visitor, had its window over the horse-block, so that he could slip out through the window without the least difficulty. Jacob, the horrible Jacob, had an awkward trick of getting up before everybody else, to stem his hunger by emptying the milk-bowl that was 'duly set' for him; but of late he had taken to sleeping in the hay-loft, and if he came into the house, it would be on the opposite side to that from which David was making his exit. There was no need to think of Jacob; yet David was liberal enough to bestow a curse on him – it was the only thing he ever did bestow gratuitously. His small bundle of clothes was ready packed, and he was soon treading lightly on the steps of the horse-block, soon walking at a smart pace across the fields towards the thicket. It would take him no more than two minutes to get out the box; he could make out the tree it was under by the pale strip where the bark was off, although the dawning light was rather dimmer in the thicket. But what, in the name of – burnt pastry – was that large body with a staff planted beside it, close at the foot of the ash-tree? David paused, not to make up his mind as to the nature of the apparition – he had not the happiness of doubting for a moment that the staff was Jacob's pitchfork – but to gather the self-command necessary for addressing his brother with a sufficiently honeyed accent. Jacob was absorbed in scratching up the earth, and had not heard David's approach.

'I say, Jacob', said David in a loud whisper, just as the tin box was lifted out of the hole.

Jacob looked up, and discerning his sweet-flavoured brother, nodded and grinned in the dim light in a way that made him seem to David like a triumphant demon. If he had been of an impetuous disposition, he would have snatched the pitchfork from the ground and impaled this fraternal demon. But David was by no means impetuous; he was a young man greatly given to calculate consequences, a habit which has been held to be the foundation of virtue. But somehow it had not precisely that effect in David: he calculated whether an action would harm himself, or whether it would only harm other people. In the former case he was very timid about satisfying his immediate desires, but in the latter he would risk the result with much courage.

'Give it *me*, Jacob', he said, stooping down and patting his brother. 'Let us see.'

Jacob, finding the lid rather tight, gave the box to his brother in perfect faith. David raised the lid, and shook his head, while Jacob put his finger in and took out a guinea to taste whether the metamorphosis into lozenges was complete and satisfactory.

'No, Jacob; too soon, too soon', said David, when the guinea had been tasted. 'Give it me; we'll go and bury it somewhere else; we'll put it in yonder', he added, pointing vaguely toward the distance.

David screwed on the lid, while Jacob, looking grave, rose and grasped his pitchfork. Then, seeing David's bundle, he snatched it, like a too officious Newfoundland, stuck his pitchfork into it and carried it over his shoulder in triumph as he accompanied David and the box out of the thicket.

What on earth was David to do? It would have been easy to frown at Jacob, and kick him, and order him to get away; but David dared as soon have kicked the bull. Jacob was quiet as long as he was treated indulgently; but on the slightest show of anger, he became unmanageable, and was liable to fits of fury which would have made him formidable even without his pitchfork. There was no mastery to be obtained over him except by kindness or guile. David tried guile.

'Go, Jacob', he said, when they were out of the thicket – pointing towards the house as he spoke; 'go and fetch me a spade – a spade. But give *me* the bundle', he added, trying to reach it from the fork, where it hung high above Jacob's tall shoulder.

But Jacob showed as much alacrity in obeying as a wasp shows in leaving a sugar-basin. Near David, he felt himself in the vicinity of lozenges: he chuckled and rubbed his brother's back, brandishing the bundle higher out of reach. David, with an inward groan, changed his tactics, and walked on as fast as he could. It was not safe to linger. Jacob would get tired of following him, or, at all events, could be eluded. If they could once get to the distant highroad, a coach would overtake them, David would mount it, having previously by some ingenious means secured his bundle, and then Jacob might howl and flourish his pitchfork as much as he liked. Meanwhile he was under the fatal necessity of being very kind to this ogre, and of providing a large breakfast for him when they stopped at a roadside inn. It was already three hours since they had started, and David was tired. Would no coach be coming up soon? he inquired. No coach for the next two hours. But there was a carrier's cart to come immediately, on its way to the next town. If he could slip out, even leaving his bundle behind, and get into the cart without Jacob! But there was a new obstacle. Jacob had recently discovered a remnant of sugar-candy in one of his brother's tail-pockets; and, since then, had cautiously kept his hold on that limb of the garment, perhaps with an expectation that there would be a further development of sugar-candy after a longer or shorter interval. Now every one who has worn a coat will understand the sensibilities that must keep a man from starting away in a hurry when there is a grasp on his coat-tail. David looked forward to being well received among strangers, but it might make a difference if he had only one tail to his coat.

He felt himself in a cold perspiration. He could walk no more: he must get into the cart and let Jacob get in with him. Presently a cheering idea occurred to him: after so large a breakfast, Jacob would be sure to go to sleep in the cart; you see at once that David meant to seize his bundle, jump out, and be free. His expectation was partly fulfilled: Jacob did go to sleep in the cart, but it was in a peculiar attitude – it was with his arms tightly fastened round his dear brother's body; and if ever David attempted to move, the grasp tightened with the force of an affectionate boa-constrictor.

'Th' innicent's fond on you', observed the carrier, thinking that David was probably an amiable brother, and wishing to pay him a compliment.

David groaned. The ways of thieving were not ways of pleasantness.[25] Oh, why had he an idiot brother? Or why, in general, was the world so constituted that a man could not take his mother's guineas comfortably? David became grimly speculative.

Copious dinner at noon for Jacob; but little dinner, because little appetite, for David. Instead of eating, he plied Jacob with beer; for through this liberality he descried a hope. Jacob fell into a dead sleep, at last, *without* having his arms round David, who paid the reckoning, took his bundle, and walked off. In another half-hour he was on the coach on his way to Liverpool, smiling the smile of the triumphant wicked. He was rid of Jacob – he was bound for the Indies, where a gullible princess awaited him. He would never steal any more, but there would be no need; he would show himself so deserving, that people would make him presents freely. He must give up the notion of his father's legacy; but it was not likely he would ever want that trifle; and even if he did – why, it was a compensation to think that in being for ever divided from his family he was divided from Jacob, more terrible than Gorgon or Demogorgon[26] to David's timid green eyes. Thank heaven, he should never see Jacob any more!

### Chapter II

It was nearly six years after the departure of Mr David Faux for the West Indies, that the vacant shop in the market-place at Grimworth was understood to have been let to the stranger with a sallow complexion and a buff cravat, whose first appearance had caused some excitement in the bar of the Woolpack, where he had called to wait for the coach.

Grimworth, to a discerning eye, was a good place to set up shopkeeping in. There was no competition in it at present; the Church-people had their own grocer and draper; the Dissenters had theirs; and the two or three butchers found a ready market for their joints without strict reference to religious persuasion – except that the rector's wife had given a general order for the veal sweetbreads and the mutton kidneys, while Mr Rodd, the Baptist minister, had requested that, so far as was compatible with the fair accommodation of other customers, the sheep's trotters might be reserved for him. And it was likely to be a growing place, for the trustees of Mr Zephaniah Crypt's Charity, under the stimulus of a late visitation by commissioners, were beginning to apply long-accumulating funds to the rebuilding of the Yellow Coat School, which was henceforth to be carried forward on a greatly-extended scale, the testator having left no restrictions concerning the curriculum, but only concerning the coat.[27]

The shopkeepers at Grimworth were by no means unanimous as to the advantages promised by this prospect of increased population and trading, being substantial men, who liked doing a quiet business in which they were sure of their customers, and could calculate their returns to a nicety. Hitherto, it had been held a point of honour by the families in Grimworth parish, to buy their sugar and their flannel at the shops where their fathers and mothers had bought before them; but, if new-comers were to bring in the system of neck-and-neck trading, and solicit feminine eyes by gown-pieces laid in fan-like folds, and surmounted by artificial flowers, giving them a factitious charm (for on what human figure would a gown sit like a fan, or what female head was like a bunch of China-asters?), or, if new grocers were to fill their windows with mountains of currants and sugar, made seductive by contrast and tickets, – what security was there for

Grimworth, that a vagrant spirit in shopping, once introduced, would not in the end carry the most important families to the larger market town of Cattleton, where, business being done on a system of small profits and quick returns, the fashions were of the freshest, and goods of all kinds might be bought at an advantage?

With this view of the times predominant among the tradespeople at Grimworth, their uncertainty concerning the nature of the business which the sallow-complexioned stranger was about to set up in the vacant shop, naturally gave some additional strength to the fears of the less sanguine. If he was going to sell drapery, it was probable that a pale-faced fellow like that would deal in showy and inferior articles – printed cottons and muslins which would leave their dye in the wash-tub, jobbed linen full of knots, and flannel that would soon look like gauze. If grocery, then it was to be hoped that no mother of a family would trust the teas of an untried grocer. Such things had been known in some parishes as tradesmen going about canvassing for custom with cards in their pockets: when people came from nobody knew where, there was no knowing what they might do. It was a thousand pities that Mr Moffat, the auctioneer and broker, had died without leaving anybody to follow him in the business, and Mrs Cleve's trustee ought to have known better than to let a shop to a stranger. Even the discovery that ovens were being put up on the premises, and that the shop was, in fact, being fitted up for a confectioner and pastry-cook's business, hitherto unknown in Grimworth, did not quite suffice to turn the scale in the new-comer's favour, though the landlady at the Woolpack defended him warmly, said he seemed to be a very clever young man, and from what she could make out, came of a very good family; indeed, was most likely a good many people's betters.

It certainly made a blaze of light and colour, almost as if a rainbow had suddenly descended into the market-place, when, one fine morning, the shutters were taken down from the new shop, and the two windows displayed their decorations. On one side, there were the variegated tints of collared and marbled meats, set off by bright green leaves, the pale brown of glazed pies, the rich tones of sauces and bottled fruits enclosed in their veil of glass – altogether a sight to bring tears into the eyes of a Dutch painter; and on the other, there was a predominance of the more delicate hues of pink, and white, and yellow, and buff, in the abundant lozenges, candies, sweet biscuits and icings, which to the eyes of a bilious person might easily have been blended into a faëry landscape in Turner's latest style.[28] What a sight to dawn upon the eyes of Grimworth children! They almost forgot to go to their dinner that day, their appetites being preoccupied with imaginary sugar-plums; and I think even Punch, setting up his tabernacle in the market-place, would not have succeeded in drawing them away from those shop-windows, where they stood according to gradations of size and strength, the biggest and strongest being nearest the window, and the little ones in the outermost rows lifting wide-open eyes and mouths towards the upper tier of jars, like small birds at meal-time.

The elder inhabitants pished and pshawed a little at the folly of the new shopkeeper in venturing on such an outlay in goods that would not keep; to be sure, Christmas was coming, but what housewife in Grimworth would not think shame to furnish forth her table[29] with articles that were not home-cooked? No, no. Mr Edward Freely, as he called himself, was deceived, if he thought Grimworth money was to flow into his pockets on such terms.

Edward Freely was the name that shone in gilt letters on a mazarine ground over the doorplace of the new shop – a generous-sounding name, that might have belonged to the open-hearted, improvident hero of an old comedy, who would have delighted in raining sugared almonds, like a new manna-gift,[30] among that small generation outside the windows. But Mr Edward Freely was a man whose impulses were kept in due subordination: he held that the desire for sweets and pastry must only be satisfied in a direct ratio with the power of paying for them. If the smallest child in Grimworth would go to him with a halfpenny in its tiny fist, he would, after ringing the halfpenny, deliver a just equivalent in 'rock'. He was not a man to cheat even the smallest child – he often said so, observing at the same time that he loved honesty, and also that he was very tender-hearted, though he didn't show his feelings as some people did.

Either in reward of such virtue, or according to some more hidden law of sequence, Mr Freely's business, in spite of prejudice, started under favourable auspices. For Mrs Chaloner, the rector's wife, was among the earliest customers at the shop, thinking it only right to encourage a new parishioner who had made a decorous appearance at church; and she found Mr Freely a most civil, obliging young man, and intelligent to a surprising degree for a confectioner; well-principled, too, for in giving her useful hints about choosing sugars he had thrown much light on the dishonesty of other tradesmen. Moreover, he had been in the West Indies, and had seen the very estate which had been her poor grandfather's property; and he said the missionaries were the only cause of the negro's discontent – an observing young man, evidently. Mrs Chaloner ordered wine-biscuits and olives, and gave Mr Freely to understand that she should find his shop a great convenience. So did the doctor's wife, and so did Mrs Gate, at the large carding-mill, who, having high connections frequently visiting her, might be expected to have a large consumption of ratafias and macaroons.

The less aristocratic matrons of Grimworth seemed likely at first to justify their husbands' confidence that they would never pay a percentage of profits on drop-cakes, instead of making their own, or get up a hollow show of liberal house-keeping by purchasing slices of collared meat when a neighbour came in for supper. But it is my task to narrate the gradual corruption of Grimworth manners from their primitive simplicity – a melancholy task, if it were not cheered by the prospect of the fine peripateia or downfall by which the progress of the corruption was ultimately checked.

It was young Mrs Steene, the veterinary surgeon's wife, who first gave way to temptation. I fear she had been rather over-educated for her station in life, for she knew by heart many passages in 'Lalla Rookh', the 'Corsair', and the 'Siege of Corinth', which had given her a distaste for domestic occupations, and caused her a withering disappointment at the discovery that Mr Steene, since his marriage, had lost all interest in the 'bulbul',[31] openly preferred discussing the nature of spavin with a coarse neighbour, and was angry if the pudding turned out watery – indeed, was simply a top-booted 'vet', who came in hungry at dinner-time; and not in the least like a nobleman turned Corsair out of pure scorn for his race, or like a renegade with a turban and crescent, unless it were in the irritability of his temper. And scorn is such a very different thing in top-boots!

This brutal man had invited a supper-party for Christmas eve, when he would expect to see mince-pies on the table. Mrs Steene had prepared her mince-meat, and had devoted much butter, fine flour, and labour, to the making of a batch of pies in the morning; but they proved to be so very heavy when they came out of the oven, that she could only think with trembling of the moment when her husband should catch sight of them on the supper-table. He would storm at her, she was certain; and before all the company; and then she should never help crying: it was so dreadful to think she had come to that, after the bulbul and everything! Suddenly the thought darted through her mind that *this once* she might send for a dish of mince-pies from Freely's: she knew he had some. But what was to become of the eighteen heavy mince-pies? Oh, it was of no use thinking about that; it was very expensive – indeed, making mince-pies at all was a great expense, when they were not sure to turn out well: it would be much better to buy them ready-made. You paid a little more for them, but there was no risk of waste.

Such was the sophistry with which this misguided young woman – enough. Mrs Steene sent for the mince-pies, and, I am grieved to add, garbled her household accounts in order to conceal the fact from her husband. This was the second step in a downward course, all owing to a young woman's being out of harmony with her circumstances, yearning after renegades and bulbuls, and being subject to claims from a veterinary surgeon fond of mince-pies. The third step was to harden herself by telling the fact of the bought mince-pies to her intimate friend Mrs Mole, who had already guessed it, and who subsequently encouraged herself in buying a mould of jelly, instead of exerting her own skill, by the reflection that 'other people' did the same sort of thing. The infection spread; soon there was a party or clique in Grimworth on the side of 'buying at Freely's'; and many husbands, kept for some time in the dark on this point, innocently swallowed at two mouthfuls a tart on which they were paying a profit of a hundred per cent, and as innocently encouraged a fatal disingenuousness in the partners of their bosoms by praising the pastry. Others, more keen-sighted, winked at the too frequent presentation on washing-days, and at impromptu suppers, of superior spiced-beef, which flattered their palates more than the cold remnants they had formerly been contented with. Every housewife who had once 'bought at Freely's' felt a secret joy when she detected a similar perversion in her neighbour's practice, and soon only two or three old-fashioned mistresses of families held out in the protest against the growing demoralisation, saying to their neighbours who came to sup with them, 'I can't offer you Freely's beef, or Freely's cheese-cakes; everything in our house is home-made; I'm afraid you'll hardly have any appetite for our plain pastry.' The doctor, whose cook was not satisfactory, the curate, who kept no cook, and the mining agent, who was a great *bon vivant*, even began to rely on Freely for the greater part of their dinner, when they wished to give an entertainment of some brilliancy. In short, the business of manufacturing the more fanciful viands was fast passing out of the hands of maids and matrons in private families, and was becoming the work of a special commercial organ.

I am not ignorant that this sort of thing is called the inevitable course of civilisation, division of labour,[32] and so forth, and that the maids and matrons may be said to have had their hands set free from cookery to add to the wealth of society in some other way. Only it happened at Grimworth, which, to be sure, was a low place, that the maids and matrons could do nothing with their hands at all better than cooking; not even those who had always made heavy cakes and leathery pastry. And so it came to pass, that the progress of civilisation at Grimworth was not otherwise apparent than in the impoverishment of men, the gossiping idleness of women, and the heightening prosperity of Mr Edward Freely.

The Yellow Coat School was a double source of profit to the calculating confectioner; for he opened an eating-room for the superior workmen employed on the new school, and he accommodated the pupils at the old school by giving great attention to the fancy-sugar department. When I think of the sweet-tasted swans and other ingenious white shapes crunched by the small teeth of that rising generation, I am glad to remember that a certain amount of calcareous food has been held good for young creatures whose bones are not quite formed; for I have observed these delicacies to have an inorganic flavour which would have recommended them greatly to that young lady of the 'Spectator's' acquaintance who habitually made her dessert on the stems of tobacco-pipes.[33]

As for the confectioner himself, he made his way gradually into Grimworth homes, as his commodities did, in spite of some initial repugnance. Somehow or other, his reception as a guest seemed a thing that required justifying, like the purchasing of his pastry. In the first place, he was a stranger, and therefore open to suspicion; secondly, the confectionery business was so entirely new at Grimworth, that its place in the scale of rank had not been distinctly ascertained. There was no doubt about drapers and grocers, when they came of good old Grimworth families, like Mr Luff and Mr Prettyman: they visited with the Palfreys, who farmed their own land, played many a game at whist with the doctor, and condescended a little towards the timber-merchant, who had lately taken to the coal-trade also, and had got new furniture; but whether a confectioner should be admitted to this higher level of respectability, or should be understood to find his associates among butchers and bakers, was a new question on which tradition threw no light. His being a bachelor was in his favour, and would perhaps have been enough to turn the scale, even if Mr Edward Freely's other personal pretensions had been of an entirely insignificant cast. But so far from this, it very soon appeared that he was a remarkable young man, who had been in the West Indies, and had seen many wonders by sea and land, so that he could charm the ears of Grimworth Desdemonas[34] with stories of strange fishes, especially sharks, which he had stabbed in the nick of time by bravely plunging overboard just as the monster was turning on his side to devour the cook's mate; of terrible fevers which he had undergone in a land where the wind blows from all quarters at once; of rounds of toast cut straight from the bread-fruit trees; of toes bitten off by land-crabs; of large honours that had been offered to him as a man who knew what was what, and was therefore particularly needed in a tropical climate; and of a Creole heiress who had wept bitterly at his departure. Such conversational talents as these, we know, will overcome disadvantages of complexion; and young Towers, whose cheeks were of the finest pink, set off by a fringe of dark whisker, was quite eclipsed by the presence of the sallow Mr Freely. So exceptional a confectioner elevated his business, and might well begin to make disengaged hearts flutter a little.

Fathers and mothers were naturally more slow and cautious in their recognition of the new-comer's merits.

'He's an amusing fellow', said Mr Prettyman, the highly respectable grocer. (Mrs Prettyman was a Miss Fothergill, and her sister had married a London mercer.) 'He's an amusing fellow; and I've no objection to his making one at the Oyster Club; but he's a bit too fond of riding the high horse. He's uncommonly knowing, I'll allow; but how came he to go to the Indies? I should like that answered. It's unnatural in a confectioner. I'm not fond of people that have been beyond seas, if they can't give a good account how they happened to go. When folks go so far off, it's because they've got little credit nearer home – that's my opinion. However, he's got some good rum; but I don't want to be hand and glove with him, for all that.'

It was this kind of dim suspicion which beclouded the view of Mr Freely's qualities in the maturer minds of Grimworth through the early months of his residence there. But when the confectioner ceased to be a novelty, the suspicions also ceased to be novel, and people got tired of hinting at them, especially as they seemed to be refuted by his advancing prosperity and importance. Mr Freely was becoming a person of influence in the parish; he was found useful as an overseer of the poor, having great firmness in enduring other people's pain, which firmness, he said, was due to his great benevolence; he always did what was good for people in the end. Mr Chaloner had even selected him as clergyman's churchwarden, for he was a very handy man, and much more of Mr Chaloner's opinion in everything about church business than the older parishioners. Mr Freely was a very regular churchman, but at the Oyster Club he was sometimes a little free in his conversation, more than hinting at a life of Sultanic self-indulgence which he had passed in the West Indies, shaking his head now and then and smiling rather bitterly, as men are wont to do when they intimate that they have become a little too wise to be instructed about a world which has long been flat and stale to them.

For some time he was quite general in his attentions to the fair sex, combining the gallantries of a lady's man with a severity of criticism on the person and manners of absent belles, which tended rather to stimulate in the feminine breast the desire to conquer the approval of so fastidious a judge. Nothing short of the very best in the department of female charms and virtues could suffice to kindle the ardour of Mr Edward Freely, who had become familiar with the most luxuriant and dazzling beauty in the West Indies. It may seem incredible that a confectioner should have ideas and conversation so much resembling those to be met with in a higher walk of life, but it must be remembered that he had not merely travelled, he had also bow-legs and a sallow, small-featured visage, so that nature herself had stamped him for a fastidious connoisseur of the fair sex.

At last, however, it seemed clear that Cupid had found a sharper arrow than usual, and that Mr Freely's heart was pierced. It was the general talk among the young people at Grimworth. But was it really love, and not rather ambition? Miss Fullilove, the timber-merchant's daughter, was quite sure that if *she* were Miss Penny Palfrey, she would be cautious; it was not a good sign when men looked so much above themselves for a wife. For it was no less a person than Miss Penelope Palfrey, second daughter of the Mr Palfrey who farmed his own land, that had attracted Mr Freely's peculiar regard, and conquered his fastidiousness; and no wonder, for the Ideal, as exhibited in the finest waxwork, was perhaps never so closely approached by the Real as in the person of the pretty Penelope. Her yellowish flaxen hair did not curl naturally, I admit, but its bright crisp ringlets were such smooth, perfect miniature tubes, that you would have longed to pass your little finger through them, and feel their soft elasticity. She wore them in a crop, for in those days, when society was in a healthier state, young ladies wore crops long after they were twenty, and Penolope was not yet nineteen. Like the waxen ideal, she had round blue eyes, and round nostrils in her little nose, and teeth such as the ideal would be seen to have, if it ever showed them. Altogether, she was a small, round thing, as neat as a pink-and-white double daisy, and as guileless; for I hope it does not argue guile in a pretty damsel of nineteen, to think that she should like to have a beau and be 'engaged', when her elder sister had already been in that position a year and a half. To be sure, there was young Towers always coming to the house; but Penny felt convinced he only came to see her brother, for he never had anything to say to her, and never offered her his arm, and was as awkward and silent as possible.

It is not unlikely that Mr Freely had early been smitten by Penny's charms, as brought under his observation at church, but he had to make his way in society a little before he could come into nearer contact with them; and even after he was well received in Grimworth families, it was a long while before he could converse with Penny otherwise than in an incidental meeting at Mr Luff's. It was not so easy to get invited to Long Meadows, the residence of the Palfreys; for though Mr Palfrey had been losing money of late years, not being able quite to recover his feet after the terrible murrain which forced him to borrow, his family were far from considering themselves on the same level even as the old-established tradespeople with whom they visited. The greatest people, even kings and queens, must visit with somebody, and the equals of the great are scarce. They were especially scarce at Grimworth, which, as I have before observed, was a low parish, mentioned with the most scornful brevity in gazetteers. Even the great people there were far behind those of their own standing in other parts of this realm. Mr Palfrey's farmyard doors had the paint all worn off them, and the front garden walks had long been merged in a general weediness. Still, his father had been called Squire Palfrey, and had been respected by the last Grimworth generation as a man who could afford to drink too much in his own house.

Pretty Penny was not blind to the fact that Mr Freely admired her, and she felt sure that it was he who had sent her a beautiful valentine; but her sister seemed to think so lightly of him (all young ladies think lightly of the gentlemen to whom they are not engaged), that Penny never dared mention him, and trembled and blushed whenever they met him, thinking of the valentine, which was very strong in its expressions, and which she felt guilty of knowing by heart. A man who had been to the Indies, and knew the sea so well, seemed to her a sort of public character, almost like Robinson Crusoe or Captain Cook; and Penny had always wished her husband to be a remarkable personage, likely to be put in Mangnall's Questions,[35] with which register of the immortals she had become acquainted during her one year at a boarding-school. Only it seemed strange that a remarkable man should be a confectioner and pastry-cook, and this anomaly quite disturbed Penny's dreams. Her brothers, she knew, laughed at men who couldn't sit on horseback well, and called them tailors; but her brothers were very rough, and were quite without that power of anecdote which made Mr Freely such a delightful companion. He was a very good man, she thought, for she had heard him say at Mr Luff's, one day, that he always wished to do his duty in whatever state of life he might be placed; and he knew a great deal of poetry, for one day he had repeated a verse of a song. She wondered if he had made the words of the valentine! – it ended in this way:

> Without thee, it is pain to live,
> But with thee, it were sweet to die.[36]

Poor Mr Freely! her father would very likely object – she felt sure he would, for he always called Mr Freely 'that sugar-plum fellow'. Oh, it was very cruel, when true love was crossed in that way, and all because Mr Freely was a confectioner: well, Penny would be true to him, for all that, and since his being a confectioner gave her an opportunity of showing her faithfulness, she was glad of it. Edward Freely was a pretty name, much better than John Towers. Young Towers had offered her a rose out of his button-hole the other day, blushing very much; but she refused it, and thought with delight how much Mr Freely would be comforted if he knew her firmness of mind.

Poor little Penny! the days were so very long among the daisies on a grazing farm, and thought is so active – how was it possible that the inward drama should not get the start of the outward? I have known young ladies, much better educated, and with an outward world diversified by instructive lectures, to say nothing of literature and highly-developed fancy-work, who have spun a cocoon of visionary joys and sorrows for themselves, just as Penny did. Her elder sister Letitia, who had a prouder style of beauty, and a more worldly ambition, was engaged to a wool-factor, who came all the way from Cattelton to see her; and everybody knows that a wool-factor takes a very high rank, sometimes driving a double-bodied gig. Letty's notions got higher every day, and Penny never dared to speak of her cherished griefs to her lofty sister – never dared to propose that they should call at Mr Freely's to buy liquorice, though she had prepared for such an incident by mentioning a slight sore throat. So she had to pass the shop on the other side of the market-place, and reflect, with a suppressed sigh, that behind those pink and white jars somebody was thinking of her tenderly, unconscious of the small space that divided her from him.

And it was quite true that, when business permitted, Mr Freely thought a great deal of Penny. He thought her prettiness comparable to the loveliest things in confectionery; he judged her to be of submissive temper – likely to wait upon him as well as if she had been a negress, and to be silently terrified when his liver made him irritable; and he considered the Palfrey family quite the best in the parish, possessing marriageable daughters. On the whole, he thought her worthy to become Mrs Edward Freely, and all the more so, because it would probably require some ingenuity to win her. Mr Palfrey was capable of horse-whipping a too rash pretender to his daughter's hand; and, moreover, he had three tall sons: it was clear that a suitor would be at a disadvantage with such a family, unless travel and natural acumen had given him a countervailing power of contrivance. And the first idea that occurred to him in the matter was, that Mr Palfrey would object less if he knew that the Freelys were a much higher family than his own. It had been foolish modesty in him hitherto to conceal the fact that a branch of the Freelys held a manor in Yorkshire, and to shut up the portrait of his great uncle the admiral, instead of hanging it up where a family portrait should be hung – over the mantelpiece in the parlour. Admiral Freely, K.C.B., once placed in this conspicuous position, was seen to have had one arm only, and one eye, – in these points resembling the heroic Nelson, – while a certain pallid insignificance of feature confirmed the relationship between himself and his grand-nephew.

Next, Mr Freely was seized with an irrepressible ambition to possess Mrs Palfrey's receipt for brawn, hers being pronounced on all hands to be superior to his own – as he informed her in a very flattering letter carried by his errand-boy. Now Mrs Palfrey, like other geniuses, wrought by instinct rather than by rule, and possessed no receipts, – indeed, despised all people who used them, observing that people who pickled by book, must pickle by weights and measures, and such nonsense; as for herself, her weights and measures were the tip of her finger and the tip of her tongue, and if you went nearer, why, of course, for dry goods like flour and spice, you went by handfuls and pinches, and for wet, there was a middle-sized jug – quite the best thing whether for much or little, because you might know how much a teacupful was if you'd got any use of your senses, and you might be sure it would take five middle-sized jugs to make a gallon. Knowledge of this kind is like Titian's colouring, difficult to communicate; and as Mrs Palfrey, once remarkably handsome, had now become rather stout and asthmatical, and scarcely ever left home, her oral teaching could hardly be given anywhere except at Long

Meadows. Even a matron is not insusceptible to flattery, and the prospect of a visitor whose great object would be to listen to her conversation, was not without its charms to Mrs Palfrey. Since there was no receipt to be sent in reply to Mr Freely's humble request, she called on her more docile daughter, Penny, to write a note, telling him that her mother would be glad to see him and talk with him on brawn, any day that he could call at Long Meadows. Penny obeyed with a trembling hand, thinking how wonderfully things came about in this world.

In this way, Mr Freely got himself introduced into the home of the Palfreys, and notwithstanding a tendency in the male part of the family to jeer at him a little as 'peaky' and bow-legged, he presently established his position as an accepted and frequent guest. Young Towers looked at him with increasing disgust when they met at the house on a Sunday, and secretly longed to try his ferret upon him, as a piece of vermin which that valuable animal would be likely to tackle with unhesitating vigour. But – so blind sometimes are parents – neither Mr nor Mrs Palfrey suspected that Penny would have anything to say to a tradesman of questionable rank whose youthful bloom was much withered. Young Towers, they thought, had an eye to her, and *that* was likely enough to be a match some day; but Penny was a child at present. And all the while Penny was imagining the circumstances under which Mr Freely would make her an offer: perhaps down by the row of damson-trees, when they were in the garden before tea; perhaps by letter – in which case, how would the letter begin? 'Dearest Penelope?' or 'My dear Miss Penelope?' or straight off, without dear anything, as seemed the most natural when people were embarrassed? But, however he might make the offer, she would not accept it without her father's consent: she would always be true to Mr Freely, but she would not disobey her father. For Penny was a good girl, though some of her female friends were afterwards of opinion that it spoke ill for her not to have felt an instinctive repugnance to Mr Freely.

But he was cautious, and wished to be quite sure of the ground he trod on. His views in marriage were not entirely sentimental, but were as duly mingled with considerations of what would be advantageous to a man in his position, as if he had had a very large amount of money spent on his education. He was not a man to fall in love in the wrong place; and so, he applied himself quite as much to conciliate the favour of the parents, as to secure the attachment of Penny. Mrs Palfrey had not been inaccessible to flattery, and her husband, being also of mortal mould, would not, it might be hoped, be proof against rum – that very fine Jamaica rum of which Mr Freely expected always to have a supply sent him from Jamaica. It was not easy to get Mr Palfrey into the parlour behind the shop, where a mild back-street light fell on the features of the heroic admiral; but by getting hold of him rather late one evening as he was about to return home from Grimworth, the aspiring lover succeeded in persuading him to sup on some collared beef which, after Mrs Palfrey's brawn, he would find the very best of cold eating.

From that hour Mr Freely felt sure of success: being in privacy with an estimable man old enough to be his father, and being rather lonely in the world, it was natural he should unbosom himself a little on subjects which he could not speak of in a mixed circle – especially concerning his expectations from his uncle in Jamaica, who had no children, and loved his nephew Edward better than any one else in the world, though he had been so hurt at his leaving Jamaica, that he had threatened to cut him off with a shilling. However, he had since written to state his full forgiveness, and though he was an eccentric old gentleman and could not bear to give away money during his life, Mr Edward Freely could show Mr Palfrey the letter which declared, plainly enough, who would be the affectionate uncle's heir. Mr Palfrey actually saw the letter, and could not help admiring the spirit of the nephew who declared that such brilliant hopes as these made no difference to his conduct; he should work at his humble business and make his modest fortune at it all the same. If the Jamaica estate was to come to him – well and good. It was nothing very surprising for one of the Freely family to have an estate left him, considering the lands that family had possessed in time gone by, – nay, still possessed in the Northumberland branch. Would not Mr Palfrey take another glass of rum? and also look at the last year's balance of the accounts? Mr Freely was a man who cared to possess personal virtues, and did not pique himself on his family, though some men would.

We know how easily the great Leviathan may be led, when once there is a hook in his nose or a bridle in his jaws.[37] Mr Palfrey was a large man, but, like Leviathan's, his bulk went against him when once he had taken a turning. He was not a mercurial man, who easily changed his point of view. Enough. Before two months were over, he had given his consent to Mr Freely's marriage with his daughter Penny, and having hit on a formula by which he could justify it, fenced off all doubts and objections, his own included. The formula was this: 'I'm not a man to put my head up an entry before I know where it leads.'

Little Penny was very proud and fluttering, but hardly so happy as she expected to be in an engagement. She wondered if young Towers cared much about it, for he had not been to the house lately, and her sister and brothers were rather inclined to sneer than to sympathise. Grimworth rang with the news. All men extolled Mr Freely's good fortune; while the women, with the tender solicitude characteristic of the sex, wished the marriage might turn out well.

While affairs were at this triumphant juncture, Mr Freely one morning observed that a stone-carver who had been breakfasting in the eating-room had left a newspaper behind. It was the 'X——shire Gazette and X——shire being a county not unknown to Mr Freely, he felt some curiosity to glance over it, and especially over the advertisements. A slight flush came over his face as he read. It was produced by the following announcement: – 'If David Faux, son of Jonathan Faux, late of Gilsbrook, will apply at the office of Mr Strutt, attorney, of Rodham, he will hear of something to his advantage.'

'Father's dead!' exclaimed Mr Freely, involuntarily. 'Can he have left me a legacy?'

## CHAPTER III

Perhaps it was a result quite different from your expectations, that Mr David Faux should have returned from the West Indies only a few years after his arrival there, and have set up in his old business, like any plain man who had never travelled. But these cases do occur in life. Since, as we know, men change their skies and see new constellations without changing their souls, it will follow sometimes that they don't change their business under those novel circumstances.

Certainly, this result was contrary to David's own expectations. He had looked forward, you are aware, to a brilliant career among 'the blacks'; but, either because they had already seen too many white men, or for some other reason, they did not at once recognise him as a superior order of human being; besides, there were no princesses among them. Nobody in Jamaica was anxious to maintain David for the mere pleasure of his society; and those hidden merits of a man which are so well known to himself were as little recognised there as they notoriously are in the effete society of the Old World. So that in the dark hints that David threw out at the Oyster Club about that life of Sultanic self-indulgence spent by him in the luxurious Indies, I really think he was doing himself a wrong; I believe he worked for his bread, and, in fact, took to cooking again, as, after all, the only department in which he could offer skilled labour. He had formed several ingenious plans by which he meant to circumvent people of large fortune and small faculty; but then he never met with exactly the right people under exactly the right circumstances. David's devices for getting rich without work had apparently no direct relation with the world outside him, as his confectionery receipts had. It is possible to pass a great many bad halfpennies and bad half-crowns, but I believe there has no instance been known of passing a halfpenny or a half-crown as a sovereign. A sharper can drive a brisk trade in this world: it is undeniable that there may be a fine career for him, if he will dare consequences; but David was too timid to be a sharper, or venture in any way among the man-traps of the law. He dared rob nobody but his mother. And so he had to fall back on the genuine value there was in him – to be content to pass as a good halfpenny, or, to speak more accurately, as a good confectioner. For in spite of some additional reading and observation, there was nothing else he could make so much money by; nay, he found in himself even a capability of extending his skill in this direction, and embracing all forms of cookery; while, in other branches of human labour, he began to see that it was not possible for him to shine. Fate was too strong for him; he had thought to master her inclination and had fled over the seas to that end; but she caught him, tied an apron round him, and snatching him from all other devices, made him devise cakes and patties in a kitchen at Kingstown. He was getting submissive to her, since she paid him with tolerable gains; but fevers and prickly heat, and other evils incidental to cooks in ardent climates, made him long for his native land; so he took ship once more, carrying his six years' savings, and seeing distinctly, this time, what were Fate's intentions as to his career. If you question me closely as to whether all the money with which he set up at Grimworth consisted of pure and simple earnings, I am obliged to confess that he got a sum or two for charitably abstaining from mentioning some other people's misdemeanours. Altogether, since no prospects were attached to his family name, and since a new christening seemed a suitable commencement of a new life, Mr David Faux thought it as well to call himself Mr Edward Freely.

But lo! now, in opposition to all calculable probability, some benefit appeared to be attached to the name of David Faux. Should he neglect it, as beneath the attention of a prosperous tradesman? It might bring him into contact with his family again, and he felt no yearnings in that direction: moreover, he had small belief that the 'something to his advantage' could be anything considerable. On the other hand, even a small gain is pleasant, and the promise of it in this instance was so surprising, that David felt his curiosity awakened. The scale dipped at last on the side of writing to the lawyer, and, to be brief, the correspondence ended in an appointment for a meeting between David and his eldest brother at Mr Strutt's, the vague 'something' having been defined as a legacy from his father of eighty-two pounds three shillings.

David, you know, had expected to be disinherited; and so he would have been, if he had not, like some other indifferent sons, come of excellent parents, whose conscience made them scrupulous where much more highly-instructed people often feel themselves warranted in following the bent of their indignation. Good Mrs Faux could never forget that she had brought this ill-conditioned son into the world when he was in that entirely helpless state which excluded the smallest choice on his part; and, somehow or other, she felt that his going wrong would be his father's and mother's fault, if they failed in one tittle of their parental duty. Her notion of parental duty was not of a high and subtle kind, but it included giving him his due share of the family property; for when a man had got a little honest money of his own, was he so likely to steal? To cut the delinquent son off with a shilling, was like delivering him over to his evil propensities. No; let the sum of twenty guineas which he had stolen be deducted from his share, and then let the sum of three guineas be put back from it, seeing that his mother had always considered three of the twenty guineas as his; and, though he had run away, and was, perhaps, gone across the sea, let the money be left to him all the same, and be kept in reserve for his possible return. Mr Faux agreed to his wife's views, and made a codicil to his will accordingly, in time to die with a clear conscience. But for some time his family thought it likely that David would never reappear; and the eldest son, who had the charge of Jacob on his hands, often thought it a little hard that David might perhaps be dead, and yet, for want of certitude on that point, his legacy could not fall to his legal heir. But in this state of things the opposite certitude – namely, that David was still alive and in England – seemed to be brought by the testimony of a neighbour, who, having been on a journey to Cattelton, was pretty sure he had seen David in a gig, with a stout man driving by his side. He could 'swear it was David', though he could 'give no account why, for he had no marks on him; but no more had a white dog, and that didn't hinder folks from knowing a white dog'. It was this incident which had led to the advertisement.

The legacy was paid, of course, after a few preliminary

disclosures as to Mr David's actual position. He begged to send his love to his mother, and to say that he hoped to pay her a dutiful visit by-and-by; but, at present, his business and near prospect of marriage made it difficult for him to leave home. His brother replied with much frankness.

'My mother may do as she likes about having you to see her, but, for my part, I don't want to catch sight of you on the premises again. When folks have taken a new name, they'd better keep to their new 'quinetance'.

David pocketed the insult along with the eighty-two pounds three, and travelled home again in some triumph at the ease of a transaction which had enriched him to this extent. He had no intention of offending his brother by further claims on his fraternal recognition, and relapsed with full contentment into the character of Mr Edward Freely, the orphan, scion of a great but reduced family, with an eccentric uncle in the West Indies. (I have already hinted that he had some acquaintance with imaginative literature; and being of a practical turn, he had, you perceive, applied even this form of knowledge to practical purposes.)

It was little more than a week after the return from his fruitful journey, that the day of his marriage with Penny having been fixed, it was agreed that Mrs Palfrey should overcome her reluctance to move from home, and that she and her husband should bring their two daughters to inspect little Penny's future abode and decide on the new arrangements to be made for the reception of the bride. Mr Freely meant her to have a house so pretty and comfortable that she need not envy even a wool-factor's wife. Of course, the upper room over the shop was to be the best sitting-room; but also the parlour behind the shop was to be made a suitable bower for the lovely Penny, who would naturally wish to be near her husband, though Mr Freely declared his resolution never to allow *his* wife to wait in the shop. The decisions about the parlour furniture were left till last, because the party was to take tea there; and, about five o'clock, they were all seated there with the best muffins and buttered buns before them, little Penny blushing and smiling, with her 'crop' in the best order, and a blue frock showing her little white shoulders, while her opinion was being always asked and never given. She secretly wished to have a particular sort of chimney ornaments, but she could not have brought herself to mention it. Seated by the side of her yellow and rather withered lover, who though he had not reached his thirtieth year, had already crow's-feet about his eyes, she was quite tremulous at the greatness of her lot in being married to a man who had travelled so much – and before her sister Letty! The handsome Letitia looked rather proud and contemptuous, thought her future brother-in-law an odious person, and was vexed with her father and mother for letting Penny marry him. Dear little Penny! She certainly did look like a fresh white-heart cherry going to be bitten off the stem by that lipless mouth. Would no deliverer come to make a slip between that cherry and that mouth without a lip?[38]

'Quite a family likeness between the admiral and you, Mr Freely', observed Mrs Palfrey, who was looking at the family portrait for the first time. 'It's wonderful! and only a grand-uncle. Do you feature the rest of your family, as you know of?'

'I can't say', said Mr Freely, with a sigh. 'My family have mostly thought themselves too high to take any notice of me.'

At this moment an extraordinary disturbance was heard in the shop, as of a heavy animal stamping about and making angry noises, and then of a glass vessel falling in shivers, while the voice of the apprentice was heard calling 'Master' in great alarm.

Mr Freely rose in anxious astonishment, and hastened into the shop, followed by the four Palfreys, who made a group at the parlour-door, transfixed with wonder at seeing a large man in a smock-frock, with a pitchfork in his hand, rush up to Mr Freely and hug him, crying out, – 'Zavy, Zavy, b'other Zavy!'

It was Jacob, and for some moments David lost all presence of mind. He felt arrested for having stolen his mother's guineas. He turned cold, and trembled in his brother's grasp.

'Why, how's this?' said Mr Palfrey, advancing from the door. 'Who is he?'

Jacob supplied the answer by saying over and over again, – 'I'se Zacob, b'other Zacob. Come 'o zee Zavy' – till hunger prompted him to relax his grasp, and to seize a large raised pie, which he lifted to his mouth.

By this time David's power of device had begun to return, but it was a very hard task for his prudence to master his rage and hatred towards poor Jacob.

'I don't know who he is; he must be drunk', he said, in a low tone to Mr Palfrey. 'But he's dangerous with that pitchfork. He'll never let it go.' Then checking himself on the point of betraying too great an intimacy with Jacob's habits, he added, '*You* watch him, while I run for the constable.' And he hurried out of the shop.

'Why, where do you come from, my man?' said Mr Palfrey, speaking to Jacob in a conciliatory tone. Jacob was eating his pie by large mouthfuls, and looking round at the other good things in the shop, while he embraced his pitchfork with his left arm and laid his left hand on some Bath buns. He was in the rare position of a person who recovers a long absent friend and finds him richer than ever in the characteristics that won his heart.

'I's Zacob – b'other Zacob – 't home. I love Zavy – b'other Zavy', he said, as soon as Mr Palfrey had drawn his attention. 'Zavy come back from z'Indies – got mother's zinnies. Where's Zavy?' he added, looking round and then turning to the others with a questioning air, puzzled by David's disappearance.

'It's very odd', observed Mr Palfrey to his wife and daughters. 'He seems to say Freely's his brother come back from th' Indies.'

'What a pleasant relation for us!' said Letitia, sarcastically. 'I think he's a good deal like Mr Freely. He's got just the same sort of nose, and his eyes are the same colour.'

Poor Penny was ready to cry.

But now Mr Freely re-entered the shop without the constable. During his walk of a few yards he had had time and calmness enough to widen his view of consequences, and he saw that to get Jacob taken to the workhouse or to the lock-up house as an offensive stranger, might have awkward effects if his family took the trouble of inquiring after him. He must resign himself to more patient measures.

'On second thoughts,' he said, beckoning to Mr Palfrey and whispering to him while Jacob's back was turned, 'he's a poor half-witted fellow. Perhaps his friends will come after him. I don't mind giving him something to eat, and letting him lie down for the night. He's got it into his head that he knows me – they do get these fancies, idiots do. He'll perhaps go away again in an hour or two, and make no more ado. I'm a kind-hearted man *myself* – I shouldn't like to have the poor fellow ill-used.'

'Why, he'll eat a sovereign's worth in no time', said Mr Palfrey, thinking Mr Freely a little too magnificent in his generosity.

'Eh, Zavy, come back?' exclaimed Jacob, giving his dear brother another hug, which crushed Mr Freely's features inconveniently against the stale of the pitchfork.

'Ay, ay', said Mr Freely, smiling, with every capability of murder in his mind, except the courage to commit it. He wished the Bath buns might by chance have arsenic in them.

'Mother's zinnies?' said Jacob, pointing to a glass jar of yellow lozenges that stood in the window. 'Zive 'em me.'

David dared not do otherwise than reach down the glass jar and give Jacob a handful. He received them in his smock-frock, which he held out for more.

'They'll keep him quiet a bit, at any rate', thought David, and emptied the jar. Jacob grinned and mowed with delight.

'You're very good to this stranger, Mr Freely', said Letitia; and then spitefully, as David joined the party at the parlour-door, 'I think you could hardly treat him better, if he was really your brother.'

'I've always thought it a duty to be good to idiots', said Mr Freely, striving after the most moral view of the subject. 'We might have been idiots ourselves – everybody might have been born idiots, instead of having their right senses.'

'I don't know where there'd ha' been victual for us all then', observed Mrs Palfrey, regarding the matter in a housewifely light.

'But let us sit down again and finish our tea', said Mr Freely. 'Let us leave the poor creature to himself.'

They walked into the parlour again; but Jacob, not apparently appreciating the kindness of leaving him to himself, immediately followed his brother, and seated himself, pitchfork grounded, at the table.

'Well', said Miss Leitia, rising, 'I don't know whether *you* mean to stay, mother; but I shall go home.'

'Oh, me too', said Penny, frightened to death at Jacob, who had begun to nod and grin at her.

'Well, I think we *had* better be going, Mr Palfrey', said the mother, rising more slowly.

Mr Freely, whose complexion had become decidedly yellower during the last half-hour, did not resist this proposition. He hoped they should meet again 'under happier circumstances'.

'It's my belief the man is his brother', said Letitia, when they were all on their way home.

'Letty, it's very ill-natured of you', said Penny, beginning to cry.

'Nonsense!' said Mr Palfrey. 'Freely's got no brother – he's said so many and many a time; he's an orphan; he's got nothing but uncles – leastwise, one. What's it matter what an idiot says? What call had Freely to tell lies?'

Letitia tossed her head and was silent.

Mr Freely, left alone with his affectionate brother Jacob, brooded over the possibility of luring him out of the town early the next morning, and getting him conveyed to Gilsbrook without further betrayals. But the thing was difficult. He saw clearly that if he took Jacob away himself, his absence, conjoined with the disappearance of the stranger, would either cause the conviction that he was really a relative, or would oblige him to the dangerous course of inventing a story to account for his disappearance, and his own absence at the same time. David groaned. There come occasions when falsehood is felt to be inconvenient. It would, perhaps, have been a longer-headed device, if he had never told any of those clever fibs about his uncles, grand and otherwise; for the Palfreys were simple people and shared the popular prejudice against lying. Even if he could·get Jacob away this time, what security was there that he would not come again, having once found the way? O guineas! O lozenges! what enviable people those were who had never robbed their mothers, and had never told fibs! David spent a sleepless night, while Jacob was snoring close by. Was this the upshot of travelling to the Indies, and acquiring experience combined with anecdote?

He rose at break of day, as he had once before done when he was in fear of Jacob, and took all gentle means to rouse this fatal brother from his deep sleep; he dared not be loud, because his apprentice was in the house, and would report everything. But Jacob was not to be roused. He fought out with his fist at the unknown cause of disturbance, turned over, and snored again. He must be left to wake as he would. David, with a cold perspiration on his brow, confessed to himself that Jacob could not be got away that day.

Mr Palfrey came over to Grimworth before noon, with a natural curiosity to see how his future son-in-law got on with the stranger to whom he was so benevolently inclined. He found a crowd round the shop. All Grimworth by this time had heard how Freely had been fastened on by an idiot, who called him 'Brother Zavy'; and the younger population seemed to find the singular stranger an unwearying source of fascination, while the householders dropped in one by one to inquire into the incident.

'Why don't you send him to the workhouse?' said Mr Prettyman. 'You'll have a row with him and the children presently, and he'll eat you up. The workhouse is the proper place for him; let his kin claim him, if he's got any.'

'Those may be *your* feelings, Mr Prettyman', said David, his mind quite enfeebled by the torture of his position.

'What! *is* he your brother, then?' said Mr Prettyman, looking at his neighbour Freely rather sharply.

'All men are our brothers, and idiots particular so', said Mr Freely, who, like many other travelled men, was not master of the English language.

'Come, come, if he's your brother, tell the truth, man', said Mr Prettyman, with growing suspicion. 'Don't be ashamed of your own flesh and blood'.

Mr Palfrey was present, and also had his eye on Freely. It is difficult for a man to believe in the advantage of a truth which will disclose him to have been a liar. In this critical moment, David shrank from this immediate disgrace in the eyes of his future father-in-law.

'Mr Prettyman,' he said, 'I take your observations as an insult. I've no reason to be otherwise than proud of my own flesh and blood. If this poor man was my brother more than all men are, I should say so.'

A tall figure darkened the door, and David, lifting his eyes in that direction, saw his eldest brother, Jonathan, on the door-sill.

'I'll stay wi' Zavy', shouted Jacob, as he, too, caught sight of his eldest brother; and, running behind the counter, he clutched David hard.

'What, he *is* here?' said Jonathan Faux, coming forward. 'My mother would have no nay, as he'd been away so long, but I must see after him. And it struck me he was very like come after you, because we'd been talking of you o' late, and where you lived.'

David saw there was no escape; he smiled a ghastly smile.

'What! is this a relation of yours, sir?' said Mr Palfrey to Jonathan.

'Ay, it's my innicent of a brother, sure enough', said honest Jonathan. 'A fine trouble and cost he is to us, in th' eating and other things, but we must bear what's laid on us.'

'And your name's Freely, is it?' said Mr Prettyman.

'Nay, nay, my name's Faux, I know nothing o' Freelys', said Jonathan, curtly. 'Come', he added, turning to David, 'I must take some news to mother about Jacob. Shall I take him with me, or will you undertake to send him back?'

'Take him, if you can make him loose his hold of me', said David, feebly.

'Is this gentleman here in the confectionery line your brother, then, sir?' said Mr Prettyman, feeling that it was an occasion on which formal language must be used.

'*I* don't want to own him', said Jonathan, unable to resist a movement of indignation that had never been allowed to satisfy itself. 'He run away from home with good reasons in his pocket years ago: he didn't want to be owned again, I reckon.'

Mr Palfrey left the shop; he felt his own pride too severely wounded by the sense that he had let himself be fooled, to feel curiosity for further details. The most pressing business was to go home and tell his daughter that Freely was a poor sneak, probably a rascal, and that her engagement was broken off.

Mr Prettyman stayed, with some internal self-gratulation that *he* had never given into Freely, and that Mr Chaloner would see now what sort of fellow it was that he had put over the heads of older parishioners. He considered it due from him (Mr Prettyman) that, for the interests of the parish, he should know all that was to be known about this 'interloper'. Grimworth would have people coming from Botany Bay[39] to settle in it, if things went on in this way.

It soon appeared that Jacob could not be made to quit his dear brother David except by force. He understood, with a clearness equal to that of the most intelligent mind, that Jonathan would take him back to skimmed milk, apple-dumpling, broad-beans, and pork. And he had found a paradise in his brother's shop. It was a difficult matter to use force with Jacob, for he wore heavy nailed boots; and if his pitchfork had been mastered, he would have resorted without hesitation to kicks. Nothing short of using guile to bind him hand and foot would have made all parties safe.

'Let him stay', said David, with desperate resignation, frightened above all things at the idea of further disturbances in his shop, which would make his exposure all the more conspicuous. '*You* go away again, and tomorrow I can, perhaps, get him to go to Gilsbrook with me. He'll follow me fast enough, I daresay', he added, with a half-groan.

'Very well', said Jonathan, gruffly. ' I don't see why *you* shouldn't have some trouble and expense with him as well as the rest of us. But mind you bring him back safe and soon, else mother'll never rest.'

On this arrangement being concluded, Mr Prettyman begged Mr Jonathan Faux to go and take a snack with him, an invitation which was quite acceptable; and as honest Jonathan had nothing to be ashamed of, it is probable that he was very frank in his communications to the civil draper, who, pursuing the benefit of the parish, hastened to make all the information he could gather about Freely common parochial property. You may imagine that the meeting of the Club at the Woolpack that evening was unusually lively. Every member was anxious to prove that he had never liked Freely, as he called himself. Faux was his name, was it? Fox would have been more suitable. The majority expressed a desire to see him hooted out of the town.

Mr Freely did not venture over his door-sill that day, for he knew Jacob would keep at his side, and there was every probability that they would have a train of juvenile followers. He sent to engage the Woolpack gig for an early hour the next morning; but this order was not kept religiously a secret by the landlord. Mr Freely was informed that he could not have the gig till seven; and the Grimworth people were early risers. Perhaps they were more alert than usual on this particular morning; for when Jacob, with a bag of sweets in his hand, was induced to mount the gig with his brother David, the inhabitants of the market-place were looking out of their doors and windows, and at the turning of the street there was even a muster of apprentices and schoolboys, who shouted as they passed in what Jacob took to be a very merry and friendly way, nodding and grinning in return. 'Huzzay, David Faux! how's your uncle?' was their morning's greeting. Like other pointed things, it was not altogether impromptu.

Even this public derision was not so crushing to David as the horrible thought that though he might succeed now in getting Jacob home again there would never be any security against his coming back, like a wasp to the honey-pot. As long as David lived at Grimworth, Jacob's return would be hanging over him. But could he go on living at Grimworth – an object of ridicule, discarded by the Palfreys, after having revelled in the consciousness that he was an envied and prosperous confectioner? David liked to be envied; he minded less about being loved.

His doubts on this point were soon settled. The mind of Grimworth became obstinately set against him and his viands, and the new school being finished, the eating-room was closed. If there had been no other reason, sympathy with the Palfreys, that respectable family who had lived in the parish time out of mind, would have determined all well-to-do people to decline Freely's goods. Besides, he had absconded with his mother's guineas: who knew what else he had done, in Jamaica or elsewhere, before he came to Grimworth, worming himself into families under false pretences? Females shuddered. Dreadful suspicions gathered round him: his green eyes, his bow-legs, had a criminal aspect. The rector disliked the sight of a man who had imposed upon him; and all boys who could not afford to purchase, hooted 'David Faux' as they passed his shop. Certainly no man now would pay anything for the 'goodwill' of Mr Freely's business, and he would be obliged to quit it without a peculium so desirable towards defraying the expense of moving.

In a few months the shop in the market-place was again to let, and Mr David Faux, *alias* Mr Edward Freely, had gone – nobody at Grimworth knew whither. In this way the demoralisation of Grimworth women was checked. Young Mrs Steene renewed her efforts to make light mince-pies, and having at last made a batch so excellent that Mr Steene looked at her with complacency as he ate them, and said that they were the best he had ever eaten in his life, she thought less of bulbuls and renegades ever after. The secrets of the finer cookery were revived in the breasts of matronly housewives, and daughters were again anxious to be initiated in them.

You will further, I hope, be glad to hear, that some purchases of drapery made by pretty Penny, in preparation for her marriage with Mr Freely, came in quite as well for her wedding with young Towers as if they had been made expressly for the latter occasion. For Penny's complexion had not altered, and blue always became it best.

Here ends the story of Mr David Faux, confectioner, and his brother Jacob. And we see in it, I think, an admirable instance of the unexpected forms in which the great Nemesis hides herself.

\*      \*      \*

If 'The Lifted Veil' is a *jeu de mélancolie*, this is a *jeu d'esprit* which may have appeared *outré* to John Blackwood. Both, he said, were 'as clever as can be', but there was 'a painful want of light' about them. The story is excellently written and deftly manipulated; it is lambent with humour and fancy, and its suspense is judiciously managed throughout. Perhaps Blackwood was puzzled that a rogue and impostor could be treated with mock-seriousness; more probably he was disturbed to find that an important role in this ironic tale is played by an idiot. The change in the title from 'Mr David Faux, Confectioner' to 'The Idiot Brother', with 'Brother Jacob' as the more discreet preference, underlines this importance; and suggests that George Eliot had been fortified in her resolve to write the story by the example of Wordsworth in 'The Idiot Boy'. Wordsworth 'never wrote anything with so much glee', and George Eliot never wrote anything with more genial light-heartedness than 'Brother Jacob'. In neither, it should be said, is fun directed against an unfortunate creature; Jacob's role as the unwitting agent of nemesis allies itself with his brotherly affection to win the reader's sympathy.

# III    Adjuncts to Major Works

## i    HOW I CAME TO WRITE FICTION

(This account was entered in George Eliot's journal in December 1857, just before the publication of *Scenes of Clerical Life*. 'Amos Barton', the first of these three stories to be written, was begun in September 1856.)

September 1856 made a new era in my life, for it was then I began to write Fiction. It had always been a vague dream of mine that some time or other I might write a novel, and my shadowy conception of what the novel was to be, varied, of course, from one epoch of my life to another. But I never went farther towards the actual writing of the novel than an introductory chapter describing a Staffordshire village and the life of the neighbouring farm houses, and as the years passed on I lost any hope that I should ever be able to write a novel, just as I desponded about everything else in my future life. I always thought I was deficient in dramatic power, both of construction and dialogue, but I felt I should be at my ease in the descriptive parts of a novel. My 'introductory chapter' was pure description though there were good materials in it for dramatic presentation. It happened to be among the papers I had with me in Germany and one evening at Berlin, something led me to read it to George.[1] He was struck with it as a bit of concrete description, and it suggested to him the possibility of my being able to write a novel, though he distrusted – indeed disbelieved in, my possession of any dramatic power. Still, he began to think that I might as well try, some time, what I could do in fiction, and by and bye when we came back to England and I had greater success than he had ever expected in other kinds of writing, his impression that it was worth while to see how far my mental power would go towards the production of a novel, was strengthened. He began to say very positively, 'You must try and write a story', and when we were at Tenby he urged

me to begin at once. I deferred it, however, after my usual fashion,
with work that does not present itself as an absolute duty. But one
morning as I was lying in bed, thinking what should be the subject
of my first story, my thoughts merged themselves into a dreamy
doze, and I imagined myself writing a story of which the title was –
'The Sad Fortunes of the Reverend Amos Barton'. I was soon wide
awake again, and told G. He said, 'O what a capital title!' and
from that time I had settled in my mind that this should be my
first story. George used to say, 'It may be a failure – it may be that
you are unable to write fiction. Or perhaps, it may be just good
enough to warrant your trying again.' Again, 'You may write a
chef-d'oeuvre at once – there's no telling.' But his prevalent
impression was that though I could hardly write a *poor* novel, my
effort would want the highest quality of fiction – dramatic
presentation. He used to say, 'You have wit, description and
philosophy – those go a good way towards the production of a
novel. It is worth while for you to try the experiment.'

We determined that if my story turned out good enough, we
would send it to Blackwood,[2] but G. thought the more probable
result was, that I should have to lay it aside and try again.

But when we returned to Richmond I had to write my article on
Silly Novels and my review of Contemporary Literature for the
Westminister; so that I did not begin my story till September 22.
After I had begun it, as we were walking in the Park, I mentioned
to G. that I had thought of the plan of writing a series of stories
containing sketches drawn from my own observations of the
Clergy, and calling them 'Scenes from Clerical Life' opening with
'Amos Barton'. He at once accepted the notion as a good one –
fresh and striking; and about a week afterwards when I read him
the early part of 'Amos', he had no longer any doubt about my
ability to carry out the plan. The scene at Cross Farm, he said,
satisfied him that I had the very element he had been doubtful
about – it was clear I could write good dialogue. There still
remained the question whether I could command any pathos, and
that was to be decided by the mode in which I treated Milly's
death. One night G. went to town on purpose to leave me a quiet
evening for writing it. I wrote the chapter from the news brought
by the shepherd to Mrs Hackit, to the moment when Amos is
dragged from the bedside and I read it to G. when he came home.
We both cried over it, and then he came up to me and kissed me,
saying 'I think your pathos is better than your fun.'

So when the story was finished G. sent it to Blackwood, who
wrote in reply, that he thought the 'Clerical reminiscences would
do', congratulated the author on being 'worthy the honours of

print and pay', but would like to see more of the series before he undertook to print. However, when G. wrote that the author was discouraged by this editorial caution, Blackwood disclaimed any distrust and agreed to print the story at once. The first part appeared in the January number 1857. Before the appearance of the Magazine – on sending me the proof, Blackwood already expressed himself with much greater warmth of admiration, and when the first part had appeared, he sent me a charming letter with a cheque for fifty guineas, and a proposal about republication of the series. When the story was concluded he wrote me word how Albert Smith[3] had sent him a letter saying he had never read anything that affected him more than Milly's death, and, added Blackwood, 'the men at the club seem to have mingled their tears and their tumblers together. It will be curious if you should be a member and be hearing your own praises!' There was clearly no suspicion that I was a woman. It is interesting, as an indication of the value there is in such conjectural criticism generally, to remember that when G. read the first part of 'Amos' to a party at Helps's,[4] they were all sure I was a clergyman – a Cambridge man. Agnes[5] thought I was the father of a family – was sure I was a man who had seen a great deal of society etc. etc. Blackwood seemed curious about the author, and when I signed my letter 'George Eliot' hunted up some old letters from Eliot Warburton's brother, to compare the handwritings, though, he said, 'Amos seems to me not in the least like what that good artillery man would write.'

Several pleasant bits of admiration came about that time: – a letter from the Rev. Mr. Swaine, saying that 'Amos' in its charming tenderness, reminded him of the 'Vicar of Wakefield', is the only one I remember just now. The adverse critics mentioned by Blackwood were Colonel Hamley and Prof. Aytoun.[6] Professor Aytoun came round afterwards, said he had been quite mistaken in his estimate of the powers of the author of 'Amos Barton', and expressed great admiration of 'Mr Gilfil's Love Story' – or rather at the conclusion of it. Colonel Hamley said I was 'a man of science, but not a practised writer'. Blackwood was eager for the second story, and much delighted with the two first parts of 'Mr Gilfil's Love Story', which I sent him together. I wrote the fourth part at Scilly – the epilogue, sitting on the Fortification Hill, one sunshiny morning. Blackwood himself wrote in entire admiration of it, and in the same letter told us that Thackeray 'thought highly of the series'. When we were at Jersey, he was in London, and wrote from thence that he heard nothing but approval of 'Mr Gilfil's Love Story'. Lord Stanley, among other people, had spoken to him about the 'Clerical Scenes' at Bulwer's,[7] and was astonished to find Blackwood in the dark as to the author.

I began 'Janet's Repentance' at Scilly and sent off the first Part from Jersey, G. declaring it to be admirable, almost better than the other stories. But to my disappointment, Blackwood did not like it so well, seemed to misunderstand the characters, and be doubtful about the treatment of clerical matters. I wrote at once to beg him to give up printing the story if he felt uncomfortable about it, and he immediately sent a very anxious, cordial letter, saying the thought of putting a stop to the series 'gave him quite a turn' – 'he didn't meet with George Eliots every day' – and so on.

One of the pleasantest little incidents at Jersey was a letter from Archer Gurney to the unknown author of 'Mr Gilfil's Love Story', expressing simply but warmly his admiration of the truth and originality he found in the Clerical Scenes. Dear G. came upstairs to me with the letter in his hands, his face bright with gladness, saying, 'Her fame's beginning already!'

I had meant to carry on the series beyond 'Janet's Repentance', and especially I longed to tell the story of the Clerical Tutor[8] but my annoyance at Blackwood's want of sympathy in the first two parts of 'Janet', (although he came round to admiration at the third part) determined me to close the series and republish them in two volumes.

The first volume is printed, and the advertisements greet our eyes every week, but we are still wondering how the public will behave to my first book.

## ii HISTORY OF 'ADAM BEDE'

(From George Eliot's journal, 30 November 1858, on completing *Adam Bede*. Her aunt Elizabeth had been converted to Wesleyanism in 1797; it was while she was a Methodist preacher that she met Robert Evans' brother, whom she married. When Mary Voce was condemned to death for child-murder in 1802 at the Nottingham assizes, she was one of two women who prayed with the prisoner the night before her execution. The girl confessed her crime, and Elizabeth was chosen to accompany her in a cart to Gallows Hill. The story was told when Elizabeth Evans visited Griff House in 1839. George Eliot's original intention was to add the story to her *Scenes of Clerical Life* series. Then she decided to blend it with 'points' in her father's early life and character, the subject she most probably had in mind when she wrote her introductory chapter to a novel set in Staffordshire (p. 104); the result was *Adam Bede*.)

The germ of 'Adam Bede' was an anecdote told me by my Methodist Aunt Samuel (the wife of my Father's younger brother): an anecdote from her own experience. We were sitting together one afternoon during her visit to me at Griffe, probably in 1839 or 40, when it occurred to her to tell me how she had visited a condemned criminal, a very ignorant girl who had murdered her child and refused to confess – how she had stayed with her praying, through the night and how the poor creature at last broke out into tears, and confessed her crime. My Aunt afterwards went with her in the cart to the place of execution, and she described to me the great respect with which this ministry of hers was regarded by the official people about the gaol. The story, told by my aunt with great feeling, affected me deeply, and I never lost the impression of that afternoon and our talk together; but I believe I never mentioned it, through all the intervening years, till something prompted me to tell it to George in December 1856, when I had begun to write the 'Scenes of Clerical Life'. He remarked that the scene in the prison would make a fine element in a story, and I afterwards began to think of blending this and some other recollections of my aunt in one story with some points in my father's early life and character. The problem of construction that remained was to make the unhappy girl one of the chief *dramatis personae* and connect her with the hero. At first I thought of making the story one of the series of 'Scenes', but afterwards, when several motives had induced me to close these with 'Janet's Repentance', I determined on making what we always called in our conversations 'My Aunt's Story', the subject of a long novel: which I accordingly began to write on the 22 October 1857.

The character of Dinah grew out of my recollections of my aunt, but Dinah is not at all like my aunt, who was a very small, black-eyed woman, and (as I was told, for I never heard her preach) very vehement in her style of preaching. She had left off preaching when I knew her, being, probably, sixty years old, and in delicate health; and she had become, as my father told me, much more gentle and subdued than she had been in the days of her active ministry and bodily strength, when she could not rest without exhorting and remonstrating in season and out of season. I was very fond of her, and enjoyed the few weeks of her stay with me greatly. She was loving and kind to me, and I could talk to her about my inward life, which was closely shut up from those usually round me. I saw her only twice again, for much shorter periods: once at her own home at Wirksworth in Derbyshire, and once at my Father's last residence, Foleshill.

The character of Adam, and one or two incidents connected with him were suggested by my ·Father's early life; but Adam is not my father any more than Dinah is my aunt. Indeed, there is not a single *portrait* in 'Adam Bede'; only the suggestions of experience wrought up into new combinations. When I began to write it, the only elements I had determined on besides the character of Dinah were the character of Adam, his relation to Arthur Donnithorne and their mutual relation to Hetty, i.e. to the girl who commits child-murder: the scene in the prison being of course the climax towards which I worked. Everything else grew out of the characters and their mutual relations. Dinah's ultimate relation to Adam was suggested by George, when I had read to him the first part of the first volume: he was so delighted with the presentation of Dinah and so convinced that the readers' interest would centre in her, that he wanted her to be the principal figure at the last. I accepted the idea at once, and from the end of the third chapter worked with it constantly in view.

The first volume was written at Richmond and given to Blackwood in March. He expressed great admiration of its freshness and vividness, but seemed to hesitate about putting it in the Magazine, which was the form of publication he, as well as myself, had previously contemplated. He still *wished* to have it for the Mag., but desired to know the course of the story; at *present*, he saw nothing to prevent its reception in Maga, but he would like to see more. I am uncertain whether his doubts rested solely on Hetty's relation to Arthur, or whether they were also directed towards the treatment of Methodism by the Church. I refused to tell my story beforehand, on the ground that I would not have it judged apart from my *treatment*, which alone determines the moral quality of art;[9] and ultimately I proposed that the notion of publication in Maga should be given up, and that the novel should be published in three volumes, at Christmas, if possible. He assented.

I began the second volume in the second week of my stay at Munich, about the middle of April. While we were at Munich, George expressed his fear that Adam's part was too passive throughout the drama, and that it was important for him to be brought into more direct collision with Arthur. This doubt haunted me, and out of it grew the scene in the Wood between Arthur and Adam: the fight came to me as a *necessity* one night at the Munich opera when I was listening to *William Tell*. Work was slow and interrupted at Munich, and when we left I had only written to the beginning of the dance on the Birthday Feast: but at Dresden, I wrote uninterruptedly and with great enjoyment in the long, quiet mornings, and there I nearly finished the second volume – all, I think, but the last chapter, which I wrote here in the old room at Richmond in the first week of September, and then sent the M.S. off to Blackwood. The opening of the third volume – Hetty's journeys – was, I think written more rapidly than the rest of the book, and was left without the slightest alteration of the first draught. Throughout the book, I have altered little, and the only cases, I think, in which George suggested more than a verbal alteration, when I read the M.S. aloud to him, were the first scene at the Farm and the scene in the Wood between Arthur and Adam, both of which he recommended me to 'space out' a little, which I did.

When, on October 29, I had written to the end of the love scene at the Farm, between Adam and Dinah, I sent the M.S. to Blackwood, since the remainder of the third volume could not affect the judgment passed on what had gone before. He wrote back in warm admiration, and offered me, on the part of the firm, £800 for four years' copyright. I accepted the offer. The last words of the third volume were written and dispatched on their way to Edinburgh November the 16th, and now on this last day of the same month I have written this slight history of my book. I love it very much and am deeply thankful to have written it, whatever the public may say to it – a result which is still in darkness, for I have at present had only four sheets of the proof. The book would have been published at Christmas, or rather, early in December, but that Bulwer's 'What will he do with it?' was to be published by Blackwoods at that time, and it was thought that this novel might interfere with mine.

### iii ADDRESS TO WORKING MEN, BY FELIX HOLT

(Although *Felix Holt* (1866) is set in the election period just after the passing of the First Reform Bill of 1832, it arose from George Eliot's reflections during the period when the demand for the Second Reform Bill was often clamant. This bill was passed in August 1867. After hearing Disraeli speak on the subject to the working men of Edinburgh at the end of October, John Blackwood suggested this address and title. George Eliot demurred at first, but began the article on 22 November, and sent it off on 4 December; it appeared in the January 1868 number of *Blackwood's Magazine*. Written in a deliberately simple style, and even blunt at times, as befits the character of Felix Holt, its main arguments and principles are as valid today as when they were written.)

Fellow-workmen, – I am not going to take up your time by complimenting you. It has been the fashion to compliment kings and other authorities when they have come into power, and to tell them that, under their wise and beneficent rule, happiness would certainly overflow the land. But the end has not always corresponded to that beginning. If it were true that we who work for wages had more of the wisdom and virtue necessary to the right use of power than has been shown by the aristocratic and mercantile classes, we should not glory much in that fact, or consider that it carried with it any near approach to infallibility.

In my opinion, there has been too much complimenting of that sort; and whenever a speaker, whether he is one of ourselves or not, wastes our time in boasting or flattery, I say, let us hiss him. If we have the beginning of wisdom, which is, to know a little truth about ourselves, we know that as a body we are neither very wise nor very virtuous. And to prove this, I will not point specially to our own habits and doings, but to the general state of the country. Any nation that had within it a majority of men – and we are the majority – possessed of much wisdom and virtue, would not tolerate the bad practices, the commercial lying and swindling, the poisonous adulteration of goods,[10] the retail cheating, and the political bribery which are carried on boldly in the midst of us. A majority has the power of creating a public opinion. We could groan and hiss before we had the franchise: if we had groaned and hissed in the right place, if we had discerned better between good and evil, if the multitude of us artisans, and factory hands, and miners, and labourers of all sorts, had been skilful, faithful, well-judging, industrious, sober – and I don't see how there can be wisdom and virtue anywhere without those qualities – we should have made an audience that would have shamed the other classes out of their share in the national vices. We should have had better members of Parliament, better religious teachers, honester tradesmen, fewer foolish demagogues, less impudence in infamous and brutal men; and we should not have had among us the abomination of men calling themselves religious while living in splendour on ill-gotten gains. I say, it is not possible for any society in which there is a very large body of wise and virtuous men to be as vicious as our society is – to have as low a standard of right and wrong, to have so much belief in falsehood, or to have so degrading, barbarous a notion of what pleasure is, or of what

justly raises a man above his fellows. Therefore, let us have done
with this nonsense about our being much better than the rest of
our countrymen, or the pretence that that was a reason why we
ought to have such an extension of the franchise as has been given
to us. The reason for our having the franchise, as I want presently
to show, lies somewhere else than in our personal good qualities,
and does not in the least lie in any high betting chance that a
delegate is a better man than a duke, or that a Sheffield grinder is a
better man than any one of the firm he works for.

However, we have got our franchise now. We have been
sarcastically called in the House of Commons the future masters of
the country;[11] and if that sarcasm contains any truth, it seems to
me that the first thing we had better think of is, our heavy
responsibility; that is to say, the terrible risk we run of working
mischief and missing good, as others have done before us.
Suppose certain men, discontented with the irrigation of a
country which depended for all its prosperity on the right
direction being given to the waters of a great river, had got the
management of the irrigation before they were quite sure how
exactly it could be altered for the better, or whether they could
command the necessary agency for such an alteration. Those men
would have a difficult and dangerous business on their hands; and
the more sense, feeling, and knowledge they had, the more they
would be likely to tremble rather than to triumph. Our situation is
not altogether unlike theirs. For general prosperity and well-being
is a vast crop, that like the corn in Egypt[12] can be come at, not at
all by hurried snatching, but only by a well-judged patient
process; and whether our political power will be any good to us
now we have got it, must depend entirely on the means and
materials – the knowledge, ability, and honesty, we have at
command. These three things are the only conditions on which we
can get any lasting benefit, as every clever workman among us
knows: he knows that for an article to be worth much there must
be a good invention or plan to go upon, there must be well-
prepared material, and there must be skilful and honest work in
carrying out the plan. And by this test we may try those who want
to be our leaders. Have they anything to offer us besides indignant
talk? When they tell us we ought to have this, that, or the other
thing, can they explain to us any reasonable, fair, safe way of
getting it? Can they argue in favour of a particular change by
showing us pretty closely how the change is likely to work? I don't
want to decry a just indignation; on the contrary, I should like it to
be more thorough and general. A wise man, more than two
thousand years ago, when he was asked what would most tend to

lessen injustice in the world, said, 'If every bystander felt as indignant at a wrong as if he himself were the sufferer'.[13] Let us cherish such indignation. But the long-growing evils of a great nation are a tangled business, asking for a good deal more than indignation in order to be got rid of. Indignation is a fine war-horse, but the war-horse must be ridden by a man: it must be ridden by rationality, skill, courage, armed with the right weapons, and taking definite aim.

We have reason to be discontented with many things, and, looking back either through the history of England to much earlier generations or to the legislation and administrations of later times, we are justified in saying that many of the evils under which our country now suffers are the consequences of folly, ignorance, neglect, or self-seeking in those who, at different times have wielded the powers of rank, office, and money. But the more bitterly we feel this, the more loudly we utter it, the stronger is the obligation we lay on ourselves to beware, lest we also, by a too hasty wresting of measures which seem to promise an immediate partial relief, make a worse time of it for our own generation, and leave a bad inheritance to our children. The deepest curse of wrong-doing, whether of the foolish, or wicked sort, is that its effects are difficult to be undone. I suppose there is hardly anything more to be shuddered at than that part of the history of disease which shows how, when a man injures his constitution by a life of vicious excess, his children and grandchildren inherit diseased bodies and minds, and how the effects of that unhappy inheritance continue to spread beyond our calculation. This is only one example of the law by which human lives are linked together; another example of what we complain of when we point to our pauperism, to the brutal ignorance of multitudes among our fellow countrymen, to the weight of taxation laid on us by blamable wars, to the wasteful channels made for the public money, to the expense and trouble of getting justice, and call these the effects of bad rule. This is the law that we all bear the yoke of, the law of no man's making, and which no man can undo. Everybody now sees an example of it in the case of Ireland. We who are living now are sufferers by the wrong-doing of those who lived before us; we are sufferers by each other's wrong-doing; and the children who come after us are and will be sufferers from the same causes. Will any man say he doesn't care for that law – it is nothing to him – what he wants is to better himself? With what face then will he complain of any injury? If he says that in politics or in any sort of social action he will not care to know what are likely to be the consequences to others besides himself, he is defending the very worst doings that have brought about his discontent. He might as well say that there is no better rule needful for men than that each should tug and rive for what will please him, without caring how that tugging will act on the fine widespread network of society in which he is fast meshed. If any man taught that as a doctrine, we should know him for a fool. But there are men who act upon it; every scoundrel, for example, whether he is a rich religious scoundrel who lies and cheats on a large scale, and will perhaps come and ask you to send him to Parliament, or a poor pocket-picking scoundrel, who will steal your loose pence while you are listening round the platform. None of us are so ignorant as not to know that a society, a nation is held together by just the opposite doctrine and action – by the dependence of men on each other and the sense they have of a common interest in preventing injury. And we working men are, I think, of all classes the last that can afford to forget this; for if we did we should be much like sailors cutting away the timbers of our own ship to warm our grog with. For what else is the meaning of our Trades-unions? What else is the meaning of every flag we carry, every procession we make, every crowd we collect for the sake of making some protest on behalf of our body as receivers of wages, if not this: that it is our interest to stand by each other, and that this being the common interest, no one of us will try to make a good bargain for himself without considering what will be good for his fellows? And every member of a union believes that the wider he can spread his union, the stronger and surer will be the effect of it. So I think I shall be borne out in saying that a working man who can put two and two together, or take three from four and see what will be the remainder, can understand that a society, to be well off, must be made up chiefly of men who consider the general good as well as their own.

Well, but taking the world as it is – and this is one way we must take it when we want to find out how it can be improved – no society is made up of a single class: society stands before us like that wonderful piece of life, the human body, with all its various parts depending on one another, and with a terrible liability to get wrong because of that delicate dependence. We all know how many diseases the human body is apt to suffer from, and how difficult it is even for the doctors to find out exactly where the seat or beginning of the disorder is. That is because the body is made up of so many various parts, all related to each other, or likely all to feel the effect if any of them goes wrong. It is somewhat the same with our old nations or societies.[14] No society ever stood long in the world without getting to be composed of different classes.

Now, it is all pretence to say that there is no such thing as Class Interest. It is clear that if any particular number of men get a particular benefit from any existing institution, they are likely to band together, in order to keep up that benefit and increase it, until it is perceived to be unfair and injurious to another large number, who get knowledge and strength enough to set up a resistance. And this, again, has been part of the history of every great society since history began. But the simple reason for this being, that any large body of men is likely to have more of stupidity, narrowness, and greed than of farsightedness and generosity, it is plain that the number who resist unfairness and injury are in danger of becoming injurious in their turn. And in this way a justifiable resistance has become a damaging convulsion, making everything worse instead of better. This has been seen so often that we ought to profit a little by the experience. So long as there is selfishness in men; so long as they have not found out for themselves institutions which express and carry into practice the truth, that the highest interest of mankind must at last be a common and not a divided interest; so long as the gradual operation of steady causes has not made that truth a part of every man's knowledge and feeling, just as we now not only know that it is good for our health to be cleanly, but feel that cleanliness is only another word for comfort, which is the under-side or lining of all pleasure; so long, I say as men wink at their own knowingness, or hold their heads high, because they have got an advantage over their fellows; so long Class Interest will be in danger of making itself felt injuriously. No set of men will get any sort of power without being in danger of wanting more than their right share. But, on the other hand, it is just as certain that no set of men will get angry at having less than their right share, and set up a claim on that ground, without falling into just the same danger of exacting too much, and exacting it in wrong ways. It's human nature we have got to work with all round, and nothing else. That seems like saying something very commonplace – nay, obvious; as if one should say that where there are hands there are mouths. Yet, to hear a good deal of the speechifying and to see a good deal of the action that goes forward, one might suppose it was forgotten.

But I come back to this: that, in our old society, there are old institutions, and among them the various distinctions and inherited advantages of classes, which have shaped themselves along with all the wonderful slow-growing system of things made up of our laws, our commerce, and our stores of all sorts, whether in material objects, such as buildings and machinery, or in knowledge, such as scientific thought and professional skill. Just as in that case I spoke of before, the irrigation of a country, which must absolutely have its water distributed or it will bear no crop; there are the old channels, the old banks, and the old pumps, which must be used as they are until new and better have been prepared, or the structure of the old has been gradually altered. But it would be fool's work to batter down a pump only because a better might be made, when you had no machinery ready for a new one: it would be wicked work, if villages lost their crops by it. Now the only safe way by which society can be steadily improved and our worst evils reduced, is not by any attempt to do away directly with the actually existing class distinctions and advantages, as if everybody could have the same sort of work, or lead the same sort of life (which none of my hearers are stupid enough to suppose), but by the turning of Class Interests into Class Functions or duties. What I mean is, that each class should be urged by the surrounding conditions to perform its particular work under the strong pressure of responsibility to the nation at large; that our public affairs should be got into a state in which there should be no impunity for foolish or faithless conduct. In this way, the public judgment would sift out incapability and dishonesty from posts of high charge, and even personal ambition would necessarily become of a worthier sort, since the desires of the most selfish men must be a good deal shaped by the opinions of those around them; and for one person to put on a cap and bells, or to go about dishonest or paltry ways of getting rich that he may spend a vast sum of money in having more finery than his neighbours, he must be pretty sure of a crowd who will applaud him. Now changes can only be good in proportion as they help to bring about this sort of result: in proportion as they put knowledge in the place of ignorance, and fellow-feeling in the place of selfishness. In the course of that substitution class distinctions must inevitably change their character; and represent the varying Duties of men, not their varying Interests. But this end will not come by impatience. 'Day will not break the sooner because we get up before the twilight.' Still less will it come by mere undoing, or change merely as change. And moreover, if we believed that it would be unconditionally hastened by our getting the franchise, we should be what I call superstitious men, believing in magic, or the production of a result by hocus-pocus. Our getting the franchise will greatly hasten that good end in proportion only as every one of us has the knowledge, the foresight, the conscience, that will make him well-judging and scrupulous in the use of it. The nature of things in this world has been determined for us beforehand, and in such a way that no ship can be expected to sail well on a difficult voyage, and reach the right port, unless it is well manned: the nature of the winds and the waves, of the timbers, the sails and the cordage, will not accommodate itself to drunken, mutinous sailors.

You will not suspect me of wanting to preach any cant to you, or of joining in the pretence that everything is in a fine way, and need not be made better. What I am striving to keep in our minds is the care, the precaution, with which we should go about making things better, so that the public order may not be destroyed, so that no fatal shock may be given to this society of ours, this living body in which our lives are bound up. After the Reform Bill of 1832 I was in an election riot, which showed me clearly, on a small scale, what public disorder must always be;[15] and I have never forgotten that the riot was brought about chiefly by the agency of dishonest men who professed to be on the people's side. Now, the danger hanging over change is great, just in proportion as it tends to produce such disorder by giving any large number of ignorant men, whose notions of what is good are of a low and brutal sort, the belief that they have got power into their hands, and may do pretty much as they like. If any one can look round us and say that he sees no signs of any such danger now, and that our national condition is running along like a clear broadening stream, safe not to get choked with mud, I call him a cheerful man: perhaps he does his own gardening, and seldom takes exercise far away from home. To us who have no gardens, and often walk abroad, it is plain that we can never get into a bit of a crowd but we must rub clothes with a set of Roughs, who have the worst vices of the worst rich – who are gamblers, sots, libertines, knaves, or else mere sensual simpletons and victims. They are the ugly crop that has sprung up while the stewards have been sleeping;[16] they are the multiplying brood begotten by parents who have been left without all teaching save that of a too craving body, without all wellbeing save the fading delusions of drugged beer and gin. They are the hideous margin of society, at one edge drawing towards it the undesigning ignorant poor, at the other darkening imperceptibly into the lowest criminal class. Here is one of the evils which cannot be got rid of quickly, and against which any of us who have got sense, decency, and instruction have need to watch. That these degraded fellow-men could really get the mastery in a persistent disobedience to the laws and in a struggle to subvert order, I do not believe; but wretched calamities would come from the very beginning of such a struggle, and the continuance of it would be a civil war, in which the inspiration on both sides might soon cease to be even a false notion of good, and might become the direct savage impulse of ferocity. We have all to see to it that we do not help to rouse what I may call the savage beast in the breasts of our generation – that we do not help to poison the nation's blood, and make richer provision for bestiality to come. We know well enough that oppressors have sinned in this way – that oppression has notoriously made men mad; and we are determined to resist oppression. But let us, if possible, show that we can keep sane in our resistance, and shape our means more and more reasonably towards the least harmful, and therefore the speediest, attainment of our end. Let us, I say, show that our spirits are too strong to be driven mad, but can keep that sober determination which alone gives mastery over the adaptation of means. And a first guarantee of this sanity will be to act as if we understood that the fundamental duty of a government is to preserve order, to enforce obedience of the laws. It has been held hitherto that a man can be depended on as a guardian of order only when he has much money and comfort to lose. But a better state of things would be, that men who had little money and not much comfort should still be guardians of order, because they had sense to see that disorder would do no good, and had a heart of justice, pity, and fortitude, to keep them from making more misery only because they felt some misery themselves. There are thousands of artisans who have already shown this fine spirit, and have endured much with patient heroism. If such a spirit spread, and penetrated us all, we should soon become the masters of the country in the best sense and to the best ends. For, the public order being preserved, there can be no government in future that will not be determined by our insistance on our fair and practicable demands. It is only by disorder that our demands will be choked, that we shall find ourselves lost amongst a brutal rabble, with all the intelligence of the country opposed to us, and see government in the shape of guns that will sweep us down in the ignoble martyrdom of fools.

It has been a too common notion that to insist much on the preservation of order is the part of a selfish aristocracy and a selfish commercial class, because among these, in the nature of things, have been found the opponents of change. I am a Radical; and, what is more, I am not a Radical with a title, or a French cook, or even an entrance into fine society. I expect great changes, and I desire them. But I don't expect them to come in a hurry, by mere inconsiderate sweeping. A Hercules with a big besom is a fine thing for a filthy stable, but not for weeding a seed-bed, where his besom would soon make a barren floor.

That is old-fashioned talk, some one may say. We know all that.

Yes, when things are put in an extreme way, most people think they know them; but, after all, they are comparatively few who see the small degrees by which those extremes are arrived at, or have the resolution and self-control to resist the little impulses by which they creep on surely towards a fatal end. Does anybody set out meaning to ruin himself, or to drink himself to death, or to waste his life so that he becomes a despicable old man, a superannuated nuisance, like a fly in winter? Yet there are plenty, of whose lot this is the pitiable story. Well now, supposing us all to have the best intentions, we working men, as a body, run some risk of bringing evil on the nation in that unconscious manner – half-hurrying, half-pushed in a jostling march towards an end we are not thinking of. For just as there are many things which we know better and feel much more strongly than the richer, softer-handed classes can know or feel them; so there are many things – many precious benefits – which we, by the very fact of our privations, our lack of leisure and instruction, are not so likely to be aware of and take into our account. Those precious benefits form a chief part of what I may call the common estate of society: a wealth over and above buildings, machinery, produce, shipping, and so on, though closely connected with these; a wealth of a more delicate kind, that we may more unconsciously bring into danger, doing harm and not knowing that we do it. I mean that treasure of knowledge, science, poetry, refinement of thought, feeling, and manners, great memories and the interpretation of great records, which is carried on from the minds of one generation to the minds of another. This is something distinct from the indulgences of luxury and the pursuit of vain finery; and one of the hardships in the lot of working men is that they have been for the most part shut out from sharing in this treasure. It can make a man's life very great, very full of delight, though he has no smart furniture and no horses: it also yields a great deal of discovery that corrects error, and of invention that lessens bodily pain, and must at last make life easier for all.

Now the security of this treasure demands, not only the preservation of order, but a certain patience on our part with many institutions and facts of various kinds, especially touching the accumulation of wealth, which from the light we stand in, we are more likely to discern the evil than the good of. It is constantly the task of practical wisdom not to say, 'This is good, and I will have it', but to say, 'This is the less of two unavoidable evils, and I will bear it.' And this treasure of knowledge, which consists in the fine activity, the exalted vision of many minds, is bound up at present with conditions which have much evil in them. Just as in the case of material wealth and its distribution we are obliged to take the selfishness and weaknesses of human nature into account, and however we insist that men might act better, are forced, unless we are fanatical simpletons, to consider how they are likely to act; so in this matter of the wealth that is carried in men's minds, we have to reflect that the too absolute predominance of a class whose wants have been of a common sort, who are chiefly struggling to get better and more food, clothing, shelter, and bodily recreation, may lead to hasty measures for the sake of having things more fairly shared, which, even if they did not fail of their object, would at last debase the life of the nation. Do anything which will throw the classes who hold the treasures of knowledge – nay, I may say, the treasure of refined needs – into the background, cause them to withdraw from public affairs, stop too suddenly any of the sources by which their leisure and ease are furnished, rob them of the chances by which they may be influential and pre-eminent, and you do something as shortsighted as the acts of France and Spain when in jealousy and wrath, not altogether unprovoked, they drove from among them races and classes that held the traditions of handicraft and agriculture. You injure your own inheritance and the inheritance of your children. You may truly say that this which I call the common estate of society has been anything but common to you; but the same may be said, by many of us, of the sunlight and the air, of the sky and the fields, of parks and holiday games. Nevertheless, that these blessings exist makes life worthier to us, and urges us the more to energetic, likely means of getting our share in them; and I say, let us watch carefully, lest we do anything to lessen this treasure which is held in the minds of men, while we exert ourselves first of all, and to the very utmost, that we and our children may share in all its benefits. Yes; exert ourselves to the utmost, to break the yoke of ignorance. If we demand more leisure, more ease in our lives, let us show that we don't deserve the reproach of wanting to shirk that industry which, in some form or other, every man, whether rich or poor, should feel himself as much bound to as he is bound to decency. Let us show that we want to have some time and strength left to us, that we may use it, not for brutal indulgence, but for the rational exercise of the faculties which make us men. Without this no political measures can benefit us. No political institution will alter the nature of Ignorance, or hinder it from producing vice and misery. Let Ignorance start how it will, it must run the same round of low appetites, poverty, slavery, and superstition. Some of us know this well – nay, I will say, feel it; for knowledge of this kind cuts deep; and to us it is one of the most painful facts belonging to our condition that there are numbers of our fellow-workmen who are so far from feeling in the same way, that they never use the imperfect opportunities already offered them for giving their children some schooling, but turn their little ones of tender age into breadwinners, often at cruel tasks, exposed to the horrible infection of childish vice. Of course, the causes of these hideous things go a long way back. Parents' misery has made parents' wickedness. But we, who are still blessed with the hearts of fathers and the consciences of men – we who have some knowledge of the curse entailed on broods of creatures in human shape, whose enfeebled bodies and dull perverted minds are mere centres of uneasiness, in whom even appetite is feeble and joy impossible – I say we are bound to use all the means at our command to help in putting a stop to this horror. Here, it seems to me, is a way in which we may use extended co-operation among us to the most momentous of all purposes, and make conditions of enrolment that would strengthen all educational measures. It is true enough that there is a low sense of parental duties in the nation at large, and that numbers who have no excuse in bodily hardship seem to think it a light thing to beget children, to bring human beings with all their tremendous possibilities into this difficult world, and then take little heed how they are disciplined and furnished for the perilous journey they are sent on without any asking of their own. This is a sin shared in more or less by all classes; but there are sins which, like taxation, fall the heaviest on the poorest, and none have such galling reasons as we working-men to try and rouse to the utmost the feeling of responsibility in fathers and mothers. We have been urged into co-operation by the pressure of common demands. In war men need each other more; and where a given point has to be defended, fighters inevitably find themselves shoulder to shoulder. So fellowship grows, so grow the rules of fellowship, which gradually shape themselves to thoroughness as the idea of a common good becomes more complete. We feel a right to say, If you will be one of us, you must make such and such a contribution – you must renounce such and such a separate advantage – you must set your face against such and such an infringement. If we have any false ideas about our common good, our rules will be wrong, and we shall be co-operating to damage each other. But now, here is a part of our good, without which everything else we strive for will be worthless – I mean, the rescue of our children. Let us demand from the members of our Unions that they fulfil their duty as parents in this definite matter, which rules can reach. Let us demand that they send their children to school, so as not to go on recklessly breeding a moral pestilence among us, just as strictly as we demand that they pay their contributions to a common fund, understood to be for a common benefit. While we watch our public men, let us watch one another as to this duty, which is also public, and more momentous even than obedience to sanitary regulations. Whilst we resolutely declare against the wickedness in high places, let us set ourselves also against the wickedness in low places, not quarrelling which came first, or which is the worse of the two – not trying to settle the miserable precedence of plague or famine, but insisting unflinchingly on remedies once ascertained, and summoning those who hold the treasure of knowledge to remember that they hold it in trust, and that with them lies the task of searching for new remedies, and finding the right methods of applying them.

To find right remedies and right methods. Here is the great function of knowledge: here the life of one man may make a fresh era straight away, in which a sort of suffering that has existed shall exist no more. For the thousands of years down to the middle of the sixteenth century that human limbs had been hacked and amputated, nobody knew how to stop the bleeding except by searing the ends of the vessels with red hot iron. But then came a man named Ambrose Paré, and said, 'Tie up the arteries!'[17] That was a fine word to utter. It contained the statement of a method – a plan by which a particular evil was for ever assuaged. Let us try to discern the men whose words carry that sort of kernel, and choose such men to be our guides and representatives – not choose platform swaggerers, who bring us nothing but the ocean to make our broth with.

To get the chief power into the hands of the wisest, which means to get our life regulated according to the truest principles mankind is in possession of, is a problem as old as the very notion of wisdom. The solution comes slowly, because men collectively can only be made to embrace principles, and to act on them, by the slow stupendous teaching of the world's events. Men will go on planting potatoes, and nothing else but potatoes, till a potatoe-disease comes and forces them to find out the advantage of a varied crop. Selfishness, stupidity, sloth, persist in trying to adapt the world to their desires, till a time comes when the world manifests itself as too decidedly inconvenient to them. Wisdom stands outside of man and urges itself upon him, like the marks of the changing seasons, before it finds a home with him, directs his actions, and from the precious effects of obedience begets a corresponding love.

But while still outside of us, wisdom often looks terrible, and wears strange forms, wrapped in the changing conditions of a struggling world. It wears now the form of wants and just demands in a great multitude of British men: wants and demands urged into existence by the forces of a maturing world. And it is in virtue of this – in virtue of this presence of wisdom on our side as a mighty fact, physical, and moral, which must enter into and shape the thoughts and actions of mankind – that we working men have obtained the suffrage. Not because we are an excellent multitude, but because we are a needy multitude.

But now, for our own part, we have seriously to consider this outside wisdom which lies in the supreme unalterable nature of things, and watch to give it a home within us and obey it. If the claims of the unendowed multitude of working men hold within them principles which must shake the future, it is not less true that the endowed classes, in their inheritance from the past, hold the precious material without which no worthy, noble future can be moulded. Many of the highest uses of life are in their keeping; and if privilege has often been abused, it also has been the nurse of excellence. Here again we have to submit ourselves to the great law of inheritance. If we quarrel with the way in which the labours and earnings of the past have been preserved and handed down, we are just as bigoted, just as narrow, just as wanting in that religion which keeps an open ear and an obedient mind to the teachings of fact, as we accuse those of being, who quarrel with the new truths and new needs which are disclosed in the present. The deeper insight we get into the causes of human trouble, and the ways by which men are made better and happier, the less we shall be inclined to the unprofitable spirit and practice of reproaching classes as such in a wholesale fashion. Not all the evils of our condition are such as we can justly blame others for; and, I repeat, many of them are such as no changes of institutions can quickly remedy. To discern between the evils that energy can remove and the evils that patience must bear, makes the difference between manliness and childishness, between good sense and folly. And more than that, without such discernment, seeing that we have grave duties towards our own body and the country at large, we can hardly escape acts of fatal rashness and injustice.

I am addressing a mixed assembly of workmen, and some of you may be as well or better fitted than I am to take up this office. But they will not think it amiss in me that I have tried to bring together the considerations most likely to be of service to us in preparing ourselves for the use of our new opportunities. I have

avoided touching on special questions. The best help towards
judging well on these is to approach them in the right temper
without vain expectation, and with a resolution which is mixed
with temperance.

*       *       *

The address emphasizes the interdependence of the various
sections of society, and the need for enlightened evolutionary
progress rather than revolutionary excesses, which may destroy
what is traditionally good, and fail to replace it by something
better. The critical necessity is the creation of widespread concern
for the welfare of the community at large and of generations to
come. With this in view, greed, envy, and hatred bred by factional
bigotry must be transcended. Without such a fundamental
change, reform in suffrage and political institutions will make
little real difference. A nation must suffer the 'inexorable law of
consequences' for better or worse. George Eliot knows the
difficulty of making radical changes in people (p. 123); only when
their best selves are activated can there be hope for progress. This
concept of the higher self comes to the fore in *The Mill on the Floss*
(1860), and it is the key note in Matthew Arnold's answer to
current problems in his *Culture and Anarchy*, a series of essays which
first appeared in 1867–8: the 'one thing needful' is 'to come to our
best at all points'. He stresses the 'besetting danger' of the
English; it lies in their faith in 'machinery', which is the mistaking
of means for ends. In all probability he had been struck by the
passage in *Felix Holt* (xxx) where the hero, speaking for his author,
says that all schemes relative to voting are 'engines', but that the
force which works them comes inevitably from 'men's passions,
feelings, desires'. Until these are wisely motivated, political
institutions will remain effectively unsatisfactory. George Eliot
believed in a religion of humanity which would permeate the
whole of one's life, work and leisure; such integrity, open-minded
and concerned for the welfare of all in an interdependent
community, was the one way to achieve national health and
sanity. Without a common cause, the ends towards which all
should be working would be obscured by the 'machinery' of
political expedients created by rancour and division. 'Knowledge
comes, but wisdom lingers', Tennyson lamented more than one
hundred and forty years ago. George Eliot retained her faith, if
only in 'the slow stupendous teaching of the world's events'. Such
events may include decline or disaster, misdirection, injustices,
unnecessary suffering, and a fearful waste of opportunities for the

common good. George Eliot believed that the artist, by stirring people's sympathies through imaginative works, could do more for mankind than the theorist or propagandist. The heroine's conflict at Transome Court in *Felix Holt*, and her rejection of a life of luxury with a Radical opportunist (cf. p. 2) for relative poverty with a genuine, far-sighted Radical, are more memorable than Felix Holt's views. Similarly in *Middlemarch*, Caleb Garth's principles, admirable as they are, have a less lasting appeal than the antithetically juxtaposed scenes which dramatize the wrecking of practical idealism by the self-seeking Rosamond, and the unwavering faith of Dorothea, even though her idealism has to accept compromise with reality (cf. p. 2).

## iv  NOTES ON *THE SPANISH GYPSY* AND TRAGEDY

(George Eliot finished *The Spanish Gypsy* at the end of April 1868. The subject had occurred to her nearly four years earlier in Venice. She intended to write a play in blank verse but, unable to devise scenes which would sustain the dramatic life of her main characters, she abandoned it after completing four acts. After writing *Felix Holt* and visiting Spain, she began the work a second time in March 1867, designing it as a poem; it contains several dramatic scenes, combined with narrative and descriptive verse. The heroine Fedalma, who had been captured in childhood and does not know her origin, is about to marry Don Silva, duke of a Spanish fortress town near the Moorish border, when she is recognized by her father Zarca, a prisoner, chief of the Zincali tribe of gipsies. He convinces her that it is her duty to join them when he escapes; she accepts her doom, and love compels Don Silva to follow her. Unwittingly, in darkness, he helps the Zincali and the Moors to storm his own citadel. When he discovers his crime, he stabs Zarca fatally, and finds that he is under a double curse, that of the Christians whose cause he has betrayed, and that of the gipsy tribe whose new leader he loves. The Moors honour their pledge to transport the Zincali to northern Africa for their assistance in battle; Fedalma departs with them, and Don Silva resolves to redeem himself by taking up the sword for Rome against the infidels.

George Eliot's 'poem' is often dramatic, and the verse is finely worked at all points; it is often taut and rich in effects. Henry James was dazzled by it, and a reviewer who thought it superior to *Aurora Leigh* showed sound judgment; by comparison, Elizabeth

Barrett Browning's poem seems improvised, diffuse, and prosaic.

The notes, undated and apparently unfinished, were found among George Eliot's papers, after her death, by her second husband John Walter Cross. They are reproduced from his *George Eliot's Life* (1885), and will be found after entries for 29 April 1868, when *The Spanish Gypsy* was finished. George Eliot had been a great admirer of Aristotle's *Poetics*, and some of his terseness seems to have entered her style. The frequency of references to her poem suggests that she had intended an essay to accompany *The Spanish Gypsy*. She may not have been satisfied with her theory of tragedy, but it is worth considering.)

The subject of 'The Spanish Gypsy' was originally suggested to me by a picture which hangs in the Scuola di San Rocco at Venice, over the door of the large Sala containing Tintoretto's frescoes. It is an Annunciation, said to be by Titian.[18] Of course I had seen numerous pictures of this subject before, and the subject had always attracted me. But in this my second visit to the Scuola di San Rocco, this small picture of Titian's, pointed out to me for the first time, brought a new train of thought. It occurred to me that there was a great dramatic motive of the same class as those used by the Greek dramatists, yet specifically differing from them. A young maiden, believing herself to be on the eve of the chief event of her life – marriage – about to share in the ordinary lot of womanhood, full of young hope, has suddenly announced to her that she is chosen to fulfil a great destiny, entailing a terribly different experience from that of ordinary womanhood. She is chosen, not by any momentary arbitrariness, but as a result of foregoing hereditary conditions: she obeys. 'Behold the handmaid of the Lord.' Here, I thought, is a subject grander than that of Iphigenia,[19] and it has never been used. I came home with this in my mind, meaning to give the motive a clothing in some suitable set of historical and local conditions. My reflections brought me nothing that would serve me except that moment in Spanish history[20] when the struggle with the Moors was attaining its climax, and when there was the gypsy race present under such conditions as would enable me to get my heroine and the hereditary claim on her among the gypsies. I required the opposition of race to give the need for renouncing the expectation of marriage. I could not use the Jews or the Moors, because the facts of their history were too conspicuously opposed to the working out of my catastrophe. Meanwhile the subject had become more and more pregnant to me. I saw it might be taken as a symbol of the part which is played in the general human lot by hereditary conditions in the largest sense, and of the fact that what we call duty is entirely made up of such conditions; for even in cases of just antagonism to the narrow view of hereditary claims, the whole background of the particular struggle is made up of our inherited nature. Suppose for a moment that our conduct at great epochs was determined entirely by reflection, without the immediate intervention of feeling which supersedes reflection, our determination as to the right would consist in an adjustment of our individual needs to the dire necessities of our lot, partly as to our natural constitution, partly as sharers of life with our fellow-beings. Tragedy consists in the terrible difficulty of this adjustment –

> 'The dire strife
> Of poor Humanity's afflicted will,
> Struggling in vain with ruthless destiny.'[21]

Looking at individual lots, I seemed to see in each the same story, wrought out with more or less of tragedy, and I determined the elements of my drama under the influence of these ideas.

In order to judge properly of the dramatic structure, it must not be considered first in the light of doctrinal symbolism, but in the light of a tragedy representing some grand collision in the human lot. And it must be judged accordingly. A good tragic subject must represent a possible, sufficiently probable, not a common action; and to be really tragic, it must represent irreparable collision between the individual and the general (in differing degrees of generality). It is the individual with whom we sympathise, and the general of which we recognise the irresistible power. The truth of this test will be seen by applying it to the greatest tragedies. The collision of Greek tragedy is often that between hereditary, entailed Nemesis, and the peculiar individual lot, awakening our sympathy, of the particular man or woman whom the Nemesis is shown to grasp with terrific force. Sometimes, as in the 'Oresteia',[22] there is the clashing of two irreconcilable requirements – two duties, as we should say in these times. The murder of the father must be avenged by the murder of the mother, which must again be avenged. These two tragic relations of the individual and general, and of two irreconcilable 'oughts', may be – will be – seen to be almost always combined. The Greeks were not taking an artificial, entirely erroneous standpoint in their art – a standpoint which disappeared altogether with their religion and their art. They had the same essential elements of life presented to them as we have, and their art symbolised these in grand schematic forms. The Prometheus[23] represents the ineffectual struggle to redeem the small and miserable race of man, against the stronger adverse ordinances that govern the frame of things with a triumphant power. Coming to modern tragedies, what is it that makes 'Othello' a great tragic subject? A story simply of a jealous husband is elevated into a most pathetic tragedy by the hereditary conditions of Othello's lot, which give him a subjective ground for distrust. Faust, Rigoletto ('Le Roi s'Amuse'), Brutus.[24] It might be a reasonable ground of objection against the whole structure of 'The Spanish Gypsy' if it were shown that the action is outrageously improbable – lying outside all that can be congruously conceived of human actions. It is *not* a reasonable ground of objection that they would have done better to act otherwise, any more than it is a reasonable objection against the 'Iphigenia' that Agamemnon would have done better not to sacrifice his daughter.

As renunciations coming under the same great class, take the renunciation of marriage, where marriage cannot take place without entailing misery on the children.

A tragedy has not to expound why the individual must give way to the general: it has to show that it is compelled to give way, the tragedy consisting in the struggle involved, and often in the entirely calamitous issue in spite of a grand submission. Silva presents the tragedy of entire rebellion: Fedalma of a grand submission, which is rendered vain by the effects of Silva's rebellion: Zarca, the struggle for a great end, rendered vain by the surrounding conditions of life.

Now, what is the fact about our individual lots? A woman, say, finds herself on the earth with an inherited organisation: she may be lame, she may inherit a disease, or what is tantamount to a disease: she may be a negress, or have other marks of race repulsive in the community where she is born, etc., etc. One may go on for a long while without reaching the limits of the commonest inherited misfortunes. It is almost a mockery to say to such human beings, 'Seek your own happiness.' The utmost approach to well-being that can be made in such a case is through large resignation and acceptance of the inevitable, with as much effort to overcome any disadvantage as good sense will show to be attended with a likelihood of success. Any one may say, that is the dictate of mere rational reflection. But calm can, in hardly any human organism, be attained by rational reflection. Happily we are not left to that. Love, pity, constituting sympathy, and generous joy with regard to the lot of our fellowmen, comes in –

has been growing since the beginning – enormously enhanced by wider vision of results – by an imagination actively interested in the lot of mankind generally; and these feelings become piety – *i.e.*, loving, willing submission, and heroic Promethean effort towards high possibilities, which may result from our individual life.

There is really no moral 'sanction' but this inward impulse. The will of God is the same thing as the will of other men, compelling us to work and avoid what they have seen to be harmful to social existence. Disjoined from any perceived good, the divine will is simply so much as we have ascertained of the facts of existence which compel obedience at our peril. Any other notion comes from the supposition of arbitrary revelation.

That favourite view, expressed so often in Clough's poems, of doing duty in blindness as to the result,[25] is likely to deepen the substitution of egoistic yearnings for really moral impulses. We cannot be utterly blind to the results of duty, since that cannot be duty which is not already judged to be for human good. To say the contrary, is to say that mankind have reached no inductions as to what is for their good or evil.

The art which leaves the soul in despair is laming to the soul, and is denounced by the healthy sentiment of an active community. The consolatory elements in 'The Spanish Gypsy' are derived from two convictions or sentiments which so conspicuously pervade it, that they may be said to be its very warp on which the whole action is woven. These are – (1) The importance of individual deeds; (2) The all-sufficiency of the soul's passions in determining sympathetic action.

In Silva is presented the claim of fidelity to social pledges; in Fedalma, the claim constituted by an hereditary lot less consciously shared.

With regard to the supremacy of Love: if it were a fact without exception that man or woman never did renounce the joys of love, there could never have sprung up a notion that such renunciation could present itself as a duty. If no parents had ever cared for their children, how could parental affection have been reckoned among the elements of life? But what are the facts in relation to this matter? Will any one say that faithfulness to the marriage tie has never been regarded as a duty, in spite of the presence of the profoundest passion experienced after marriage? Is Guinevere's conduct[26] the type of duty?

\* \* \*

The theory that tragedy depends on the conflict between the

individual and the general (duties, expectations, codes of honour and morality) is an interesting one. It applies very markedly to *The Spanish Gypsy*, and it is manifest in the peculiar lot of the individual in the *Oresteia*, where revenge as a form of filial duty runs counter to law. The tragedy of such a conflict may precede unlawful action, as in *Othello*, briefly but agonizingly in *Macbeth*, and at full length in *Hamlet*. It is evident in the lives of Mrs Transome (FH) and of Bulstrode (M); it reaches almost terrifying proportions in the Gwendolen Harleth story (DD); and it is relevant to the final tragedy of Maggie Tulliver. George Eliot's comment on tragedy in *The Mill on the Floss* (VI.vi) is excellent; she agrees with Novalis that destiny depends on character, but insists that it depends equally on circumstances, illustrating her contention strikingly with reference to *Hamlet*. For a humanist like Hardy, who sees heredity as inescapable and at times uncontrollable, tragedy is mainly a matter of chance, as he demonstrates at large in *Tess of the d'Urbervilles*. Here, as in *The Mill on the Floss*, the heroine suffers from the inhumanity of orthodoxy. There may therefore be an implicit (sometimes explicit) protest against convention in the tragedy of conflict, as in Ibsen and some later dramatists. No formula provides a general key to tragedies in all their variety. Nevertheless, George Eliot's views deserve attention, and may have a wider significance than is at first suspected.

One sentence, 'The art which leaves the soul in despair is laming to the soul, and is denounced by the healthy sentiment of an active community', recalls the positive aims which inspired George Eliot's anti-egoistical fiction. No one familiar with her works would suggest that she encourages facile optimism; she expects great writers to inspire manliness and concerted action in the face of adversity. She supports views expressed by Matthew Arnold (not always in the best terms) at the opening of his preface to the 1853 edition of his poems. Discussing subjects from which 'no poetical enjoyment can be derived', he writes:

> They are those . . . in which a continuous state of mental distress is prolonged, unrelieved by incident, hope, or resistance; in which there is everything to be endured, nothing to be done. In such situations there is inevitably something morbid, in the description of them something monotonous. When they occur in actual life, they are painful, not tragic; the representation of them in poetry is painful also.

# IV  Poems

## i  'O MAY I JOIN THE CHOIR INVISIBLE

(Uncertainty about life after death makes it the more imperative to do everything possible for the welfare of humanity in this life (cf. p. 22 and the preceding comments on Young's ignoble reaction to the thought that there can be no other-worldly immortality). The 'miserable aims that end with self' underlines one of the main themes of George Eliot's novels; 'vaster issues' reminds one of Lydgate and Dorothea Brooke (the poem was written in Germany in the summer of 1867, more than three years before her story was begun) and the ultimate fate of Fedalma and of Daniel Deronda. For another view of this humanist idea of immortality on earth, see Thomas Hardy's 'His Immortality' and 'The To-Be-Forgotten' in *Poems of the Past and the Present*.)

*Longum illud tempus, quum non ero, magis me movet, quam hoc exiguum.*
Cicero, ad Att., xii, 18.[1]

> O may I join the choir invisible
> Of those immortal dead who live again
> In minds made better by their presence: live
> In pulses stirred to generosity,
> In deeds of daring rectitude, in scorn
> For miserable aims that end with self,
> In thoughts sublime that pierce the night like stars,
> And with their mild persistence urge man's search
> To vaster issues.
>         So to live is heaven:
> To make undying music in the world,
> Breathing as beauteous order that controls
> With growing sway the growing life of man.
> So we inherit that sweet purity

For which we struggled, failed, and agonised
With widening retrospect that bred despair.
Rebellious flesh that would not be subdued,
A vicious parent shaming still its child
Poor anxious penitence, is quick dissolved;
Its discords, quenched by meeting harmonies,
Die in the large and charitable air.
And all our rarer, better, truer self,
That sobbed religiously in yearning song,
That watched to ease the burthen of the world,
Laboriously tracing what must be,
And what may yet be better — saw within
A worthier image for the sanctuary,
And shaped it forth before the multitude
Divinely human, raising worship so
To higher reverence more mixed with love —
That better self shall live till human Time
Shall fold its eyelids, and the human sky
Be gathered like a scroll within the tomb
Unread for ever.
                    This is life to come,
Which martyred men have made more glorious
For us who strive to follow. May I reach
That purest heaven, be to other souls
The cup of strength in some great agony,
Enkindle generous ardour, feed pure love,
Beget the smiles that have no cruelty —
Be the sweet presence of a good diffused,
And in diffusion ever more intense.
So shall I join the choir invisible
Whose music is the gladness of the world.


## ii  HOW LISA LOVED THE KING

(Work on *The Spanish Gypsy* encouraged George Eliot to compose
verse epigraphs for chapters in her last three novels (FH, M, DD),
and to write other poems. Based on a story in Boccaccio's *Il
Decamerone* (X.vii), 'How Lisa Loved the King' is hardly a
translation; freely rendered and amplified, it displays originality
throughout. The subject (easily marred in the hands of an inferior
writer) is gracefully controlled, and redolent of the courtly

noblesse of the period, the 'honour and curteisie' which the
author knew well in Chaucer, whose verse medium she uses,
varying it artfully with alexandrines to bring paragraphs to a
close. The envoy (farewell to the reader) is in the traditional
medieval style; *eyne*: eyes; *Perdicone*: 4-syllabled, ending '*o-nay*'.)


Six hundred years ago, in Dante's time,
Before his cheek was furrowed by deep rhyme –
When Europe, fed afresh from Eastern story,[2]
Was like a garden tangled with the glory
Of flowers hand-planted and of flowers air-sown,
Climbing and trailing, budding and full-blown,
Where purple bells are tossed amid pink stars,
And springing blades, green troops in innocent wars,
Crowd every shady spot of teeming earth,
Making invisible motion visible birth –
Six hundred years ago, Palermo town
Kept holiday. A deed of great renown,
A high revenge, had freed from it the yoke
Of hated Frenchmen, and from Calpe's rock[3]
To where the Bosporus caught the earlier sun,
'Twas told that Pedro, King of Aragon,
Was welcomed master of all Sicily,
A royal knight, supreme as kings should be
In strength and gentleness that make high chivalry.

Spain was the favourite home of knightly grace,
Where generous men rode steeds of generous race;
Both Spanish, yet half Arab, both inspired
By mutual spirit, that each motion fired
With beauteous response, like minstrelsy
Afresh fulfilling fresh expectancy.
So when Palermo made high festival,
The joy of matrons and of maidens all
Was the mock terror of the tournament,
Where safety, with the glimpse of danger blent,
Took exaltation as from epic song,
Which greatly tells the pains that to great life belong.

And in all eyes King Pedro was the king
Of cavaliers: as in a full-gemmed ring
The largest ruby, or as that bright star[4]
Whose shining shows us where the Hyads are.
His the best jennet, and he sat it best;

His weapon, whether tilting or in rest,
Was worthiest watching, and his face once seen
Gave to the promise of his royal mien
Such rich fulfilment as the opened eyes
Of a loved sleeper, or the long-watched rise
Of vernal day, whose joy o'er stream and meadow flies.

But of the maiden forms that thick enwreathed
The broad piazza and sweet witchery breathed,
With innocent faces budding all arow
From balconies and windows high and low,
Who was it felt the deep mysterious glow,
The impregnation with supernal fire
Of young ideal love – transformed desire,
Whose passion is but worship of that Best
Taught by the many-mingled creed of each young breast?

'Twas gentle Lisa, of no noble line,
Child of Bernardo, a rich Florentine,
Who from his merchant-city hither came
To trade in drugs; yet kept an honest fame,
And had the virtue not to try and sell
Drugs that had none. He loved his riches well,
But loved them chiefly for his Lisa's sake,
Whom with a father's care he sought to make
The bride of some true honourable man: –
Of Perdicone (so the rumour ran),
Whose birth was higher than his fortunes were;
For still your trader likes a mixture fair
Of blood that hurries to some higher strain
Than reckoning money's loss and money's gain.
And of such mixture good may surely come:
Lords' scions so may learn to cast a sum,
A trader's grandson bear a well-set head,
And have less conscious manners, better bred;
Nor, when he tries to be polite, be rude instead.

'Twas Perdicone's friends made overtures
To good Bernardo: so one dame assures
Her neighbour dame who notices the youth
Fixing his eyes on Lisa; and in truth
Eyes that could see her on this summer day
Might find it hard to turn another way.
She had a pensive beauty, yet not sad;
Rather, like minor cadences that glad

The hearts of little birds amid spring boughs;
And oft the trumpet or the joust would rouse
Pulses that gave her cheek a finer glow,
Parting her lips that seemed a mimic bow
By chiselling Love for play in coral wrought,
Then quickened by him with the passionate thought,
The soul that trembled in the lustrous night
Of slow long eyes. Her body was so slight,
It seemed she could have floated in the sky,
And with the angelic choir made symphony;
But in her cheek's rich tinge, and in the dark
Of darkest hair and eyes, she bore a mark
Of kinship to her generous mother earth,
The fervid land that gives the plumy palm-trees birth.

She saw not Perdicone; her young mind
Dreamed not that any man had ever pined
For such a little simple maid as she:
She had but dreamed how heavenly it would be
To love some hero noble, beauteous, great,
Who would live stories worthy to narrate,
Like Roland, or the warriors of Troy,
The Cid, or Amadis, or that fair boy
Who conquered everything beneath the sun,
And somehow, some time, died at Babylon⁵
Fighting the Moors. For heroes all were good
And fair as that archangel who withstood
The Evil One, the author of all wrong –
That Evil One who made the French so strong;
And now the flower of heroes must be he
Who drove those tyrants from dear Sicily,
So that her maids might walk to vespers tranquilly.

Young Lisa saw this hero in the king,
And as wood-lilies that sweet odours bring
Might dream the light that opes their modest eyne
Was lily-odoured, – and as rites divine,
Round turf-laid altars, or 'neath roofs of stone,
Draw sanctity from out the heart alone
That loves and worships, so the miniature
Perplexed of her soul's world, all virgin pure,
Filled with heroic virtues that bright form,
Raona's royalty, the finished norm
Of horsemanship – the half of chivalry:
For how could generous men avengers be,

Save as God's messengers on coursers fleet? –
These, scouring earth, made Spain with Syria meet
In one self world where the same right had sway,
And good must grow as grew the blessed day.
No more; great Love his essence had endued
With Pedro's form, and entering subdued
The soul of Lisa, fervid and intense,
Proud in its choice of proud obedience
To hardship glorified by perfect reverence.

Sweet Lisa homeward carried that dire guest,
And in her chamber through the hours of rest
The darkness was alight for her with sheen
Of arms, and plumèd helm, and bright between
Their commoner gloss, like the pure living spring
'Twixt porphyry lips, or living bird's bright wing
'Twixt golden wires, the glances of the king
Flashed on her soul, and waked vibrations there
Of known delights love-mixed to new and rare:
The impalpable dream was turned to breathing flesh,
Chill thought of summer to the warm close mesh
Of sunbeams held between the citron-leaves,
Clothing her life of life. Oh, she believes
That she could be content if he but knew
(Her poor small self could claim no other due)
How Lisa's lowly love had highest reach
Of wingèd passion, whereto wingèd speech
Would be scorched remnants left by mounting flame.
Though, had she such lame message, were it blame
To tell what greatness dwelt in her, what rank
She held in loving? Modest maidens shrank
From telling love that fed on selfish hope;
But love, as hopeless as the shattering song
Wailed for loved beings who have joined the throng
Of mighty dead ones. . . . Nay, but she was weak –
Knew only prayers and ballads – could not speak
With eloquence save what dumb creatures have,
That with small cries and touches small boons crave.

She watched all day that she might see him pass
With knights and ladies; but she said, 'Alas!
Though he should see me, it were all as one
He saw a pigeon sitting on the stone
Of wall or balcony : some coloured spot
His eye just sees, his mind regardeth not.

I have no music-touch that I could bring nigh
My love to his soul's hearing. I shall die,
And he will never know who Lisa was –
The trader's child, whose soaring spirit rose
As hedge-born aloe-flowers that rarest years disclose.

'For were I now a fair deep-breasted queen
A-horseback, with blonde hair, and tunic green
Gold-bordered, like Costanza, I should need
No change within to make me queenly there;
For they the royal-hearted women are
Who nobly love the noblest, yet have grace
For needy suffering lives in lowliest place,
Carrying a choicer sunlight in their smile,
The heavenliest ray that pitieth the vile.
My love is such, it cannot choose but soar
Up to the highest; yet for evermore,
Though I were happy, throned beside the king,
I should be tender to each little thing
With hurt warm breast, that had no speech to tell
Its inward pang, and I would soothe it well
With tender touch and with a low soft moan
For company: my dumb love-pang is lone,
Prisoned as topaz-beam within a rough-garbed stone.'

So, inward-wailing, Lisa passed her days.
Each night the August moon with changing phase
Looked broader, harder on her unchanged pain;
Each noon the heat lay heavier again
On her despair; until her body frail
Shrank like the snow that watchers in the vale
See narrowed on the height each summer morn;
While her dark glance burnt larger, more forlorn,
As if the soul within her all on fire
Made of her being one swift funeral pyre.
Father and mother saw with sad dismay
The meaning of their riches melt away:
For without Lisa what would sequins buy?
What wish were left if Lisa were to die?
Through her they cared for summers still to come,
Else they would be as ghosts without a home
In any flesh that could feel glad desire.
They pay the best physicians, never tire
Of seeking what will soothe her, promising
That aught she longed for, though it were a thing

Hard to be come at as the Indian snow,
Or roses that on alpine summits blow –
It should be hers. She answers with low voice,
She longs for death alone – death is her choice;
Death is the King who never did think scorn,
But rescues every meanest soul to sorrow born.

Yet one day, as they bent above her bed
And watched her in brief sleep, her drooping head
Turned gently, as the thirsty flowers that feel
Some moist revival through their petals steal,
And little flutterings of her lids and lips
Told of such dreamy joy as sometimes dips
A skyey shadow in the mind's poor pool.
She oped her eyes, and turned their dark gems full
Upon her father, as in utterance dumb
Of some new prayer that in her sleep had come.
'What is it, Lisa?' 'Father, I would see
Minuccio, the great singer; bring him me.'
For always, night and day, her unstilled thought,
Wandering all o'er its little world, had sought
How she could reach, by some soft pleading touch,
King Pedro's soul, that she who loved so much
Dying, might have a place within his mind –
A little grave which he would sometimes find
And plant some flower on it – some thought, some memory
    kind.
Till in her dream she saw Minuccio
Touching his viola, and chanting low
A strain that, falling on her brokenly,
Seemed blossoms lightly blown from off a tree,
Each burthened with a word that was a scent –
Raona, Lisa, love, death, tournament;
Then in her dream she said, 'He sings of me –
Might be my messenger; ah, now I see
The king is listening –' Then she awoke,
And, missing her dear dream, that new-born longing spoke.

She longed for music: that was natural;
Physicians said it was medicinal;
The humours might be schooled by true consent
Of a fine tenor and fine instrument;
In brief, good music, mixed with doctor's stuff,
Apollo with Asklepios – enough![6]
Minuccio, entreated, gladly came.

(He was a singer of most gentle fame –
A noble, kindly spirit, not elate
That he was famous, but that song was great –
Would sing as finely to this suffering child
As at the court where princes on him smiled.)
Gently he entered and sat down by her,
Asking what sort of strain she would prefer –
The voice alone, or voice with viol wed;
Then, when she chose the last, he preluded
With magic hand, that summoned from the strings
Aerial spirits, rare yet vibrant wings
That fanned the pulses of his listener,
And waked each sleeping sense with blissful stir.
Her cheek already showed a slow faint blush,
But soon the voice, in pure full liquid rush,
Made all the passion, that till now she felt,
Seem but cool waters that in warmer melt.
Finished the song, she prayed to be alone
With kind Minuccio; for her faith had grown
To trust him as if missioned like a priest
With some high grace, that when his singing ceased
Still made him wiser, more magnanimous
Than common men who had no genius.

So laying her small hand within his palm,
She told him how that secret glorious harm
Of loftiest loving had befallen her;
That death, her only hope, most bitter were,
If when she died her love must perish too
As songs unsung and thoughts unspoken do,
Which else might live within another breast.
She said, 'Minuccio, the grave were rest,
If I were sure, that lying cold and lone,
My love, my best of life, had safely flown
And nestled in the bosom of the king;
See, 'tis a small weak bird, with unfledged wing.
But you will carry it for me secretly,
And bear it to the king, then come to me
And tell me it is safe, and I shall go
Content, knowing that he I love my love doth know.'

Then she wept silently, but each large tear
Made pleasing music to the inward ear
Of good Minuccio. 'Lisa, trust in me',
He said, and kissed her fingers loyally;

'It is sweet law to me to do your will,
And ere the sun his round shall thrice fulfil,
I hope to bring you news of such rare skill
As amulets have, that aches in trusting bosoms still.'

He needed not to pause and first devise
How he should tell the king; for in nowise
Were such love-message worthily bested
Save in fine verse by music renderèd.
He sought a poet-friend, a Siennese,
And 'Mico, mine,' he said, 'full oft to please
Thy whim of sadness I have sung thee strains
To make thee weep in verse: now pay my pains,
And write me a canzòn divinely sad,
Sinlessly passionate and meekly mad
With young despair, speaking a maiden's heart
Of fifteen summers, who would fain depart
From ripening life's new-urgent mystery –
Love-choice of one too high her love to be –
But cannot yield her breath till she has poured
Her strength away in this hot-bleeding word
Telling the secret of her soul to her soul's lord.'

Said Mico, 'Nay, that thought is poesy,
I need but listen as it sings to me.
Come thou again to-morrow.' The third day,
When linkèd notes had perfected the lay,
Minuccio had his summons to the court
To make, as he was wont, the moments short
Of ceremonious dinner to the king.
This was the time when he had meant to bring
Melodious message of young Lisa's love:
He waited till the air had ceased to move
To ringing silver, till Falernian wine[7]
Made quickened sense with quietude combine,
And then with passionate descant made each ear incline.

*Love, thou didst see me, light as morning's breath,*
*Roaming a garden in a joyous error,*
*Laughing at chases vain, a happy child,*
*Till of thy countenance the alluring terror*
*In majesty from out the blossoms smiled,*
*From out their life seeming a beauteous Death.*

*O Love, who so didst choose me for thine own,*
*Taking this little isle to thy great sway,*

*See now, it is the honour of thy throne*
*That what thou gavest perish not away,*
*Nor leave some sweet remembrance to atone*
*By life that will be for the brief life gone:*
*Hear, ere the shroud o'er these frail limbs be thrown —*
*Since every king is vassal unto thee,*
*My heart's lord needs must listen loyally —*
*O tell him I am waiting for my Death!*

*Tell him, for that he hath such royal power*
*'Twere hard for him to think how small a thing,*
*How slight a sign, would make a wealthy dower*
*For one like me, the bride of that pale king*
*Whose bed is mine at some swift-nearing hour.*
*Go to my lord, and to his memory bring*
*That happy birthday of my sorrowing*
*When his large glance made meaner gazers glad,*
*Entering the bannered lists: 'twas then I had*
*The wound that laid me in the arms of Death.*

*Tell him, O Love, I am a lowly maid,*
*No more than any little knot of thyme*
*That he with careless foot may often tread;*
*Yet lowest fragrance oft will mount sublime*
*And cleave to things most high and hallowèd,*
*As doth the fragrance of my life's springtime,*
*My lowly love, that soaring seeks to climb*
*Within his thought, and make a gentle bliss,*
*More blissful than if mine, in being his:*
*So shall I live in him and rest in Death.*

The strain was new. It seemed a pleading cry,
And yet a rounded perfect melody,
Making grief beauteous as the tear-filled eyes
Of little child at little miseries.
Trembling at first, then swelling as it rose,
Like rising light that broad and broader grows,
It filled the hall, and so possessed the air
That not one breathing soul was present there,
Though dullest, slowest, but was quivering
In music's grasp, and forced to hear her sing.
But most such sweet compulsion took the mood
Of Pedro (tired of doing what he would).
Whether the words which that strange meaning bore
Were but the poet's feigning or aught more,

Was bounden question, since their aim must be
At some imagined or true royalty.
He called Minuccio and bade him tell
What poet of the day had writ so well;
For though they came behind all former rhymes,
The verses were not bad for these poor times.
'Monsignor, they are only three days old',
Minuccio said; 'but it must not be told
How this song grew, save to your royal ear.'
Eager, the king withdrew where none was near,
And gave close audience to Minuccio,
Who meetly told that love-tale meet to know.
The king had features pliant to confess
The presence of a manly tenderness –
Son, father, brother, lover, blent in one,
In fine harmonic exaltation –
The spirit of religious chivalry.
He listened, and Minuccio could see
The tender, generous admiration spread
O'er all his face, and glorify his head
With royalty that would have kept its rank
Though his brocaded robes to tatters shrank.
He answered without pause, 'So sweet a maid
In nature's own insignia arrayed,
Though she were come of unmixed trading blood
That sold and bartered ever since the Flood,
Would have the self-contained and single worth
Of radiant jewels born in darksome earth.
Raona were a shame to Sicily,
Letting such love and tears unhonoured be:
Hasten, Minuccio, tell her that the king
To-day will surely visit her when vespers ring.'

Joyful, Minuccio bore the joyous word,
And told at full, while none but Lisa heard,
How each thing had befallen, sang the song,
And like a patient nurse who would prolong
All means of soothing, dwelt upon each tone,
Each look, with which the mighty Aragon
Marked the high worth his royal heart assigned
To that dear place he held in Lisa's mind.
She listened till the draughts of pure content
Through all her limbs like some new being went –
Life, not recovered, but untried before,

From out the growing world's unmeasured store
Of fuller, better, more divinely mixed.
'Twas glad reverse: she had so firmly fixed
To die, already seemed to fall a veil
Shrouding the inner glow from light of senses pale.

Her parents wondering see her half arise –
Wondering, rejoicing, see her long dark eyes
Brimful with clearness, not of 'scaping tears,
But of some light ethereal that enspheres
Their orbs with calm, some vision newly learnt
Where strangest fires erewhile had blindly burnt.
She asked to have her soft white robe and band
And coral ornaments, and with her hand
She gave her locks' dark length a backward fall,
Then looked intently in a mirror small,
And feared her face might perhaps displease the king;
'In truth', she said, 'I am a tiny thing;
I was too bold to tell what could such visit bring.'
Meanwhile the king, revolving in his thought
That virgin passion, was more deeply wrought
To chivalrous pity; and at vesper bell,
With careless mien which hid his purpose well,
Went forth on horseback, and as if by chance
Passing Bernardo's house, he paused to glance
At the fine garden of this wealthy man,
This Tuscan trader turned Palermitan:
But, presently dismounting, chose to walk
Amid the trellises, in gracious talk
With this same trader, deigning even to ask
If he had yet fulfilled the father's task
Of marrying that daughter whose young charms
Himself, betwixt the passages of arms,
Noted admiringly. 'Monsignor, no,
She is not married; that were little woe,
Since she has counted barely fifteen years;
But all such hopes of late have turned to fears;
She droops and fades; though for a space quite brief –
Scarce three hours past – she finds some strange relief.'

The king advised: ' 'Twere dole to all of us,
The world should lose a maid so beauteous;
Let me now see her; since I am her liege lord,
Her spirits must wage war with death at my strong word.'
In such half-serious playfulness, he wends,

With Lisa's father and two chosen friends,
Up to the chamber where she pillowed sits
Watching the open door, that now admits
A presence as much better than her dreams,
As happiness than any longing seems.
The king advanced, and, with a reverent kiss
Upon her hand, said, 'Lady, what is this?
You, whose sweet youth should others' solace be,
Pierce all our hearts, languishing piteously.
We pray you, for the love of us, be cheered,
Nor be too reckless of that life, endeared
To us who know your passing worthiness,
And count your blooming life as part of our life's bliss.'
Those words, that touch upon her hand from him
Whom her soul worshipped, as far seraphim
Worship the distant glory, brought some shame
Quivering upon her cheek, yet thrilled her frame
With such deep joy she seemed in paradise,
In wondering gladness, and in dumb surprise
That bliss could be so blissful: then she spoke –
'Signor, I was too weak to bear the yoke,
The golden yoke of thoughts too great for me;
That was the ground of my infirmity.
But now, I pray your grace to have belief
That I shall soon be well, nor any more cause grief.'

The king alone perceived the covert sense
Of all her words, which made one evidence
With her pure voice and candid loveliness,
That he had lost much honour, honouring less
That message of her passionate distress.
He stayed beside her for a little while
With gentle looks and speech, until a smile
As placid as a ray of early morn
On opening flower-cups o'er her lips was borne.
When he had left her, and the tidings spread
Through all the town how he had visited
The Tuscan trader's daughter, who was sick,
Men said, it was a royal deed and catholic.

And Lisa? She no longer wished for death;
But as a poet, who sweet verses saith
Within his soul, and joys in music there,
Nor seeks another heaven, nor can bear
Disturbing pleasures, so was she content,

Breathing the life of grateful sentiment.
She thought no maid betrothed could be more blest;
For treasure must be valued by the test
Of highest excellence and rarity,
And her dear joy was best as best could be;
There seemed no other crown to her delight
Now the high loved one saw her love aright.
Thus her soul thriving on that exquisite mood,
Spread like the May-time all its beauteous good
O'er the soft bloom of neck, and arms, and cheek,
And strengthened the sweet body, once so weak,
Until she rose and walked, and, like a bird
With sweetly rippling throat, she made her spring joys heard.

The king, when he the happy change had seen,
Trusted the ear of Constance, his fair queen,
With Lisa's innocent secret, and conferred
How they should jointly, by their deed and word,
Honour this maiden's love, which, like the prayer
Of loyal hermits, never thought to share
In what it gave. The queen had that chief grace
Of womanhood, a heart that can embrace
All goodness in another woman's form;
And that same day, ere the sun lay too warm
On southern terraces, a messenger
Informed Bernardo that the royal pair
Would straightway visit him and celebrate
Their gladness at his daughter's happier state,
Which they were fain to see. Soon came the king
On horseback, with his barons, heralding
The advent of the queen in courtly state;
And all, descending at the garden gate,
Streamed with their feathers, velvet, and brocade,
Through the pleached alleys, till they, pausing, made
A lake of splendour 'mid the aloes grey –
When, meekly facing all their proud array,
The white-robed Lisa with her parents stood,
As some white dove before the gorgeous brood
Of dapple-breasted birds born by the Colchian flood.[8]

The king and queen, by gracious looks and speech,
Encourage her, and thus their courtiers teach
How this fair morning they may courtliest be
By making Lisa pass it happily.
And soon the ladies and the barons all

Draw her by turns, as at a festival
Made for her sake, to easy, gay discourse,
And compliment with looks and smiles enforce;
A joyous hum is heard the gardens round;
Soon there is Spanish dancing and the sound
Of minstrel's song, and autumn fruits are pluckt;
Till mindfully the king and queen conduct
Lisa apart to where a trellised shade
Made pleasant resting. Then King Pedro said –
'Excellent maiden, that rich gift of love
Your heart hath made us, hath a worth above
All royal treasures, nor is fitly met
Save when the grateful memory of deep debt
Lies still behind the outward honours done:
And as a sign that no oblivion
Shall overflood that faithful memory,
We while we live your cavalier will be,
Nor will we ever arm ourselves for fight,
Whether for struggle dire or brief delight
Of warlike feigning, but we first will take
The colours you ordain, and for your sake
Charge the more bravely where your emblem is;
Nor will we ever claim an added bliss
To our sweet thoughts of you save one sole kiss.
But there still rests the outward honour meet
To mark your worthiness, and we entreat
That you will turn your ear to proferred vows
Of one who loves you, and would be your spouse.
We must not wrong yourself and Sicily
By letting all your blooming years pass by
Unmated: you will give the world its due
From beauteous maiden and become a matron true.'

Then Lisa, wrapt in virgin wonderment
At her ambitious love's complete content,
Which left no further good for her to seek
Than love's obedience, said with accent meek –
'Monsignor, I know well that were it known
To all the world how high my love had flown,
There would be few who would not deem me mad,
Or say my mind the falsest image had
Of my condition and your lofty place.
But heaven has seen that for no moment's space
Have I forgotten you to be the king,

Or me myself to be a lowly thing –
A little lark, enamoured of the sky,
That scared to sing, to break its breast, and die.
But, as you better know than I, the heart
In choosing chooseth not its own desert,
But that great merit which attracteth it;
'Tis law, I struggled, but I must submit,
And having seen a worth all worth above,
I loved you, love you, and shall always love.
But that doth mean, my will is ever yours,
Not only when your will my good insures,
But if it wrought me what the world calls harm –
Fire, wounds, would wear from your dear will a charm.
That you will be my knight is full content,
And for that kiss – I pray, first for the queen's consent.'

Her answer, given with such firm gentleness,
Pleased the queen well, and made her hold no less
Of Lisa's merit than the king had held.
And so, all cloudy threats of grief dispelled,
There was betrothal made that very morn
'Twixt Perdicone, youthful, brave, well-born,
And Lisa, whom he loved; she loving well
The lot that from obedience befell.
The queen a rare betrothal ring on each
Bestowed, and other gems, with gracious speech.
And that no joy might lack, the king, who knew
The youth was poor, gave him rich Ceffalù
And Cataletta, large and fruitful lands –
Adding much promise when he joined their hands.
At last he said to Lisa, with an air
Gallant yet noble: 'Now we claim our share
From your sweet love, a share which is not small:
For in the sacrament one crumb is all.'
Then taking her small face his hands between,
He kissed her on the brow with kiss serene,
Fit seal to that pure vision her young soul had seen.

Sicilians witnessed that King Pedro kept
His royal promise: Perdicone stept
To many honours honourably won,
Living with Lisa in true union.
Throughout his life the king still took delight
To call himself fair Lisa's faithful knight;

And never wore in field or tournament
A scarf or emblem save by Lisa sent.

Such deeds made subjects loyal in that land:
They joyed that one so worthy to command,
So chivalrous and gentle, had become
The king of Sicily, and filled the room
Of Frenchmen, who abused the Church's trust,
Till, in a righteous vengeance on their lust,
Messina rose, with God, and with the dagger's thrust.

L'envoi

*Reader, this story pleased me long ago*
*In the bright pages of Boccaccio,*
*And where the author of a good we know,*
*Let us not fail to pay the grateful thanks we owe.*


### iii   BROTHER AND SISTER

(The early chapters of *The Mill on the Floss* were drawn from the author's memories of childhood with her brother Isaac. The sonnets indicate that some of these memories were fictionalized: fishing in the canal was transferred to the deep Round Pool, which had been created in the remote past by the flooding of the Floss. These poems were written in the summer of 1869, the last just before *Middlemarch* was begun.)


I

I cannot choose but think upon the time
When our two lives grew like two buds that kiss
At lightest thrill from the bee's swinging chime,
Because the one so near the other is.
He was the elder and a little man
Of forty inches, bound to show no dread,
And I the girl that puppy-like now ran,
Now lagged behind my brother's larger tread.
I held him wise, and when he talked to me
Of snakes and birds, and which God loved the best,
I thought his knowledge marked the boundary
Where men grew blind, though angels knew the rest.
   If he said 'Hush!' I tried to hold my breath;
   Wherever he said 'Come!' I stepped in faith.

## II

Long years have left their writing on my brow,
But yet the freshness and the dew-fed beam
Of those young mornings are about me now,
When we two wandered toward the far-off stream
With rod and line. Our basket held a store
Baked for us only, and I thought with joy
That I should have my share, though he had more,
Because he was the elder and a boy.
The firmaments of daisies since to me
Have had those mornings in their opening eyes,
The bunchèd cowslip's pale transparency
Carries that sunshine of sweet memories,
   And wild-rose branches take their finest scent
   From those blest hours of infantine content.

## III

Our mother bade us keep the trodden ways,
Stroked down my tippet, set my brother's frill,
Then with the benediction of her gaze
Clung to us lessening, and pursued us still
Across the homestead to the rookery elms,
Whose tall old trunks had each a grassy mound,
So rich for us, we counted them as realms
With varied products: here were earth-nuts found,
And here the Lady-fingers in deep shade;
Here sloping toward the Moat the rushes grew,
The large to split for pith, the small to braid;
While over all the dark rooks cawing flew,
   And made a happy strange solemnity,
   A deep-toned chant from life unknown to me.

## IV

Our meadow-path had memorable spots:
One where it bridged a tiny rivulet,
Deep hid by tangled blue Forget-me-nots;
And all along the waving grasses met
My little palm, or nodded to my cheek,
When flowers with upturned faces gazing drew
My wonder downward, seeming all to speak
With eyes of souls that dumbly heard and knew.
Then came the copse, where wild things rushed unseen,
And black-scathed grass betrayed the past abode

Of mystic gypsies, who still lurked between
Me and each hidden distance of the road.
   A gypsy once had startled me at play,
   Blotting with her dark smile my sunny day.


### V

Thus rambling we were schooled in deepest lore,
And learned the meanings that give words a soul,
The fear, the love, the primal passionate store,
Whose shaping impulses make manhood whole.
Those hours were seed to all my after good;
My infant gladness, through eye, ear, and touch,
Took easily as warmth a various food
To nourish the sweet skill of loving much.
For who in age shall roam the earth and find
Reasons for loving that will strike out love
With sudden rod from the hard year-pressed mind?
Were reasons sown as thick as stars above,
   'Tis love must see them, as the eye sees light:
   Day is but Number to the darkened sight.


### VI

Our brown canal was endless to my thought;
And on its banks I sat in dreamy peace,
Unknowing how the good I loved was wrought,
Untroubled by the fear that it would cease.
Slowly the barges floated into view
Rounding a grassy hill to me sublime
With some Unknown beyond it, whither flew
The parting cuckoo toward a fresh spring time.
The wide-arched bridge,[9] the scented elder-flowers,
The wondrous watery rings that died too soon,
The echoes of the quarry, the still hours
With white robe sweeping-on the shadeless noon,
   Were but my growing self, are part of me,
   My present Past, my root of piety.


### VII

Those long days measured by my little feet
Had chronicles which yield me many a text;
Where irony still finds an image meet
Of full-grown judgments in this world perplext.
One day my brother left me in high charge,
To mind the rod, while he went seeking bait,

And bade me, when I saw a nearing barge,
Snatch out the line, lest he should come too late.
Proud of the task, I watched with all my might
For one whole minute, till my eyes grew wide,
Till sky and earth took on a strange new light
And seemed a dream-world floating on some tide –
   A fair pavilioned boat for me alone
    Bearing me onward through the vast unknown.

### VIII

But sudden came the barge's pitch-black prow,
Nearer and angrier came my brother's cry,
And all my soul was quivering fear, when lo!
Upon the imperilled line, suspended high,
A silver perch! My guilt that won the prey,
Now turned to merit, had a guerdon rich
Of hugs and praises, and made merry play,
Until my triumph reached its highest pitch
When all at home were told the wondrous feat,
And how the little sister had fished well.
In secret, though my fortune tasted sweet,
I wondered why this happiness befell.
   'The little lass had luck', the gardener said:
    And so I learned, luck was with glory wed.

### IX

We had the self-same world enlarged for each
By loving difference of girl and boy:
The fruit that hung on high beyond my reach
He plucked for me, and oft he must employ
A measuring glance to guide my tiny shoe
Where lay firm stepping-stones, or call to mind
This thing I like my sister may not do,
For she is little, and I must be kind.
Thus boyish Will the nobler mastery learned
Where inward vision over impulse reigns,
Widening its life with separate life discerned,
A Like unlike, a Self that self restrains.
   His years with others must the sweeter be
    For those brief days he spent in loving me.

### X

His sorrow was my sorrow, and his joy
Sent little leaps and laughs through all my frame;

My doll seemed lifeless and no girlish toy
Had any reason when my brother came.
I knelt with him at marbles, marked his fling
Cut the ringed stem and make the apple drop,
Or watched him winding close the spiral string
That looped the orbits of the humming top.
Grasped by such fellowship my vagrant thought
Ceased with dream-fruit dream-wishes to fulfil;
My aëry-picturing fantasy was taught
Subjection to the harder, truer skill
    That seeks with deeds to grave a thought-tracked line
    And by 'What is', 'What will be' to define.

## XI

School parted us; we never found again
That childish world where our two spirits mingled
Like scents from varying roses that remain
One sweetness, nor can evermore be singled.
Yet the twin habit of that early time
Lingered for long about the heart and tongue:
We had been natives of one happy clime,
And its dear accent to our utterance clung.
Till the dire years whose awful name is Change
Had grasped our souls still yearning in divorce,
And pitiless shaped them in two forms that range
Two elements which sever their life's course.
    But were another childhood-world my share,
    I would be born a little sister there.

\*     \*     \*

Although heaven does not lie round the infancy of Tom and Maggie Tulliver, George Eliot saw her own in the light of Wordsworth's 'Intimations of Immortality' (see the last two paragraphs of MF.v. The first is comparable with the opening of DD.iii; the second echoes the *May* day, the pansy *at my feet*, the bird notes, the *sunshine*, and the *splendour in the grass* of Wordsworth's ode.) The sonnets show other Wordsworthian similarities or influences. George Eliot ascribes her moral development to childhood experiences fostering love and fear (v.3–5); they were the 'seed' of her 'after good' (cf. *The Prelude*, I.301ff.) or root of her piety (vi; cf. Wordsworth's 'My heart leaps up'). The 'touch' of childhood (v.6) augments the Wordsworthian world of eye and ear in 'Lines' (written above Tintern Abbey). The adult rift between brother and sister (p. 152) is alluded to in the pitiless 'Change' of the final sonnet.

## iv  STRADIVARIUS

(Written in 1873, before *Daniel Deronda* was begun.)

Your soul was lifted by the wings to-day
Hearing the master of the violin:
You praised him, praised the great Sebastian too
Who made that fine Chaconne;[10] but did you think
Of old Antonio Stradivari?[11] – him
Who a good century and half ago
Put his true work in that brown instrument
And by the nice adjustment of its frame
Gave it responsive life, continuous
With the master's finger-tips and perfected
Like them by delicate rectitude of use.
Not Bach alone, helped by fine precedent
Of genius gone before, nor Joachim[12]
Who holds the strain afresh incorporate
By inward hearing and notation strict
Of nerve and muscle, made our joy to-day:
Another soul was living in the air
And swaying it to true deliverance
Of high invention and responsive skill: –
That plain white-aproned man who stood at work
Patient and accurate full fourscore years,
Cherished his sight and touch by temperance,
And since keen sense is love of perfectness
Made perfect violins, the needed paths
For inspiration and high mastery.

No simpler man than he: he never cried,
'Why was I born to this monotonous task
Of making violins?' or flung them down
To suit with hurling act a well-hurled curse
At labour on such perishable stuff.
Hence neighbours in Cremona held him dull,
Called him a slave, a mill-horse, a machine,
Begged him to tell his motives or to lend

A few gold pieces to a loftier mind.
Yet he had pithy words full fed by fact;
For Fact, well-trusted, reasons and persuades,
Is gnomic, cutting, or ironical,
Draws tears, or is a tocsin to arouse –
Can hold all figures of the orator
In one plain sentence; has her pauses too –
Eloquent silence at the chasm abrupt
Where knowledge ceases. Thus Antonio
Made answers as Fact willed, and made them strong.

Naldo, a painter of eclectic school,
Taking his dicers, candlelight and grins
From Caravaggio,[13] and in holier groups
Combining Flemish flesh with martyrdom –
Knowing all tricks of style at thirty-one,
And weary of them, while Antonio
At sixty-nine wrought placidly his best
Making the violin you heard to-day –
Naldo would tease him oft to tell his aims.
'Perhaps thou hast some pleasant vice to feed –
The love of louis d'ors in heaps of four,
Each violin a heap – I've nought to blame;
My vices waste such heaps. But then, why work
With painful nicety? Since fame once earned
By luck or merit – oftenest by luck –
(Else why do I put Bonifazio's name[14]
To work that "*pinxit Naldo*" would not sell?)
Is welcome index to the wealthy mob
Where they should pay their gold, and where they pay
There they find merit – take your tow for flax,
And hold the flax unlabelled with your name,
Too coarse for sufferance.'
                              Antonio then:
'I like the gold – well, yes – but not for meals.
And as my stomach, so my eye and hand,
And inward sense that works along with both,
Have hunger that can never feed on coin.
Who draws a line and satisfies his soul,
Making it crooked where it should be straight?
An idiot with an oyster-shell may draw
His lines along the sand, all wavering,
Fixing no point or pathway to a point;
An idiot one remove may choose his line,

Straggle and be content; but God be praised,
Antonio Stradivari has an eye
That winces at false work and loves the true,
With hand and arm that play upon the tool
As willingly as any singing bird
Sets him to sing his morning roundelay,
Because he likes to sing and likes the song.'

Then Naldo: 'Tis a petty kind of fame
At best, that comes of making violins;
And saves no masses, either. Thou wilt go
To purgatory none the less.'
                          But he:
' 'Twere purgatory here to make them ill;
And for my fame – when any master holds
'Twixt chin and hand a violin of mine,
He will be glad that Stradivari lived,
Made violins, and made them of the best.
The masters only know whose work is good:
They will choose mine, and while God gives them skill
I give them instruments to play upon,
God choosing me to help Him.'
                         'What ! were God
At fault for violins, thou absent?'
                         'Yes;
He were at fault for Stradivari's work.'

'Why, many hold Giuseppe's violins
As good as thine.'
                'May be: they are different.
His quality declines: he spoils his hand
With over-drinking. But were his the best,
He could not work for two. My work is mine,
And, heresy or not, if my hand slacked
I should rob God – since He is fullest good –
Leaving a blank instead of violins.
I say, not God Himself can make man's best
Without best men to help Him. I am one best
Here in Cremona, using sunlight well
To fashion finest maple till it serves
More cunningly than throats, for harmony.
'Tis rare delight: I would not change my skill
To be the Emperor with bungling hands,
And lose my work, which comes as natural
As self at waking.'

'Thou art little more
Than a deft potter's wheel, Antonio;
Turning out work by mere necessity
And lack of varied function. Higher arts
Subsist on freedom – eccentricity –
Uncounted inspirations – influence
That comes with drinking, gambling, talk turned wild,
Then moody misery and lack of food –
With every dithyrambic fine excess:
These make at last a storm which flashes out
In lightning revelations. Steady work
Turns genius to a loom; the soul must lie
Like grapes beneath the sun till ripeness comes
And mellow vintage. I could paint you now
The finest Crucifixion; yesternight
Returning home I saw it on a sky
Blue-black, thick-starred. I want two louis d'ors
To buy the canvas and the costly blues –
Trust me a fortnight.'
                    'Where are those last two
I lent thee for thy Judith? – her thou saw'st
In saffron gown, with Holofernes' head[15]
And beauty all complete?
                    'She is but sketched:
I lack the proper model – and the mood.
A great idea is an eagle's egg,
Craves time for hatching; while the eagle sits
Feed her.'
          'If thou wilt call thy pictures eggs
I call the hatching, Work. 'Tis God gives skill,
But not without men's hands: He could not make
Antonio Stradivari's violins
Without Antonio. Get thee to thy easel.'

\*        \*        \*

Influenced by the dramatic style of Browning, 'Stradivarius' shows deftness and economy in admirable conversational style. The value of excellent workmanship to the human race (a theme which begins with Adam Bede and is echoed by Caleb Garth) has Positivist overtones, by implication: 'I say, not God Himself can make man's best/Without best men to help Him'; 'God gives skill,/But not without men's hands: He could not make/Antonio

Stradivari's violins/Without Antonio.' The romantic view that
artistic excellence is fostered by freedom and spontaneity,
eccentricity and extravagant living – 'drinking, gambling, talk
turned wild' or 'moody misery and lack of food', combining with
'every dithyrambic fine excess' – is that of the young Ladislaw
(M.x), and is here rejected for insistence on the discipline of art,
with attention to craftsmanship in every detail.

# V   Late Essays

## i   DEBASING THE MORAL CURRENCY

(Like the next essay, this is from *Impressions of Theophrastus Such*, George Eliot's last published work. The moral argument becomes more valid in an age of mass-media when, by a kind of Gresham's Law, the lowest tastes are appealed to, and thereby developed, for commercial exploitation, most damagingly in television, where the appeal is to eye and ear. George Eliot's image of the new Famine or cultural impoverishment which threatens recalls W. B. Yeats's 'The Second Coming'; barbarism is never far off, the nineteenth-century writer Sainte-Beuve observes (p. 162); it may be obvious in crises, but the preservation of civilization demands vigilance at all times.)

'Il ne faut pas mettre un ridicule où il n'y en a point: c'est se gâter le goût, c'est corrompre son jugement et celui des autres. Mais le ridicule qui est quelque part, il faut l'y voir, l'en tirer avec grâce et d'une manière qui plaise et qui instruise.'

I am fond of quoting this passage from La Bruyère,[1] because the subject is one where I like to show a Frenchman on my side, to save my sentiments from being set down to my peculiar dulness and deficient sense of the ludicrous, and also that they may profit by that enhancement of ideas when presented in a foreign tongue, that glamour of unfamiliarity conferring a dignity on the foreign names of very common things, of which even a philosopher like Dugald Stewart[2] confesses the influence. I remember hearing a fervid woman attempt to recite in English the narrative of a begging Frenchman who described the violent death of his father in the July days.[3] The narrative had impressed her, through the mists of her flushed anxiety to understand it, as something quite grandly pathetic; but finding the facts turn out meagre, and her audience cold, she broke off, saying, 'It sounded so much finer in

French – *j'ai vu le sang de mon père,* and so on – I wish I could repeat it in French.' This was a pardonable illusion in an old-fashioned lady who had not received the polyglot education of the present day; but I observe that even now much nonsense and bad taste win admiring acceptance solely by virtue of the French language, and one may fairly desire that what seems a just discrimination should profit by the fashionable prejudice in favour of La Bruyère's idiom. But I wish he had added that the habit of dragging the ludicrous into topics where the chief interest is of a different or even opposite kind is a sign not of endowment, but of deficiency. The art of spoiling is within reach of the dullest faculty: the coarsest clown with a hammer in his hand might chip the nose off every statue and bust in the Vatican, and stand grinning at the effect of his work. Because wit is an exquisite product of high powers, we are not therefore forced to admit the sadly confused inference of the monotonous jester that he is establishing his superiority over every less facetious person, and over every topic on which he is ignorant or insensible, by being uneasy until he has distorted it in the small cracked mirror which he carries about with him as a joking apparatus. Some high authority is needed to give many worthy and timid persons the freedom of muscular repose under the growing demand on them to laugh when they have no other reason than the peril of being taken for dullards; still more to inspire them with the courage to say that they object to the theatrical spoiling for themselves and their children of all affecting themes, all the grander deeds and aims of men, by burlesque associations adapted to the taste of rich fishmongers in the stalls and their assistants in the gallery. The English people in the present generation are falsely reputed to know Shakspere (as, by some innocent persons, the Florentine mule-drivers are believed to have known the *Divina Commedia*, not, perhaps excluding all the subtle discourses in the *Purgatorio* and *Paradiso*);[4] but there seems a clear prospect that in the coming generation he will be known to them through burlesques, and that his plays will find a new life as pantomimes. A bottle-nosed Lear will come on with a monstrous corpulence from which he will frantically dance himself free during the midnight storm; Rosalind and Celia will join in a grotesque ballet with shepherds and shepherdesses; Ophelia in fleshings and a voluminous brevity of grenadine will dance through the mad scene, finish with the famous 'attitude of the scissors' in the arms of Laertes; and all the speeches in 'Hamlet' will be so ingeniously parodied that the originals will be reduced to a mere *memoria technica* of the improver's puns – premonitory signs of a hideous millennium, in which the lion will have to lie down with the lascivious monkeys whom (if we may trust Pliny)[5] his soul naturally abhors.

I have been amazed to find that some artists whose own works have the ideal stamp, are quite insensible to the damaging tendency of the burlesquing spirit which ranges to and fro and up and down on the earth, seeing no reason (except a precarious censorship) why it should not appropriate every sacred, heroic, and pathetic theme which serves to make up the treasure of human admiration, hope, and love. One would have thought that their own half-despairing efforts to invest in worthy outward shape the vague inward impressions of sublimity, and the consciousness of an implicit deal in the commonest scenes, might have made them susceptible of some disgust or alarm at a species of burlesque which is likely to render their compositions no better than a dissolving view, where every noble form is seen melting into its preposterous caricature. It used to be imagined of the unhappy medieval Jews that they parodied Calvary by crucifying dogs; if they had been guilty they would at least have had the excuse of the hatred and rage begotten by persecution. Are we on the way to a parody which shall have no other excuse than the reckless search after fodder for degraded appetites – after the pay to be earned by pasturing Circe's herd[6] where they may defile every monument of that growing life which should have kept them human?

The world seems to me well supplied with what is genuinely ridiculous: wit and humour may play as harmlessly or beneficently round the changing facets of egoism, absurdity, and vice, as the sunshine over the rippling sea or the dewy meadows. Why should we make our delicious sense of the ludicrous, with its invigorating shocks of laughter and its irrepressible smiles which are the outglow of an inward radiation as gentle and cheering as the warmth of morning, flourish like a brigand on the robbery of our mental wealth? – or let it take its exercise as a madman might, if allowed a free nightly promenade, by drawing the populace with bonfires which leave some venerable structure a blackened ruin or send a scorching smoke across the portraits of the past, at which we once looked with a loving recognition of fellowship, and disfigure them into butts of mockery? – nay, worse – use it to degrade the healthy appetites and affections of our nature as they are seen to be degraded in insane patients whose system, all out of joint, finds matter for screaming laughter in mere topsy-turvy, makes every passion preposterous or obscene, and turns the hard-won order of life into a second chaos hideous enough to make one wail that the first was ever thrilled with light?

This is what I call debasing the moral currency: lowering the value of every inspiring fact and tradition so that it will command less and less of the spiritual products, the generous motives which sustain the charm and elevation of our social existence – the something besides bread by which man saves his soul alive. The bread-winner of the family may demand more and more coppery shillings, or assignats, or greenbacks for his day's work, and so get the needful quantum of food; but let that moral currency be emptied of its value – let a greedy buffoonery debase all historic beauty, majesty, and pathos, and the more you heap up the desecrated symbols the greater will be the lack of the ennobling emotions which subdue the tyranny of suffering, and make ambition one with social virtue.[7]

And yet, it seems, parents will put into the hands of their children ridiculous parodies (perhaps with more ridiculous 'illustrations') of the poems which stirred their own tenderness or filial piety, and carry them to make their first acquaintance with great men, great works, or solemn crises through the medium of some miscellaneous burlesque which, with its idiotic puns and farcical attitudes, will remain among their primary associations, and reduce them throughout their time of studious preparation for life to the moral imbecility of an inward giggle at what might have stimulated their high emulation or fed the fountains of compassion, trust, and constancy. One wonders where these parents have deposited that stock of morally educating stimuli which is to be independent of poetic tradition, and to subsist in spite of the finest images being degraded and the finest words of genius being poisoned as with some befooling drug.

Will fine wit, will exquisite humour prosper the more through this turning of all things indiscriminately into food for a gluttonous laughter, an idle craving without sense of flavours? On the contrary. That delightful power which La Bruyère points to – 'le ridicule qui est quelque part, il faut l'y voir, l'en tirer avec grâce et d'une manière qui plaise et qui instruise' – depends on a discrimination only compatible with the varied sensibilities which give sympathetic insight, and with the justice of perception which is another name for grave knowledge. Such a result is no more to be expected from faculties on the strain to find some small hook by which they may attach the lowest incongruity to the most momentous subject, than it is to be expected of a sharper, watching for gulls in a great political assemblage, that he will notice the blundering logic of partisan speakers, or season his observation with the salt of historical parallels. But after all our psychological teaching, and in the midst of our zeal for education, we are still, most of us, at the stage of believing that mental powers and habits have somehow, not perhaps in the general statement, but in any particular case, a kind of spiritual glaze against conditions which we are continually applying to them. We soak our children in habits of contempt and exultant gibing, and yet are confident that – as Clarissa one day said to me – 'We can always teach them to be reverent in the right place, you know.' And doubtless if she were to take her boys to see a burlesque Socrates, with swollen legs, dying in the utterance of cockney puns, and were to hang up a sketch of this comic scene among their bedroom prints, she would think this preparation not at all to the prejudice of their emotions on hearing their tutor read that narrative of the *Apology*,[8] which has been consecrated by the reverent gratitude of ages. This is the impoverishment that threatens our posterity : – a new Famine, a meagre fiend with lewd grin and clumsy hoof, is breathing a moral mildew over the harvest of our human sentiments. These are the most delicate elements of our too easily perishable civilisation. And here again I like to quote a French testimony. Sainte Beuve, referring to a time of insurrectionary disturbance, says: 'Rien de plus prompt à baisser que la civilisation dans des crises comme celle-ci ; on perd en trois semaines la résultat de plusieurs siècles. La civilisation, la *vie* est une chose apprise et inventée, qu'on le sache bien : "*Inventas aut qui vitam excoluere per artes.*" Les hommes après quelques années de paix oublient trop cette verité : ils arrivent à croire que la *culture* est chose innée, qu'elle est la même chose que la *nature*. La sauvagerie est toujours là à deux pas, et, dès qu'on lâche pied, elle recommence.'[9] We have been severely enough taught (if we were willing to learn) that our civilisation, considered as a splendid material fabric, is helplessly in peril without the spiritual police of sentiments or ideal feelings. And it is this invisible police which we had need, as a community, strive to maintain in efficient force. How if a dangerous 'Swing' were sometimes disguised in a versatile entertainer devoted to the amusement of mixed audiences ? And I confess that sometimes when I see a certain style of young lady, who checks our tender admiration with rouge and henna and all the blazonry of an extravagant expenditure, with slang and bold *brusquerie* intended to signify her emancipated view of things, and with cynical mockery which she mistakes for penetration, I am sorely tempted to hiss out '*Pétroleuse!*'[10] It is a small matter to have our palaces set aflame compared with the misery of having our sense of a noble womanhood, which is the inspiration of a purifying shame, the promise of life-penetrating affection, stained and blotted out by images of repulsiveness.

These things come – not of higher education, but – of dull ignorance fostered into pertness by the greedy vulgarity which reverses Peter's visionary lesson and learns to call all things common and unclean.[11] It comes of debasing the moral currency.

The Tirynthians, according to an ancient story reported by Athenaeus,[12] becoming conscious that their trick of laughter at everything and nothing was making them unfit for the conduct of serious affairs, appealed to the Delphic oracle for some means of cure. The god prescribed a peculiar form of sacrifice, which would be effective if they could carry it through without laughing. They did their best; but the flimsy joke of a boy upset their unaccustomed gravity, and in this way the oracle taught them that even the gods could not prescribe a quick cure for a long vitiation, or give power and dignity to a people who in a crisis of the public wellbeing were at the mercy of a poor jest.

## ii MORAL SWINDLERS

It is a familiar example of irony in the degradation of words that 'what a man is worth' has come to mean how much money he possesses; but there seems a deeper and more melancholy irony in the shrunken meaning that popular or polite speech assigns to 'morality' and 'morals'. The poor part these words are made to play recalls the fate of those pagan divinities who, after being understood to rule the powers of the air and the destinies of men, came down to the level of insignificant demons, or were even made a farcical show for the amusement of the multitude.

Talking to Melissa in a time of commercial trouble, I found her disposed to speak pathetically of the disgrace which had fallen on Sir Gavial Mantrap, because of his conduct in relation to the Eocene Mines, and to other companies ingeniously devised by him for the punishment of ignorance in people of small means: a disgrace by which the poor titled gentleman was actually reduced to live in comparative obscurity on his wife's settlement of one or two hundred thousand in the consols.

'Surely your pity is misapplied', said I, rather dubiously, for I like the comfort of trusting that a correct moral judgment is the strong point in woman (seeing that she has a majority of about a million in our islands), and I imagined that Melissa might have some unexpressed grounds for her opinion. 'I should have thought you would rather be sorry for Mantrap's victims – the widows, spinsters, and hard-working fathers whom his unscrupulous haste to make himself rich has cheated of all their savings, while he is eating well, lying softly, and after impudently justifying himself before the public, is perhaps joining in the General Confession with a sense that he is an acceptable object in the sight of God, though decent men refuse to meet him.'

'Oh, all that about the Companies, I know, was most unfortunate. In commerce people are led to do so many things, and he might not know exactly how everything would turn out. But Sir Gavial made a good use of his money, and he is a thoroughly *moral* man.'

'What do you mean by a thoroughly moral man?' said I.

'Oh, I suppose every one means the same by that', said Melissa, with a slight air of rebuke. 'Sir Gavial is an excellent family man – quite blameless there; and so charitable round his place at Tiptop. Very different from Mr Barabbas, whose life, my husband tells me, is most objectionable, with actresses and that sort of thing. I think a man's morals should make a difference to us. I'm not sorry for Mr Barabbas, but *I am* sorry for Sir Gavial Mantrap.'

I will not repeat my answer to Melissa, for I fear it was offensively brusque, my opinion being that Sir Gavial was the more pernicious scoundrel of the two, since his name for virtue served as an effective part of a swindling apparatus; and perhaps I hinted that to call such a man moral showed rather a silly notion of human affairs. In fact, I had an angry wish to be instructive, and Melissa, as will sometimes happen, noticed my anger without appropriating my instruction, for I have since heard that she speaks of me as rather violent-tempered, and not over strict in my views of morality.

I wish that this narrow use of words which are wanted in their full meaning were confined to women like Melissa. Seeing that Morality and Morals under their *alias* of Ethics are the subject of voluminous discussion, and their true basis a pressing matter of dispute – seeing that the most famous book ever written on Ethics, and forming a chief study in our colleges, allies ethical with political science or that which treats of the constitution and prosperity of States, one might expect that educated men would find reason to avoid a perversion of language which lends itself to no wider view of life than that of village gossips. Yet I find even respectable historians of our own and of foreign countries, after showing that a king was treacherous, rapacious, and ready to sanction gross breaches in the administration of justice, end by praising him for his pure moral character, by which one must suppose them to mean that he was not lewd nor debauched, not the European twin of the typical Indian potentate whom Macaulay[13] describes as passing his life in chewing bang and fondling dancing-girls. And since we are sometimes told of such maleficent kings that they were religious, we arrive at the curious result that the most serious wide-reaching duties of man lie quite outside both Morality and Religion – the one of these consisting in not keeping mistresses (and perhaps not drinking too much), and the other in certain ritual and spiritual transactions with God which can be carried on equally well side by side with the basest conduct towards men. With such a classification as this it is no wonder, considering the strong reaction of language on thought, that many minds, dizzy with indigestion of recent science and philosophy, are far to seek for the grounds of social duty, and without entertaining any private intention of committing a perjury which would ruin an innocent man, or seeking gain by supplying bad preserved meats to our navy, feel themselves speculatively obliged to inquire why they should not do so, and are inclined to measure their intellectual subtlety by their dissatisfaction with all answers to this 'Why?' It is of little use to theorise in ethics while our habitual phraseology stamps the larger part of our social duties as something that lies aloof from the deepest needs and affections of our nature. The informal definitions of popular language are the only medium through which theory really affects the mass of minds even among the nominally educated; and when a man whose business hours, the solid part of every day, are spent in an unscrupulous course of public or private action which has every calculable chance of causing widespread injury and misery, can be called moral because he comes home to dine with his wife and children and cherishes the happiness of his own hearth, the augury is not good for the use of high ethical and theological disputation.

Not for one moment would one willingly lose sight of the truth that the relation of the sexes and the primary ties of kinship are the deepest roots of human wellbeing, but to make them by themselves the equivalent of morality is to cut off the channels of feeling through which they are the feeders of that wellbeing. They are the original fountains of a sensibility to the claims of others, which is the bond of societies; but being necessarily in the first instance a private good, there is always the danger that individual selfishness will see in them only the best part of its own gain; just as knowledge, navigation, commerce, and all the conditions which are of a nature to awaken men's consciousness of their mutual dependence and to make the world one great society,[14] are the occasions of selfish, unfair action, of war and oppression, so long as the public conscience or chief force of feeling and opinion is not uniform and strong enough in its insistence on what is demanded by the general welfare. And among the influences that must retard a right public judgment, the degradation of words which involve praise and blame will be reckoned worth protesting against by every mature observer. To rob words of half their meaning, while they retain their dignity as qualifications, is like allowing to men who have lost half their faculties the same high and perilous command which they won in their time of vigour; or like selling food and seeds after fraudulently abstracting their best virtues: in each case what ought to be beneficently strong is fatally enfeebled, if not empoisoned. Until we have altered our dictionaries and have found some other word than *morality* to stand in popular use for the duties of man to man, let us refuse to accept as moral the contractor who enriches himself by using large machinery to make pasteboard soles pass as leather for the feet of unhappy conscripts fighting at miserable odds against invaders: let us rather call him a miscreant, though he were the tenderest, most faithful of husbands, and contend that his own experience of home happiness makes his reckless infliction of suffering on others all the more atrocious. Let us refuse to accept as moral any political leader who should allow his conduct in relation to great issues to be determined by egoistic passion, and boldly say that he would be less immoral even though he were as lax in his personal habits as Sir Robert Walpole,[15] if at the same time his sense of the public welfare were supreme in his mind, quelling all pettier impulses beneath a magnanimous impartiality. And though we were to find among that class of journalists who live by recklessly reporting injurious rumours, insinuating the blackest motives in opponents, descanting at large and with an air of infallibility on dreams which they both find and interpret, and stimulating bad feeling between nations by abusive writing which is as empty of real conviction as the rage of a pantomime king, and would be ludicrous if its effects did not make it appear diabolical – though we were to find among these a man who was benignancy itself in his own circle, a healer of private differences, a soother in private calamities, let us pronounce him nevertheless flagrantly immoral, a root of hideous cancer in the commonwealth, turning the channels of instruction into feeders of social and political disease.

In opposite ways one sees bad effects likely to be encouraged by this narrow use of the word *morals*, shutting out from its meaning half those actions of a man's life which tell momentously on the wellbeing of his fellow-citizens, and on the preparation of a future for the children growing up around him. Thoroughness of workmanship, care in the execution of every task undertaken, as if

it were the acceptance of a trust which it would be a breach of
faith not to discharge well, is a form of duty so momentous that if
it were to die out from the feeling and practice of a people, all
reforms of institutions would be helpless to create national
prosperity and national happiness. Do we desire to see public spirit
penetrating all classes of the community and affecting every
man's conduct, so that he shall make neither the saving of his soul
nor any other private saving an excuse for indifference to the
general welfare? Well and good. But the sort of public spirit that
scamps its bread-winning work, whether with the trowel, the pen,
or the overseeing brain, that it may hurry to scenes of political or
social agitation, would be as baleful a gift to our people as any
malignant demon could devise. One best part of educational
training is that which comes through special knowledge and
manipulative or other skill, with its usual accompaniment of
delight, in relation to work which is the daily bread-winning
occupation – which is a man's contribution to the effective wealth
of society in return for what he takes as his own share. But this
duty of doing one's proper work well, and taking care that every
product of one's labour shall be genuinely what it pretends to be,
is not only left out of morals in popular speech, it is very little
insisted on by public teachers, at least in the only effective way – by
tracing the continuous effects of ill-done work. Some of them
seem to be still hopeful that it will follow as a necessary
consequence from week-day services, ecclesiastical decoration,
and improved hymn-books; others apparently trust to descanting
on self-culture in general, or to raising a general sense of faulty
circumstances; and meanwhile lax, make-shift work from the
high conspicuous kind to the average and obscure, is allowed to
pass unstamped with the disgrace of immorality, though there is
not a member of society who is not daily suffering from it
materially and spiritually, and though it is the fatal cause that
must degrade our national rank and our commerce in spite of all
open markets and discovery of available coal-seams.

I suppose one may take the popular misuse of the words
Morality and Morals as some excuse for certain absurdities which
are occasional fashions in speech and writing – certain old lay
figures, as ugly as the queerest Asiatic idol, which at different
periods get propped into loftiness, and attired in magnificent
Venetian drapery, so that whether they have a human face or not is
of little consequence. One is, the notion that there is a radical,
irreconcilable opposition between intellect and morality. I do not
mean the simple statement of fact, which everybody knows, that
remarkably able men have had very faulty morals, and have

outraged public feeling even at its ordinary standard; but the supposition that the ablest intellect, the highest genius, will see through morality as a sort of twaddle for bibs and tuckers, a doctrine of dulness, a mere incident in human stupidity. We begin to understand the acceptance of this foolishness by considering that we live in a society where we may hear a treacherous monarch, or a malignant and lying politician, or a man who uses either official or literary power as an instrument of his private partiality or hatred, or a manufacturer who devises the falsification of wares, or a trader who deals in virtueless seed-grains, praised or compassionated because of his excellent morals. Clearly if morality meant no more than such decencies as are practised by these poisonous members of society, it would be possible to say, without suspicion of light-headedness, that morality lay aloof from the grand stream of human affairs, as a small channel fed by the stream and not missed from it. While this form of nonsense is conveyed in the popular use of words, there must be plenty of well-dressed ignorance at leisure to run through a box of books, which will feel itself initiated in the freemasonry of intellect by a view of life which might take for a Shaksperian motto –

> Fair is foul and foul is fair,
> Hover through the fog and filthy air–[16]

and will find itself easily provided with striking conversation by the rule of reversing all the judgments on good and evil which have come to be the calendar and clock-work of society. But let our habitual talk give morals their full meaning as the conduct which, in every human relation, would follow from the fullest knowledge and the fullest sympathy – a meaning perpetually corrected and enriched by a more thorough appreciation of dependence in things, and a finer sensibility to both physical and spiritual fact – and this ridiculous ascription of superlative power to minds which have no effective awe-inspiring vision of the human lot, no response of understanding to the connection between duty and the material processes by which the world is kept habitable for cultivated man, will be tacitly descredited without any need to cite the immortal names that all are obliged to take as the measure of intellectual rank and highly-charged genius.

Suppose a Frenchman – I mean no disrespect to the great

French nation, for all nations are afflicted with their peculiar parasitic growths, which are lazy, hungry forms, usually characterised by a disproportionate swallowing apparatus: suppose a Parisian who should shuffle down the Boulevard with a soul ignorant of the gravest cares and the deepest tenderness of manhood, and a frame more or less fevered by debauchery, mentally polishing into utmost refinement of phrase and rhythm verses which were an enlargement on that Shaksperian motto, and worthy of the most expensive title to be furnished by the vendors of such antithetic ware as *Les marguerites de l'Enfer*, or *Les délices de Béelzébuth*. This supposed personage might probably enough regard his negation of those moral sensibilities which make half the warp and woof of human history, his indifference to the hard thinking and hard handiwork of life, to which he owed even his own gauzy mental garments with their spangles of poor paradox, as the royalty of genius, for we are used to witness such self-crowning in many forms of mental alienation; but he would not, I think, be taken, even by his own generation, as a living proof that there can exist such a combination as that of moral stupidity and trivial emphasis of personal indulgence with the large yet finely discriminating vision which marks the intellectual masters of our kind. Doubtless there are many sorts of transfiguration, and a man who has come to be worthy of all gratitude and reverence may have had his swinish period, wallowing in ugly places; but suppose it had been handed down to us that Sophocles or Virgil had at one time made himself scandalous in this way: the works which have consecrated their memory for our admiration and gratitude are not a glorifying of swinishness, but an artistic incorporation of the highest sentiment known to their age.

All these may seem to be wide reasons for objecting to Melissa's pity for Sir Gavial Mantrap on the ground of his good morals; but their connection will not be obscure to any one who has taken pains to observe the links uniting the scattered signs of our social development.

*     *     *

The potentiality of women in forwarding civilization is hinted at (p. 163), but the essay turns on the narrow English sense of 'morality'. There can be no genuine or stable progress until it affects the whole of our lives. The importance of integrity in journalism is stressed, but the strongest attack is reserved for dishonesty and incompetence in production. Substitute 'North

Sea oil' for 'coal seams' at the end of the passage on pages 166–7, and it sounds ominously modern.

## iii  'A FINE EXCESS'.[17] FEELING IS ENERGY

(This passage may be regarded as the nucleus of an essay in the making.)

One can hardly insist too much, in the present stage of thinking, on the efficacy of feeling in stimulating to ardent co-operation, quite apart from the conviction that such co-operation is needed for the achievement of the end in view. Just as hatred will vent itself in private curses no longer believed to have any potency, and joy, in private singing far out among the woods and fields, so sympathetic feeling can only be satisfied by joining in the action which expresses it, though the added 'Bravo!' the added push, the added penny, is no more than a grain of dust on a rolling mass. When students take the horses out of a political hero's carriage, and draw him home by the force of their own muscle, the struggle in each is simply to draw or push, without consideration whether his place would not be as well filled by somebody else, or whether his one arm be really needful to the effect. It is under the same inspiration that abundant help rushes towards the scene of a fire, rescuing imperilled lives, and labouring with generous rivalry in carrying buckets. So the old blind King John of Bohemia at the battle of Creçy begged his vassals to lead him into the fight that he might strike a good blow, though his own stroke, possibly fatal to himself, could not turn by a hair's-breadth the imperious course of victory.[18]

The question, 'Of what use is it for me to work towards an end confessedly good?' comes from that sapless kind of reasoning which is falsely taken for a sign of supreme mental activity, but is really due to languor, or incapability of that mental grasp which makes objects strongly present, and to a lack of sympathetic emotion. In the 'Spanish Gypsy' Fedalma says –

> The grandest death! to die in vain – for Love
> Greater than sways the forces of the world, –

referring to the image of the disciples throwing themselves, consciously in vain, on the Roman spears.[19] I really believe and mean this, – not as a rule of general action, but as a possible grand instance of determining energy in human sympathy, which even in particular cases, where it has only a magnificent futility, is more adorable, or as we say divine, than unpitying force, or than a prudent calculation of results. Perhaps it is an implicit joy in the resources of our human nature which has stimulated admiration for acts of self-sacrifice which are vain as to their immediate end. Marcus Curtius was probably not imagined as concluding to himself that he and his horse would so fill up the gap as to make a smooth *terra firma*.[20] The impulse and act made the heroism, not the correctness of adaptation. No doubt the passionate inspiration which prompts and sustains a course of self-sacrificing labour in the light of soberly estimated results gathers the highest title to our veneration, and makes the supreme heroism. But the generous leap of impulse is needed too to swell the flood of sympathy in us beholders, that we may not fall completely under the mastery of calculation, which in its turn may fail of ends for want of energy got from ardour. We have need to keep the sluices open for possible influxes of the rarer sort.

* * *

Like Auguste Comte, George Eliot felt that an awareness of problems is not enough; the right feelings need to be cultivated to generate the will for reform. For this reason, she could think of nothing finer than the last lines of Wordsworth's 'magnificent sonnet on Toussaint l'Ouverture':

> Thou hast left behind
> Powers that will work for thee; air, earth, and skies;
> There's not a breathing of the common wind
> That will forget thee; thou hast great allies;
> Thy friends are exultations, agonies,
> And love, and man's unconquerable mind.

The cogency of views similar to George Eliot's main argument must have been in Shakespeare's mind when, in *Julius Caesar* (III.ii), he showed ironically how the reason of the idealist Brutus is defeated by the stirring appeals of the crafty politician Mark Antony. The only motive to true moral action, George Eliot wrote, is 'the immediate impulse of love and justice'; and this, she felt, could be roused most effectively, not by reason or argument (which she thought offensive), but by the 'aesthetic teaching' of great literature (15.viii.66). 'My function', she claimed, 'is that of the *aesthetic*, not the doctrinal teacher – the rousing of the nobler emotions, which make mankind desire the social right, not the prescribing of special measures, concerning which the artistic mind, however strongly moved by social sympathy, is often not the best judge' (18.vii.78).

# NOTES

1. Francis Bacon in his dedication to the 1625 edition of his essays said that they were widely read because they 'come home to men's business and bosoms'.
2. Milton's 'On the Morning of Christ's Nativity': 'And kings sat still with awful eye,/As if they surely knew their sov'reign Lord was by.'
3. Isaac Newton (1642–1727), scientist and mathematician, discovered the law of gravitation; Frederick Herschel (1738–1822), astronomer, made important discoveries in the solar system and the Milky Way.
4. This reference to fossils exemplifies the author's scientific interests, and her way of drawing on them for incidental illustrations.
5. In his *Novum Organum* Bacon distinguishes between four types of *idola* or mental habits which lead to erroneous conclusions; the *idola theatri* arise from accepted systems of thought or philosophy.
6. During her widowhood Madame de Sablé (1599–1678) held, at her residence in the Place Royale, a salon which was attended by men and women of distinction, including Pascal and La Rochefoucauld. Discussions ranged from theology, physics, metaphysics, and morals to society and topical questions.
7. On 7 September 1838, with her father William Darling, lighthouse keeper on one of the Farne Islands off the Northumbrian coast.
8. David Teniers (1610–90), Flemish; Murillo (1618–82), Spanish.
9. One of Holman Hunt's pre-Raphaelite works (1852).
10. The picture has not be identified. The popular and profuse poetess Letitia Elizabeth Landon (1802–38) was best known as L. E. L. from her contributions to magazines and to such annuals as *The Keepsake* (cf. M.xxvii). For *primo tenore*, compare the passage on opera peasants (p. 13).
11. The sentence alludes to familiar lines in Thomas Gray's 'Elegy' and Milton's 'L'Allegro'.
12. *Modern Painters*, III, v. 13 (1856).
13. Scott, *The Antiquary* (1816) xxvi (Elspeth Mucklebackit; 'Luckie' was a familiar name for an elderly woman, especially a grandmother) and *Chronicles of Canongate*, First Series (1827);Wordsworth, 'The Reverie of Poor Susan'; Charles Kingsley, *Alton Locke* (1850) xi; 'The Little Chimney-Sweep' by Joseph Hornung, a Swiss painter (1792–1870).

14. By Lady Caroline Lucy Scott (1856).
15. Harriet Beecher Stowe became famous with her first anti-slavery novel *Uncle Tom's Cabin*; her second, *Dred*, appeared in 1856, and was reviewed by Marian Evans in the same number of *The Westminster Review* as that in which 'Silly Novels' appeared.
16. *Night Thoughts* had been Mary Evans' favourite poem in her youth. She refers to 'The Last Day' as one of Young's first two poetical performances, both bombastic.
17. This alludes to the wild hopes of speculators in the 'South Sea Bubble', which passed their peak in 1720, when, after numerous imitation companies had proved fraudulent, shares in the South Sea Company fell rapidly, and many investors were ruined.
18. *Night Thoughts*: viii,738–43 and iii,375–93.
19. If there is no reward in heaven for pain and endurance, then virtue is contrary to reason, Young argues, rather like St Paul, I Corinthians, xv.32: 'what advantageth it me, if the dead rise not? let us eat and drink; for tomorrow we die'.
20. George Eliot's revision of this sentence (as it appears in the 1884 edition) is preferred for directness and clarity.
21. In their belief that the penitent could attain salvation, the Arminians rejected the Calvinist doctrine of eternal damnation for the non-elect. To the former, predestination was conditional; to the Calvinists, absolute.

### CHAPTER II  TWO CONTRASTING STORIES

1. The original (28.ii.73) has 'save' (1.3) for 'beyond'; 'heaven' (l.c.) has been retained, since it expresses the author's intention.
2. Inscription on the tomb of Jonathan Swift: 'where fierce indignation can no longer tear the heart'.
3. Recollected from Byron's *Manfred*, III.iv.
4. Robert Potter, *The Tragedies of Aeschylus* (2 vols, translation, 1777) 6th ed. (1833). Philip Francis's translation of Horace (1757).
5. Satire is implied not only in the name 'Letherall' but also in his phrenological aptitude tests. George Eliot's interest in the subject had been stimulated by Charles Bray's enthusiasm after reading George Combe's *Elements of Phrenology*. The originator of this 'science' was Franz Joseph Gall (1758–1828).
6. Rousseau, on the Bieler See (le Lac de Bienne). See his fifth 'promenade' in *Rêveries du Promeneur Solitaire* (1782).
7. In which Elijah 'went up by a whirlwind into heaven' (II Kings, ii.11).
8. The pen-name of Friedrich von Hardenberg (1772–1801), a poet who died of consumption and was regarded as the 'prophet' of Romanticism. George Eliot knew enough about his life and work to draw her own conclusion.
9. Antonio Canale, Venetian painter (1697–1768).

10. One possessed by an evil spirit (cf. M.xlvi), from Scott's *The Abbot*, xxxxii: '*Energumene* or possessed demoniac'.
11. The authenticity of many works attributed to the Italian painter Giorgione (c. 1478–1511) has been disputed. Lucrezia Borgia (1480–1519), though respected by her subjects, has been represented as the embodiment of wantonness and crime.
12. An allusion to the story of Dr Faustus (see Marlowe's play).
13. For the same image, compare *Jane Eyre* (xi); it probably derives from the parable of the sower (Matthew, xiii.3–8) and the opening words of Bunyan's *The Pilgrim's Progress*.
14. Italian poet (1544–95).
15. With this incidental detail compare the more elaborate parallel in natural surroundings when Dorothea and Casaubon return from their honeymoon in Rome (M.xxviii), a scene which probably inspired Hardy to write a similar but more intensified and dramatic scene in *Far from the Madding Crowd* (xi).
16. From 'Le Renard et la Cicogne', one of the fables of La Fontaine (1621–95): 'Deceivers, I write for you; expect a similar fate.'
17. They provided books for the education of workers.
18. A popular story in England, France, and Germany, based on Richard Steele's in the eleventh paper of *The Spectator* (1711–14), where Thomas Inkle appears to be a man after David Faux's heart: he remembers to put self-interest first, selling Yarico, the North American Indian girl who has loved him devotedly, to a Barbadian merchant, as soon as they reach English territory and his mercenary ambition returns.
19. From *biens* (Fr.), goods, property; here, substance; usually, money.
20. The Chubb firm was well known for the locks it patented.
21. The 'mind free from guilt' (adapted from Virgil, *Aeneid*, I.604).
22. Nephew of Napoleon, and Emperor of France when this story was written.
23. Shakespeare, *The Tempest*, II.ii.
24. Honoré de Balzac (1799–1850) wrote numerous novels, including *Le Père Goriot* and *Eugénie Grandet*.
25. Cf. Proverbs, iii.17 (on wisdom), 'Her ways are ways of pleasantness, and all her paths are peace.'
26. Gorgon is not one of the three-headed monsters of Greek mythology, but a creation of the Christian era, the same as Demogorgon. Spenser describes him in *The Faerie Queene* (I.i.37) as 'Great Gorgon, Prince of darknesse and dead night', and Milton associates 'the dreaded name' of Demogorgon with Night in *Paradise Lost* (II.961–5).
27. A long robe worn as a uniform in some of the charity schools for boys.
28. More and more J. M. W. Turner (1775–1851) chose his subjects to show amazing colour effects produced by light.
29. Cf. *Hamlet*, I.ii.180–1: 'The funeral bak'd-meats/Did coldly furnish forth the marriage tables.'

30. Food from heaven (Exodus, xvi.1–15).
31. The nightingale of the East, associated with romance. When Byron set the fashion with oriental tales in verse ('The Corsair' and 'The Siege of Corinth' among them), Thomas Moore followed suit with *Lalla Rookh* (1817).
32. An allusion to Adam Smith's *Inquiry into the Nature and Causes of the Wealth of Nations* (1776), where 'division of labour' implies specialization.
33. Although Joseph Addison wrote most of *The Spectator* papers (see 18 above), this refers to another by Richard Steele (no. 431, 15 July 1712).
34. The passage that follows reads almost like a parody of a speech in *Othello*. The irony here, as in the 'flat and stale' allusion to *Hamlet* (I.ii.133–4) which follows, derives from the association of an unprepossessing scoundrel with men of heroic mould. The valiant blackamoor Othello charmed Desdemona, daughter of a Venetian senator, with stories of his feats and strange encounters abroad (I.iii.128–69).
35. Richmal Mangnall (1769–1820), who became headmistress of Crofton Hall, a girls school near Wakefield, wrote *Historical and Miscellaneous Questions for the use of Young People* (1800). By 1857 this general knowledge book had reached its 84th impression.
36. Cunning Faux had adapted lines from the popular hymn 'Sun of my Soul, Thou Saviour dear' (from 'Evening' in John Keble's *The Christian Year*, 1827).
37. Leviathan . . . hook . . . bridle: a mock-serious allusion to Job, xli.
38. Compare the old proverb: 'There's many a slip 'twixt cup and lip.'
39. In New South Wales, and once a penal settlement to which British felons were transported.

CHAPTER III    ADJUNCTS TO MAJOR WORKS

1. George Henry Lewes. See p. ix.
2. John Blackwood, publisher, Edinburgh.
3. An author and popular London lecturer (1816–60).
4. After being a private secretary to ministers of the Crown, Arthur Helps (1813–75) was made Clerk of the Privy Council in 1860; he was one of Lewes's friends.
5. Agnes Jervis Lewes, wife of G. H. Lewes; see p. ix.
6. William E. Aytoun, poet and friend of John Blackwood, was Professor of Rhetoric and Belles Lettres at Edinburgh University for a period, and on Blackwood's staff.
7. Edward George Lytton Bulwer–Lytton's; he was a prestigious novelist and playwright (1803–73).
8. This may have been transmuted into the story of Casaubon and Dorothea Brooke (M), a subject which the author had regarded as one of her 'possible themes' ever since she began to write fiction.
9. George Eliot sensibly pointed out that Scott's *The Heart of Midlothian*

would probably have been rejected had it been judged on a preliminary outline.

10. Cf. 'Moral Swindlers' (pp. 164–8) and M.xiii.

11. Robert Lowe, thinking of the development of working-class power as a result of the 1867 Reform Bill, said it was necessary to educate 'our future masters', a remark which helped to make elementary education obligatory through the Education Act of 1870.

12. The prospect of plenty (Genesis, xlii.2).

13. A similar thought was expressed by Epicurus (the Vatican Collection of Maxims, 61).

14. The same political analogy is presented in the first scene of *Coriolanus*; it originates from St Paul, I Corinthians, xii.7–26.

15. Adapted fictionally (FH.xxxiii) from the author's recollections of rioting at Nuneaton in 1832, at the election which followed the passing of the First Reform Bill.

16. An allusion to the parable of the tares, Matthew, xiii.24–30.

17. A French army surgeon who substituted ligature of the arteries for cauterization after amputation.

18. Tintoretto and Titian were two great Venetian painters of the sixteenth century. For George Eliot's interest in the works of the latter, see DD.xvii,xl. The subject of the Annunciation, with Mary's 'Behold the handmaid of the Lord', is given in Luke, i.26–38.

19. A reference to Euripides' play *Iphigenia in Aulis*.

20. Near the end of the fifteenth century.

21. Wordsworth (who has 'dread' for 'dire'), *The Excursion*, VI.555–7.

22. A tragic trilogy by Aeschylus. When the Greek fleet, bound for war with Troy, was held back by the winds, Agamemnon was persuaded to sacrifice his daughter Iphigenia to the gods. On his return from Troy, his wife Clytemnestra murdered him in revenge. Electra, Agamemnon's daughter, then incited her brother Orestes (charged by Apollo to avenge his father's death) to murder his mother. Pursued by the Furies, he was finally acquitted by Athena, who appealed for maintenance of the law.

23. Aeschylus, *Prometheus Bound*, from the old myth in which Zeus punishes Prometheus for bringing enlightenment to men.

24. The notes are the first clear indication of an unfinished essay. The references are to Goethe's play, to the opera drawn from Victor Hugo's *Le Roi s'Amuse*, and to Shakespeare's *Julius Caesar*.

25. Arthur Hugh Clough (1819–61), friend of Matthew Arnold. For an example of 'doing duty in blindness as to the result', see his poem 'All Is Well'. The problem for a secular age ('egoistic yearnings' replacing 'really moral impulses') had been raised by George Eliot in her essay on Young; cf. note 19 (Pre-Novel Writings).

26. A subject familiar to Victorian readers of Tennyson's *Idylls of the King*.

CHAPTER IV    POEMS

1. 'The thought of that long age, after my death, moves me more than this brief one.'
2. The Renaissance had its precursor in the Middle Ages when an intellectual and cultural revival spread through western Europe from the Levant, creating the climate in which writers like Dante, Petrarch, Boccaccio, and Chaucer were to flourish.
3. Calpe is the ancient name for Gibraltar.
4. Aldebaran, one of the first-magnitude stars, by comparison with which the apparently neighbouring constellation the Hyades is inconspicuous.
5. Roland, a legendary hero who died for Charlemagne in the Pyrenees; the Cid, a Spanish hero who won renown fighting against the Moors; Amadis, the subject of heroic romance (of uncertain origin), a knight-errant and constant lover. The 'fair boy' who died at Babylon is Alexander the Great (355–323 B.C.)
6. Aesculapius was the Greek god of medicine, and Apollo the god of the fine arts, including music. The mediaeval belief that illness was due to an upset in the balance of humours (the four fluids of the body – blood, phlegm, yellow bile, and black bile – according to the ancient Greek physician Hippocrates) is indicated in Chaucer's description of the doctor (*The Canterbury Tales*, Prologue, 411–44).
7. From Falernus (near Capua); celebrated by ancient Roman poets, notably Horace.
8. The pheasant (*phasianus colchicus*) takes its name from its place of origin, the Phasis river in Colchis (east of the Black Sea and below the Caucasus), a country famous in classical legend from the story of Jason.
9. Over the Coventry Canal, not far from Griff House.
10. Originally the chaconne was a slow Spanish dance. The term was used by Johann Sebastian Bach (1685–1750) to indicate the style of the last movement of his D minor Suite, the '2nd Partita' for unaccompanied violin.
11. Or Stradivarius (*c.* 1644–1737), a famous Italian violin maker of Cremona.
12. Joseph Joachim (1831–1907), a Hungarian violinist whom George Eliot heard play several times in London and thought 'amazing'.
13. An Italian painter (1569–1609), born at Caravaggio, whose work expresses his wild, gloomy character.
14. That of the painter Veronese de Pitati Bonifazio (c. 1487–1553).
15. A subject, from 'Judith' in the Old Testament *Apocrypha*, presented by several Italian painters, including Tintoretto and Paolo Veronese.

CHAPTER V    LATE ESSAYS

1. From the ending of 'Des Ouvrages de l'Esprit', the first chapter of *Les Caractères* (1688).

2. A Scottish philosopher (1753–1828) who admitted psychological considerations to his philosophy·of the mind.

3. The final days of the Reign of Terror during the French Revolution, which reached their peak with the execution of Robespierre on 27 July (Thermidor 9th) 1794.

4. Dante was one of George Eliot's favourite poets in her later years.

5. See Book VIII,xix.52 of the *Natural History* by Pliny the Elder (27–79 A.D.), the only surviving work of this Roman scholar.

6. Circe's potions turned Ulysses' men into swine.

7. Adapted from *Othello*, III.iii.350–1.

8. Plato's *Apology* or 'defence', an account of that made by the Athenian philosopher at his trial in 399 B.C.

9. Civilization owes much to 'those who have enriched life through cultivating the arts' (Virgil, *Aeneid*, VI.663).

10. A woman who uses petroleum for incendiary purposes; the term was first heard during the Paris Commune of 1871.

11. See Acts, x.28.

12. Athenaeus (d. 194 A.D.) left a miscellaneous work which, with its comments and anecdotes, throws light on ancient manners; the Tyrinthians were the people of Tyrinthus, a town in southern Greece.

13. See an early passage in the essay 'Lord Clive' on the decline in India after the death of Aurungzebe; Macaulay gives 'concubines' for 'dancing girls'.

14. Views expressed by Caleb Garth (M.xxiv) are here extended to the world. The basic theme of George Eliot's works is 'the growing good of the world' (a phrase from the final paragraph of *Middlemarch*) and its promotion.

15. Until his resignation in 1742, he had virtually ruled Great Britain for the Hanoverian George II; 'his coarseness, his love of a lecherous sally, grew rather than diminished with the years' (J. H. Plumb).

16. Uttered by the three witches, embodiments of the temptation to evil, at the opening of *Macbeth*.

17. From Keats's letter, 27.ii.18: 'I think poetry should surprise by a fine excess . . .'.

18. George Eliot read this early in 1878 at the end of the first volume of J. R. Green's *A Short History of the English People*.

19. Near the end of Book I, when, after discovering her paternity on the eve of her wedding, she renounces her lover Don Silva to serve her father (his enemy) in the struggle to obtain liberty for their gipsy tribe.

20. When the oracle declared that a chasm in the forum could be filled only by the greatest treasure of Rome, a youth named Mettus or Metius (not Marcus) Curtius leapt into it on horseback, and the chasm closed over him.

# Index

P3